Codification of Muslim Personal Law

Codification of Muslim Personal Law

A RESEARCH PROJECT BY

Dr Asghar Ali Engineer

(Chairman and Research Director)

Ms Qutub Jehan Kidwai

(Associate Research Director)

KALPAZ

First Published, 2019

Published by

Kalpaz Publications
C-30, Satyawati Nagar,
Delhi – 110052
E-mail: kalpaz@hotmail.com
Ph.: 9212142040

Printed at: G. Print Process, Delhi

Cataloging in Publication Data—DK
Courtesy: D.K. Agencies (P) Ltd. <docinfo@dkagencies.com>

Engineer, Asghar Ali, 1939-2013, **author.**
Codification of Muslim personal law / a research project by Dr. Asghar Ali Engineer, Ms. Qutub Jehan Kidwai.
pages cm
ISBN 9789353240806 (PB)

1. Islamic law. 2. Domestic relations (Islamic law) 3. Muslims—Legal status, laws, etc. I. Kidwai, Qutub Jehan, author. II. Title.

LCC KBP144.E54 2018 | DDC 340.59 23

Contents

Preface

This publication is a report of the project titled "Codification of Muslim Personal Law" which was undertaken by Centre for Study of Society and Secularism (CSSS) in the year 2008-09. Research director of the project was highly acclaimed Islamic scholar, Dr. Asghar Ali Engineer, the then Chairperson of CSSS and Ms. Qutub Jehan Kidwai was the Associate Research Director of the project.

Thisreport discusses thoroughly the codification of Muslim Personal Law through critical analysis of different Madhabs and their approaches. The methodology for the research included exhaustive questionnaires to get responses from adherents of all facets of Madhabs, in depth interviews with religious leaders, Imams and Muftis for their perspectives on the provisions of the Shariat. The project report also presents a comparative study of family laws of different countries, highlighting divergent views, features, cases and its position vis-a-vis international instruments and organizations.

The present BJP led government is taking small steps towards Uniform Civil Code (UCC). They had mentioned in their 2014 manifesto that they would strive for UCC for National Integration which now they're clothing under the narrative of gender justice. These intentions of the government were also evident when recently the government proposed a legislation criminalizing triple talaq which was opposed by overwhelming majority of the community. The report mentions a need to reform the Muslim personal law rather than such gender unjust generalized laws. With this background in mind, we decided to publish this project report in the form of a publication as we thought it is extremely relevant to the current discourse around Muslim Personal Law.

This publication is also a tribute to Dr. Asghar Ali Engineer. The project, within the framework of Shariat Law and Constitution, proposes a rough and broad draft for codification of the personal law.

We would like to thank Indian Council of Social Science Research (ICSSR) for funding the project. We are thankful to Anwar Hussain for helping us carry out the surveys and interviews. Gopakumar has been assisting in the project at various levels for which we are extremely thankful to him. Last, we extend our gratitude to Kalpaz Publications for publishing this book when it is most needed.

Irfan Engineer
Director
Centre for Study of Society and Secularism

Introduction

The Muslim Personal Law in India for decades has been in debate for its vagueness and misconception. In my earlier book Gender Empowerment and Reforms in Personal Law, I discovered that the existing Muslim law is in fact a Anglo-Mohammedan law evolved by the colonial courts in their effort to apply the laws of the Quran (in cases where the parties were Muslims) also began to be construed as a part of the Shariah. These laws, the handiwork of those who were not even nominally Muslims, were justified through the legal fiction that the courts were not interpreting the Shariah but merely applying it. It is important to understand the history of its emergence in India. Under the British East India Company, sphere of their influence gradually expanded from settlements which were major cities like Bombay, Calcutta and Madras to other small districts and villages.

English laws was originally introduced into the metropolitan areas, where British staff and their famlies lived and worked so that indigeneous law would not apply to the Europeans. However, problems arose when disputes involving an European and a local person took place. And this made British to involve more in legal administration and adjudication, they had to evolve new methods of dealing with various South Asian legal systems. In this context it is significant that the indigenous laws were recognised as laws, while at the same time Western legal system were perceived as superior.[1] Already in 1668, the East Indian Company was required in a charter to enact laws, "consonant to reason and not repugnant or contrary to the English laws and as near as may be agreeable to "such laws"[2] At this early stage too, traditional caste courts or *Panchayats* were recognised. The 1718 Proclamation marked the beginning of the official involvement of the colonial court in the administration of local justice. Eventually a picture emerged that the caste court were not often used and the Indian complainants prefered the Mayor's court. Such observation were often used to justify the extension of the colonial courts. In 1765, the East India Company obtained *diwani* rights over some part of Bengal, which meant that it now acted as a local authority under continued Mughal supremacy.[3]

In the series of proclamations between 1772 and 1793, the East India Company confirmed its policy that Hindus and Muslims were to be governed by their own laws (but not administered in their own courts) in disputes relating to the inheritance, succession, marriage and caste and other religious usages. The assumption was that Hindu laws were 'the laws of the Shastras' and Muslim laws 'the laws of the Quran'. This focus on scriptural law was soon modified and by 1793 the Regulations referred to 'Hindu laws' and 'Mohammadan laws.' Significantly, in the actual administration of justice, from 1772 until 1786, Hindu and Muslim experts or assesors (pandits and moulavis) were enlisted to instruct the courts as to the nature of Hindu and Muslim laws.[4]

The dawn of codification era commenced with the Code of Civil Procedure 1859, followed by Limitation Act 1859, The Indian Penal Code 1860 and the Code of Criminal Procedure 1861. The Trust Act of 1882 shows the acceptance of Personal Laws because British believed at this time that the personal laws were so interconnected with the religious feelings that any attempt to large scale reforms, or any endeavour to codify will upset their colonial motto and creating grounds for anti-colonial agitation.[5]

After 1864 indigenous legal advisors were dispensed with and the British judges began learning Sanskrit or Persian or Urdu, and interpret and pronounce upon Hindu and Muslim laws, while increasingly drawing on English legal principles and procedures to work through these customary laws, usage and *shastric* laws.[6] Often the colonial courts simply interpreted for purposes of specific judgments rather than to reform existing practices. Precedents and case laws were built up this way. The consequence in practice was that sometimes the laws were stretched too far towards customary practices which even the community found diverging from their own law. At other times English common law wisdom subverted indigenous inclination or preferences on the pretext that ancient usages stand in the way of social progress and utilitarian objectives.

In course of time the government in British India had inherited the power to appoint Qazis from the Mughal rulers but had abdicated it in 1864. On the demand of Muslim leadership led by the great Sir Syed Ahmad Khan, the power was resumed by enacting the Qazis Act 1880. The Qazis Act 1880, reveals that a Qazi, in the sub-continent, not only exercised the power of a court but also manage public religious or charitable trusts, attestation and registration of documents. During the British rule, Qazis were replaced by the Judges and Magistrates and the judicial office of Qazi and Qazi-ul-Kazaat were abolished by Act No. XI of 1864. Latter on by the present Act the British Government no longer recognising the judicial function of the Qazi revived the appointment of Qazi for performing religious rituals marriage etc amongst the Muslim community in the British India. The Qazi's Act 1880 provides that the Provincial Government shall appoint a Qazi after consulting the principal Muslim residents of a local area for performance of Muslim marriages and certain other rites and ceremonies.[7]

Although the personal law have governed a narrower area of personal or private community conduct - pertaining to family law, marriage, inheritance, kinship, adoption, succession, collective property title, and so on - they nevertheless have specific implications for thinking on issues of citizenship, rights and obligations including the duty of the

State towards its citizens within varying social and cultural contexts. The Indian Divorce Act 1869 put a ceiling on the maintenance amount to be given to the estranged wife (one-fifth of the average husband's income; and even then Muslim Personal Law might override this according to its own Qur'anic or al-Hidaya ordinances. The Registration of Mohammedan Marriages and Divorces Act 1876 made registration of Muslim marriages, *nikah-nama*, voluntary or good enough if records are kept with the Qazi (judge) in the *masjid* or mosque precinct, etc.[8]

Further the emerging colonial administration recognised Muslim Law as an operative legal system. This process was not restricted to Shariah law but gradually extended to incorporate to some extent the various customs of the Muslims in South Asia. Customary practices was recognised as relevant in situation where the courts were directed to apply the personal law of the parties as governing laws.

In the early leading case on this matter is a complex litigation involving Khojas and Memons, decided in Bombay in 1847. In that case strong evidence of customs was soon found. It turn out that there was little or no conflicting testimony regarding the existence of a custom as stated in the plea. The principal question then arose that whether such customs was valid or not. The judgement contains a brief sketch of the Khoja community, which states as follows,[9]

" The Khojas are a small caste in Western India, who appears to have originally come from Sindh or Cutch; and who, by their own traditions, which are probably correct, were converted from Hinduism about four hundred years ago ......their religion is Mohammedan, their dress, appearance and manners, for the most part, Hindu."[10]

The plaintiff in the action, the daughter of the intestate, claimed a share in the inheritance of her father on the grounds that Muslim law governed the dispute and under Muslim law she was entitled, as a daughter, to a share in the inheritanc. The defendants countered the claim of the plaintiff on the ground that although the Khojas are a Muslim community and normally Muslim law would govern them, nonetheless, there are Khoja customs whereby females are not entitled to any share of the father's property on his death.

The judgement concludes as "It appears to me that if a custom has been proved to exist from time whereof the memory of man runneth not to the contrary, if it does not conflict with any express law of the ruling power, such a custom is entitled to receive the sanction of a court of law".[11]

The obvious issue in this case was whether such a custom among the Muslims would be valid despite being contrary to the Quranic principles of Muslim law. Here the petition of the daughter failed because judge restricted the application of Muslim Personal Law against the Customary law. If a customs is proved, then there is no doubt that the Muslim Personal Law is not applicable. This also proves how the precedence made by the British court under Muslim law can completely misled and cannot be termed as Islamic law.

There was a desire by the religious leadership of the Muslim community to reduce the role of local, Hindu influenced customs. As a direct result of appeals by the Muslim community, the Muslim Personal Law Shariah Application Act 1937 was enacted in British India in order to reduce the instances where custom could become the rule of decision. The text of the Act lays down that in a number of specified areas of law regarding intestate succession and the laws of marriage and divorce, in case where the parties are Muslims shall be the Muslim Personal Law. The 1937 Act was sonsequently extended to all parts of independent India but does not apply in Jammu and Kashmir.[12] There have been several amendments to the Shariah Act were carried out by many states and wider extension has been introduced for example Muslim Personal Law (Shariah Application Kerala Amendment Act 1963) (Act 42 of 1963) for the state of Kerala, which provides as follows:[13]

"2. Application of personal law to Muslim – Notwithstanding any custom or usage to the contrary, in all questions regarding intestate succession, special property of females incuding personal property inherited or obtained under contract or gift or any other provision of personal law, marriage, dissolution of marriage, including *talaq, ila, zihar, lian, khula* and *mubaraat*, maintenance, dower, guardianship, gifts, trusts and trust properties and wakfs, (other than charities and charitable institutions and charitable and religious endowments) the rule of decision in cases where the parties are Muslim, shll be the Muslim Personal law (Shariah)."[14]

The application of Muslim law, rather than local custom, has been strenthened by a series of enactments. The West Punjab Muslim Personal Law (Shariah) Application Act 1948 and the Punjab Muslim Personal Law (Shariah) Application (Amendment) Act 1951 put the spotlight on the agriculture heartland of the Punjab. The 1948 Act stated that in all question regarding succession including agricultural land, where the parties are Muslims shall be the Muslim personal law. Complications were experienced in applying the 1948 Act, in ascertaining the meanig of the word "succession". Did it include both intestate and testate succession or was it restricted to intestate succession as in the parent Act? This problem was overcome by the Punjab Muslim Personal Law (Shariah) Application (Ammendment) Act 1951, which stated that notwithstanding any rule of customary usage, whether testate or intestate, the rule of decision shall be the Muslim personal law, in cases wher the parties are Muslims. [15]

Muslim leaders in the 1930s demanded codification of their laws. Some redress came for the Muslim community with the enactment of the Shariah Act 1937 which declared that Muslims prefer to be governed by their own Shariah or canon law of Islam as interpreted by their moulavis and ulama (theologists-cleric body) and legal experts *(fuqaha)* who drafted legal codes and injunctions from the extensive moral guide that includes the Quran, Sunnah and Hadith.

Henceforth this law would apply univocally to all Muslims, their minors and descendants.

But what is Shariah has remained vague, undefined in terms of what a modern nation-state takes *law* to be with its more pragmatic if not secular nuance; nor did much specific codification on the thorny areas within Personal Law actually take place, and uniformity across the plethora of Islamic sects was not achieved. The Shariah Act recognises inheritance of family property for women, which was not allowed under customary law or Hindu law as understood in colonial times. The Indian Muslim League backed this move and Muslim community saw itself as progressive and pro-women. And it had the support of Muslim women's organisations. In 1939 the British administration passed the Dissolution of Muslim Marriage Act, which gave non-Muslim judges the right to dissolve Muslim marriages.

In a secular constitutional democracy, the Muslim Personal law remain of great importance and practical relevance to the substantial Muslim minority of India. Since this personal law has remained largely uncodified, it means in practice that the laws on marriage, divorce and many other matter are decided in accordance with traditional Shariah which also involves the recourse to Angl-Mohammadan Law. However, there is strong body of opinion that this has allowed certain un-Islamic customs which damaged womens' rights.

We also need to look in to the ongoing widening communal divide in India due to thoughtless politicisation of Muslim issues. Since independence communalism has now reached a stage when it is getting out of hand making polarisation between the two major religious communities more and more beyond the realm of possibility. Totally depending on elite and Ulama of their community for guidance, the Muslim masses do not appear to be looking anything beyond Islam, which is viewed by them as a complete way of life. Even though the Muslim community is divided into innumerable sects and groups due to different interpretations of Islamic texts, they are found to be united in getting agitated over even a rational change on certain issues linked to their community. Communal riots and bloating communal biasness found in the government system and bureaucracy has led to much rigidity and skeptical thinking among the Muslim minorities.

Contrary to the changes in Islamic rules that occurred in various Muslim countries, the Muslim leadership in India with the support of some Islamic institutions are propagating that change in Muslim Personal Law is tantamount to infringement of the religious rights of the followers of Islam. They have gone to the extent of declaring that any change would amount to an attempt of Hinduisation of Muslims. By and large Indian Muslims have linked their religio-cultural identity with issues like Personal Law, Babri Masjid, Urdu, and minority character of Aligarh Muslim University, family planning, right to prayer in archaeologically protected mosques, madrasa education, *waqf* and *haj* subsidy. Any attempt to rationalise these issues is viewed by Islamic radicals as a danger to the identity of the community. Though, such issues may not have much relevance to the modern concept of civilisation as well as the spiritual aspect of Islam, their politicisation by right wings, self-seeking Muslim leaders and 'secular' politicians since Independence have often resulted in political quibblings causing irreparable damage to the society and to national integration.

There are some historical and social reasons behind these issues but their politicisation has been largely responsible for the aloofness of Muslims from the national mainstream in the post colonial democratic polity. Dr. Asghar Ali Engineer mentioned in his article that Muslims are undoubtedly quite backward as very well brought out by Sachar Committee report[16] and blame does not lie with Muslims for their backwardness except in limited sense. It is more due to neglect of successive governments and it is as much responsibility of Government as that of Muslim leaders to pull them out of this backwardness.[17]

As we have learned from the above historical aspect of the Muslim Personal Law in India that it has been a vague and partially codified. There is strong need to rethink and reframe a new draft of Shariah and to place it for codification. Any law when thought about what is important is to understand its need. Why Muslim Personal Law in India need to be completely codified? The answer is the growing misuse of Islamic law perpetuating injustice and criminal offence especially with the women on the one hand and on the other codification will put check on the politicisation of the Muslim issues.

There are cases of oral triple divorce which are rampant and goes unreported as a result many women suffers the wrath of the Ulama and community if they confront such practice and those who don't confront and submit to such action are left destitute. In Bihar, just because wife of a person did not vote for the candidate of his choice in the Lok Sabha election he pronounced triple divorce and threw out his wife. Again just a few days ago, a husband came drunk in Bhadrak, Orissa, and had a tiff with his wife and pronounced talaq thrice but in the morning he realised his mistake and wanted to take back his wife but leaders of the Muslim community separated them insisting that it is irrevocable divorce and they cannot live together as husband and wife.[18] Recently we came across the news of couple being separated after a husband while chatting with his wife on skype from Kuwait jokingly pronounced divorce and it was declared valid. In another incident husband sent a mobile message mentioning divorce and it is also accepted and proclaimed valid and *fatawa* were issued by our learned Ulama.

Our Ulama accept and declare oral triple divorce as *Talaq-e-bid'at* (innovation in Islam which is '*Haram*') but ironically supports such un-Islamic practice out rightly. A sinful practice enforced in the name of divine law. Allow me to explain this form of divorce which has been popularly practiced by the Muslims in India and how it contradicts Quranic principles justice and compassion and Quranic form of Divorce.

The name *Talaq-e-bid'at,* which is translated in English as irregular *talaq.*[19] *Bid'at* means innovation or something new or something unprecedented. In *Mufradatul Quran* by Imam Raghib Isfahani *bid'at* means to admit an innovation in the religion which may not be traceable to any utterance or action of the Prophet Muhammad PBUH nor is proved from the earlier Muslim or from the (established) principles of Shariah. It is related that all innovation are bid'at and each bid'at or new thing is a deviation from truth and each deviation is in fire.[20] Thus, it is clear that any *bid'at* cannot be the *Sunnah* or the act of Prophet PBUH. Secondly, talaq-e-bid'at is irrevocable and it is accepted even if given during menstruation. If the husband addresses his wife that he has divorced her thrice, according to the Sunnah and the intention is that three divorces should take place at a time upon the instant pronouncements whether she be in her course or in *tuhr.*[21]

Though it is completely contradicting *Sunnah* but still in Hedaya it is said that it is a part of *Sunnah.* Ulama sanctions such Talaq even if pronounced in state of anger, intoxication, if one has dreamt about it and they have stretched it to illogical and un-Quranic approach. Does it comply with the Quranic Principle justice? The Quran is clear and pronounce the law on Divorce imperatively which render justice and benevolence. The women are not ignored in this law. They are given affirmative status and hence any such unilateral decision cannot be acceptable within the Islamic framework of legal system. The Quran says when there is a rift between husband and wife then both are free to appoint an arbitrator and every effort of reconciliation should be made and if the arbitrator fail in their effort then a divorce is pronounced in the presence of the two witnesses. The details of the Divorce as given in Quran will be discussed in the analysis chapter which will not only highlight the procedure of divorce but will expose the practice which is sanctioned under the name of Shariah completely negate Quran, which is one of the important and authentic source of Islamic law.

Another major issue in the Muslim community is the practice of Polygamy, i.e. having more than one wife and a man is permitted to have four wives according to Shariah. Firstly, Islam defines marriage as contract. It is a solemn and sacred social contract between bride and groom. This contract is a strong covenant *mithaqun ghalithun* as expressed in Quran[22]. The marriage contract in Islam is not a sacrament. It is revocable. Secondly, it is contract with consent of the partners i.e. bride and groom is must. Islam permits polygamy. Shariah has allowed four wives at a time and has enjoined equality in treatment of all wives. It should be remembered that polygamy is not a compulsory thing nor is it advocated. It is just permission with certain limitation and conditions. It is meant for maintaining the wives and upholding their rights. Dr Mrs Annie Besant, the renowned English leader of the Theosophical Movement wrote on this subject:

"There is pretended monogamy in the West, but there is real polygamy without responsibility. The mistress is cast off when the man is weary of her and she sinks gradually to be the woman of the street: for the first lover has no responsibility for her future: and she is hundred times worse off than a sheltered wife and the mother in the polygamous home. When we see thousands of miserable women, who crowd the streets of Western towns during the night, we must surely feel that it does not lie in Western mouths to reproach Islam for its polygamy. It is better for a woman, happier for a woman, more respectable for a woman to live in Islamic polygamy united to one man only with the legitimate child in her arms and surrounded with respect, than to be seduced, cast out in the streets perhaps with an illegitimate child, outside the pale of law, un-sheltered and uncared for, to become a victim of any passerby, night after night, rendered incapable of motherhood, despised by all."[23]

However, polygamy as in practice has major social disadvantage and it is not in conformity to the Quranic principle of justice. We have seen that many women loose their rights and are deserted by their husbands. Due to polygamy the family problems and marital disputes are multiplied and life of the first wife and children remains in uncertainties. The financial and psychological burden to maintain one or more wives results in gross inequality and injustice. In India, the economic status of Muslim is far from satisfactory. In most cases which occur among lower class Muslims often husband desert their first wife along with the children from the first marriage. There is no question of claiming maintenance from a husband who himself is not capable and earns a meager wage as a labourer. Though to check polygamy conditions are introduced and one of the major requirements after first wife's consent is whether husband can afford to maintain all the wives equally? Since this law remain uncodified it gives free hand to any Muslim men to acquire second wife whether he is fulfilling the require conditions or not. In Shariah law marrying four wives is permissible so it cannot declare other marriages as invalid. No doubt it is giving birth to another social challenge by creating a group of vulnerable women and children deprived of their rights to live with dignity.

I would also like to highlight the misuse of this practice by the non-Muslims in India. Many Hindu men who want to have another wife simply convert into Islam and perform Nikah to declare second marriage as legal and valid. In Hindu Law the Hindu marriage is not really a social contract but a religious sacrament. It results in a more or less permanent relationship between a man and woman. As marriage is said to be sacred it is irrevocable, other parties to the marriage can't dissolve it at will. Each is bound to the other until the death of either of them and the wife is supposed to be bound to her husband even after his death.[24] Concept of marriage, that it is, indissoluble, is a lofty one because it means that the husband and wife after marriage

age to adjust their tastes and temper their ideas and interest, instead of breaking with each other when they find that these differ.

Many Hindu men dodge the Bigamy law by to acquire another wife MORE than two decades ago, popular Bollywood stars Dharmendra and Hema Malini married secretly. Hindus could contract a second marriage only after the death of their first wife or divorce. Not otherwise. Only followers of Islam were allowed to have more than one wife. And for the sake of giving their union a legal cover, there are so many non-Muslim couples embrace Islam for e.g. Dharmendra and Hema Malini embraced Islam, a fact they hid from the public. A few years later, Bollywood stars Raj Babbar and the late Smita Patil also converted to Islam and got married. Again, it was second marriage for Raj and first for the vivacious actor, Smita.

Whether it was the growing tendency of people to exploit the Islamic marriage laws to contract second marriages or otherwise, the fact is that the Hindu marriage law was changed to allow close relations of the aggrieved wife to lodge a criminal complaint against her bigamous husband. However, after conversion to Islam, an already married man can still solemnise a second marriage. And the aggrieved wife cannot seek relief from the authorities. This is precisely what Haryana's deputy chief minister, Chander Mohan, did a few weeks ago. Son of the veteran Haryana politician, Bhajan Lal, he had gone missing from his ministerial office for over a month, causing media speculation about his whereabouts. One day, as suddenly as he had disappeared, he surfaced, only to announce to the whole world that he had married the state's high ranking law officer, Anuradha Bali. He had now embraced Islam and his name was Chand Mohammed. Therefore, it is definitely an issue to be seriously discussed and highlighted.

Polygamy is not for Hindus. It is banned by the law of the land. Second marriage, during the subsistence of the first marriage, is illegal in India and the relationship arising from the same does not have any validity. The second wives in India have little protection under the law. The social stigma attached with being a second wife, the absence of any legal status to the relationship, and the enormous pain of being cheated into the marriage are undoubtedly extremely depressing for a woman. Even though there is no recognition given to a second wife, due to the judicial interpretation of existing law as discussed above, she may have some chances of getting maintenance. In the absence of any clear provisions under the law, her chances of claiming her rights are largely dependent on the discretion of the judges. Even under the criminal law, it is extremely difficult to prove bigamy, as the marriage has to be validly performed to prove the offence of bigamy. Usually these loopholes in the law are exploited by men to defend themselves in such cases.

With the commencement of Hindu Marriage Act, 1955 (HMA), one of the condition provided for a valid marriage was that neither party should have a spouse living at the time of the marriage. Under the old law, there was a bar against a woman marrying a second husband while her first husband is alive unless custom permitted her. There was no such bar against men, till some States passed laws for prevention of bigamous marriages, and introduce the principle of monogamy among Hindus.

Interestingly, when it was found that an increasing number of Hindu men have been showing a propensity to convert to Islam whenever they wanted a second wife; the Indian Supreme Court plugged this legal loophole for all potential Hindu bigamists. In a historic ruling, on May 5, 2000, the apex court said that if it is found that a newly converted Muslim has embraced the faith only to embrace another wife or two, he should be prosecuted under the Hindu Marriage Act and the Indian Penal Code. Thus, bigamy for all Hindus was ultimately outlawed.[25]

There has been so far no direct legislative reform of Muslim Personal Law in India on the subject of polygamy.

Majority of Muslims don't register their marriage under Special Marriage Act which invokes monogamous union. Muslims solemnise their marriages in the classical religious form, mentioning the details of the bride and bridegroom in the Nikahnama's. These Nikahnama's are not registered in the court. However, they are valid under Shariah Application Act of 1937. Here there is more potential of acquiring polygamous marriage. Husbands may make arrangements for polygamy over which the wife has legally very little control unless she has put relevant stipulation into her marriage contract.

In the post-independence India, the much noted decision by Dhavan. J in *Itwari v. Asghari,* A.I.R . 1960 AI.684 went much beyond technical interpretations.[26] It defined the Muslim husband's unilateral action of taking another wife not only as inequitable treatment in Qur'anic terms but also as cruelty to the first wife for the purpose of the 1939 Act of Dissolution of Muslim Marriage Act. The *Itwari v. Asghari* was the husband's suits for restitution of conjugal rights against the first wife, who had refused to live with the husband after he had taken a second wife. The learned judge found that the Muslim law permits polygamy but does not encourage it, since the Quranic injunction showed that achieving perfect equality in the treatment of co-wives is practically impossible. It was held at page 686:

"....Muslim law as enforced in India has considered polygamy as an institution to be tolerated but not encouraged, and has not conferred upon the husband any fundamental right to compel the first wife to share his consortium with another woman in all circumstances. A Muslim husband has the legal right to take a second wife even while the first marriage subsists, but if he does so, and then seek the assistance of the civil court to compel the first wife to live with him against her wishes on pain of severe penalties including attachment of property, she is entitled to raise the question whether the court as a court of equity, ought to compel her to submit to co-inhabitation with such a husband.

In that case the circumstances in which his second marriage took place are relevant and material in deciding whether his conduct in taking a second wife was in itself an act of cruelty to the first."[27]

There is ample evidence in the legal history that various courts in India have taken a serious view of polygamous marriage. The Calcutta High Court in particular, took a strong stance against polygamous marriages and treated them from early on, as a 'continuing wrong' to the first wife.[28] In one of the case under the Kerala High Court, a Muslim wife had refused to live with her husband after he had married another woman and the husband had then failed to maintain her and the four children, so this was a criminal case regarding maintenance under Section 488 of the Criminal Procedure Code 1898, Justice Krishna Iyer J, refered during his course of judgment in strong terms to the duty of the Indian state to enforce maintenance provisions for women and children. Referring to a number of earlier cases which discussed the position of Muslim wives in a polygamous marriage and their entitlement to separate residence and maintenance the learned judge, in his usual forthright manner, doubted whether Muslim law actually permitted "multi-marriage".

Thus, in India what can be said by way of conclusion in the light of the above discussion is that there is still no agreement among Muslim scholars and intellectuals on the issue of reforms and codification in the existing Muslim law. The court is trying its best to render justice but many a times fails due to lack of codified rules in the personal laws. Unfortunately, sometimes court has to rely upon Fatwas which again is the most controversial instrument when it comes to its legality. There are several legal concepts in Islamic jurisprudence and its principles that can be brought into discussion concerning family law and keeping in view with the serious problems arising out of arbitrary practice of Islamic law. But the post-Independence era have yet not witnessed any initiative by the Islamic Fiqh experts and

State to reform existing Anglo-Mohammadan Law and introduce a complete codified Shariah law. Let us not skip the role of Muslim Personal Law Board in deterring any step towards reforms. The AIMPLB unfortunately the Ulama representing the Board is completely against any reform or codification. They resist any change in law and proclaim it is divine and unchangeable. The Law practiced in court is the enactment of the British authorities and hence the court has to use those enactments. The Ulama arouses the sentiment of the community by promoting Anglo-Mohammadan Law as divine law which is not true, as we have seen in the above mentioned history of Muslim law in India.

The next chapter deals with the evolution of Shariah law during its Islamic era and the formulation is not stopped but it is ongoing in many Muslim countries except few. The reforms and the law drafted under *zarurah* (necessities) by the Islamic jurist prove that law needs to be updated or changed under changing circumstances. The Quran sets down basic standards of human conduct, but does not provide a detailed law code. Only a few verses deal with legal matters. Prophet Muhammad PBUH helped clarify the law by interpreting provisions in the Quran and acting as a judge in legal cases. Islamic law, the Shariah, grew along with the expanding Muslim Empire. Following a period of revolts and civil war, the Umayyads were overthrown and replaced by the Abbasid dynasty. During the 500-year rule of the Abbasids, Shariah reached its full development. The process involved and the methodologies introduced during the formulation of Islamic law itself prove that it is not a complete divine law but has human efforts in the form of *Ijma* (consensus) and *Ijtihad* (reasoning) and as a result has undergone several changes in the past since its inception.

References

1. Sir Charles Fawcett, The first century of British justice in India. Oxford: Clarendon Press; London: Humphrey Milford. 1934. p. 267.
2. *Ibid*, p. 6.

3. David Pearl and Werner Men ski, Muslim Family Law, Brite Books, 1998, p. 37.
4. Derrett, On the litigiousness of South Asians, 1968, London: Faber & Faber, p. 286.
5. David Pearl and Werner Menski, Muslim Family Law, Brite Books, 1998, p. 38.
6. *Ibid.,* p. 39.
7. The Kazi Act 1880, Report No. 86 (3), www.ljcp.gov.pk
8. David Pearl and Werner Menski, Muslim Family Law, Brite Books, 1998, p. 39.
9. Perry's Oriental Cases 110, Hirbae and others vs Sonabae (1847), Cases illustrative of Oriental Life and the Application of English law in to India (1853), p. 110.
10. *Ibid,* p. 111.
11. Perry's Oriental Cases 110, Hirbae and others vs Sonabae (1847), Cases illustrative of Oriental Life and the Application of English law in to India (1853), p. 110.
12. www.lawsinindia.com
13. Muslim Personal Law Shariat Kerala Amendment Act 1963 , www.lawsinindia.com
14. *Ibid.*
15. David Pearl and Werner Menski, Muslim Family Law, Brite Books, 1998, p. 40.
16. The Rajinder Sachar Committee, appointed by the Prime Minister Manmohan Singh of India, was a high level committee for preparation of a report on the social, economic and educational status of the Muslim community of India.
17. Dr. Asghar Ali Engineer, Mainstreaming Minorities, Secular Perspective, February 16-28, 2007 published by CSSS, Mumbai.
18. Dr. Asghar Ali Engineer, Tripple Divorce- Need for Change, Secular Perspective, June 16-30, 2004 published by CSSS, Mumbai.
19. Thomas Patrick Hughes, Dictionary of Islam, London, W.H. Allen and Co,1895, pp. 87.
20. Imam Raghib Isfahani, *Mufradatul Quran*, (Urdu Translation) by Sheikhul Hadiths Moulana Abduh Ferozpuri, Ahl-e-Hadith, Lahore, 1971.
21. Hamilton Charles, Hedaya or Guide, Premier Book House, 1963, pp. 75.
22. The Holy Quran; Chapter 4- An Nisa: Verse: 21.

23. Annie Besant, The Life and Teachings of Muhammad, Madras, 1932, p. 3.
24. www.sociologyguide.com
25. http://supremecourtofindia.nic.in/
26. David Pearl and Werner Menski, Muslim Family Law, Brite Books, 1998, p. 249.
27. *Ibid;* Key passage from the judgment are reproduced in Hodkinson (1984), pp. 172-182.
28. David Pearl and Werner Menski, Muslim Family Law, Brite Books, 1998, p. 251.

1

Evolution of Shariah Law

Definition of Fiqh

The science of Source Methodology in Islamic Jurisprudence *Usul al Fiqh* has been defined as the aggregate, of legal proofs and evidence that, when studied properly, will lead either to certain knowledge of a Shari'ah ruling.[1] As its subject matter, this science deals with the proofs in the Shari'ah source-texts, viewing them from the perspective of how, by means of Ijtihad, legal judgments are derived from their particulars; though after, in cases where texts may appear mutually contradictory, preference has been established.[2]

The science of *Usul al Fiqh* is in fact an independent and autonomous field. It is, however, based on certain fundamental predications *muqaddamat*, knowledge of which the Islamic legal scholar cannot do without. These predications have been derived from several other disciplines:

(a) Some are derived from the science of Aristotelian logic which the philosopher-theologian writers' *mutakallimun (Academic discussions)* had discussed in the introductions to their works. These academic discussions dealt, for example, with the ways in which words convey meanings, the division of subjects into present and predicable. The need for, and varieties of, discourse depending on conceptual principles taken from interpretations and definitions. And how inductive reasoning done and its validity. Also several discussions about evidence and how it may be used to prove the claims of the one who is adducing it, or to refute contradictions, and so on.

(b) Some are derived from *Ilm al Kalam* (Scholastic Theology), and include discussions of such questions as the nature of the Sovereign *Hakim*. In the sense whether it is the Shari'ah itself or reason which decides what is right and what is wrong; or whether one can have knowledge of right and wrong before revelation. Or whether rendering thanks to the Bounteous Creator is a duty derived from the Shari'ah or from human reasoning.

(c) Some are general linguistic rules which the scholars of *al Usul* developed through linguistic research and presented in a crystallised form. For example, research dealing with languages and their origins, the classification of words into metaphorical and literal, discussions of etymology, synonymy, emphasis, generalisation, specification, and the meanings of grammatical particles and so on.

(d) Some are derived from the classical sciences of the Qur'an and the Sunnah. Like discussions concerning the transmission of Hadith by a single narrator *Ahad*, or by an impeccable plurality of narrators *Tawatur*. The non-standard recitations of the Qur'an. The criteria for the *Ta'dil* (acceptance) or *Jarh* (rejection) of narrators of Hadith, abrogation of legislation *al Nasikh wa al Mansukh,* the condition of the text of a Hadith and its chain of narrators, and so on.[3]

(e) Finally, the examples cited by the scholars of *al Usul* in illustration of their arguments are derived from the specifics of Fiqh, and from the detailed evidence for the same as taken from the Qur'an and the Sunnah.

The issues with which the scholars of *al Usul* are primarily concerned include the following:

- o Logic and its predications
- o Linguistics
- o Commands and Prohibitions
- o Comprehensive *al 'Amm* and particular terms *al Khass*
- o Inconclusive *al Mujmall* and Determined concepts *al Mubayyan*
- o Abrogation *al Naskh*
- o Deeds (in particular, those of the Prophet, upon whom be peace, and their significance)
- o Consensus *al Ijma'*
- o Narrations relating to the Sunnan
- o Analogical reasoning *al Qiyas*
- o Indicating preference in cases of apparent contradiction
- o Exercising legal acumen and scholarship Ijtihad
- o Following a specific school of legal thought *Taqlid*
- o Disputed Sources (those other than the four "agreed" sources).[4]

Origins and Development of Usul Al Fiqh

It is difficult to attempt a study of *Usul al Fiqh* and its development without considering the history of Fiqh, the practical precepts of Shari'ah that have been derived from detailed source-evidence.

The lexical meaning of Usul is foundation, or basis *Asl*; plural *Usul* or that upon which something else is built. In the legal system of Islam, Fiqh is built upon and stems from the bases *Usul* which constitute its source-evidence. Hence, in order to understand the origins of *Usul al Fiqh*, we need to have a general idea of the history of Islamic legislation *Tashri'*.

Quran has provided articulate proofs and clear source-evidence in order that the believers should have no trouble in finding their way to the particulars of His legislation, or *Ahkam*. with reference to some of this source-evidence, the Islamic Ummah (Muslims) has agreed on its validity and its relevance to the *Ahkam*, and has accepted it as such. However, there are differences with regard to other source-evidence.[5]

The source-evidence upon which the Muslims fully agrees, and on the validity of which there is general consensus, comprises the two sources that formed the basis of legislation at the time of the Prophet PBUH. These two sources of legislation are:

1. The Qur'an: This may be defined as the words revealed to the Prophet PBUH the recitation of which itself constitutes an act of worship, the shortest *Surah* of which is a challenge to mankind to produce anything the like thereof, every letter of which has been transmitted to us via an indisputably authentic chain of authority *Tawatur*; which is written between the two covers of the Holy Book *Mushaf* beginning with *Surat al Fatihah* "The Opening Chapter" and ending with the *Surat al Nas*.

2. The Sunnah: This includes everything, other than the Qur'an, which has been transmitted from the Prophet PBUH; what he said, did, and agreed to.

Thus, every utterance of the Prophet PBUH, apart from the Qur'an, and his every deed, from the beginning of his mission to the last moment of his life, constitute his Sunnah. In the general sense whether these establish a ruling which is generally applicable to all Muslims, or a ruling which applies only to the Prophet PBUH himself or to some of his *Sahaabah (Prophet's Companion)*.

During the lifetime of the Prophet PBUH, all the legal rulings, such as principal and derived rulings, teachings on the fundaments of the faith, and regulations regarding personal practice and legalities, were derived from these two sources, the Qur'an and the Sunnah.

3. Ijtihad was practiced by the Prophet PBUH and by those of his companions with legal proclivities *Ahl al Nazar*. The Prophet's Ijtihad was sometimes confirmed by the Qur'an and sometimes not; in which case it was explained that the better solution was other than that which he had adopted.

The Ijtihad made by the Companions was always in response to situations which actually occurred to them. Later, when they met the Prophet PBUH, they would explain what happened and tell him what they had decided. Sometimes he PBUH approved of their Ijtihad, and such decisions of theirs (having gained the approval of the Prophet) became a part of the Sunnah. If he PBUH disapproved of their Ijtihad, his explanation of the correct procedure would become the Sunnah.[6]

Thus, we can say that at that stage legislation depended on the two forms of Divine revelation *Wahi*:

1. Recited revelation *Wahi Matlu*; or the Qur'an with its absolute inimitability *I'jaz*.
2. Non-recited revelation *Wahi Ghair Matlu*; or the Sunnah of the Prophet PBUH.

Indeed, the Ijtihad made by the Prophet PBUH set a precedent for his *Sahaabah* and later Muslims, that clearly proved the legitimacy of Ijtihad, so that when they could not find an express legal ruling in the Qur'an or Sunnah, they were to make use of Ijtihad in order to arrive at a judgments on their own.[7]

Moreover; probably to reinforce and establish this concept, the Prophet PBUH used to order certain of his Companions to make Ijtihad concerning certain matters in his presence. Then he would tell them who was correct and who was mistaken.

The First Stage: Foundation (609 – 632 AD)

The first stage in the development covers the era of the Prophet Muhammad ibn'Abdullah's apostleship during which the only source of Islamic law was divine revelation in the form of either Quran or Sunnah, the saying and action of the Prophet PBUH. The Quran represented the blueprint in his day-to-day life, acted as a detailed explanation of the general principles outlined in the Quran as well as a practical demonstration of their application.

Sections of the holy Quran were continuously revealed to the Prophet PBUH from the beginning of his prophethood in the year 609 AD until shortly before his death in 632 AD, a period of approximately twenty three years. The various sections of the Quran were generally revealed to solve the problems which confronted the Prophet PBUH and his followers in Mecca and Madina. A number of Quranic verses are direct answers to questions raised by Muslims as well as non-Muslims during the era of Prophethood. Many of these verses actually begin with the phrase for example "They ask you about wine and gambling, say, there are great evil in them as well as benefit to man. But the evil is greater than the benefit."[8]

A number of other verses were revealed due to particular incidents which took place during the era of Prophet PBUH. There were verses related to marriages, Dower (Mehr), property rights and inheritance etc. Some of these contextual verses were revealed to resolve the problems during that period. For example, in case of Hilal ibn Umayyah who came before the Prophet PBUH and accused his wife of adultery with another of the Prophet's companions. The Prophet PBUH replied "Either you will receive the fixed punishment of eighty lashes on your back." Hilal said, "Oh Messenger of Allah! If any of us saw a man on top of his wife, would he go looking for witnesses?" However, the Prophet repeated his demand for proof and this verse was revealed which says, "As for those who accuse their wives and have no evidence but their own, their witness can be four declaration with oath by Allah and they are truthful and a fifth invoking Allah's curse on themselves if they are lying. But the punishments will be averted from the wife if she bears witness four times with oath by Allah that he is lying and a fifth oath invoking Allah's curse on herself if he is telling the truth".[9]

Meccan and Madinan revelations contain wide-ranging themes and diverse styles on theological and sociological topics. The Qur'an took the unusual step of presenting to the Arab pagans the idea of an afterlife in which there would be consequences for moral transgressions during one's life. Thus, even if one could get away with an action there was now an ultimate moral authority to which one would have to answer.

This ultimate authority, God, is presented as the Creator (87:2, 95:4, 96:1-2), a being of infinitely more power than even the greatest earthly strongman (86:10, 96:17-18). It is He who taught mankind all that they know (96:5) and He that will hold them accountable (82:13-15, 83:5-6, 99:7-8).[10] Thus, Quran checked the action by bringing transcending values to stop any unjust and immoral practices.

The Meccan surahs address a number of social injustices which stemmed from the Meccan socio-economic structure. Sociologically there were (allegedly) few protections in pre-Islamic Arab society for the poor or for orphans, widows, or those without a clan. In addition, it would seem that ethical standards of trade (presumably with people of tribes other than one's own) were lacking. These issues are addressed with admonitions to do what is right, or face the consequences on the coming Day of Judgment.

Perhaps one of the best known and most striking examples of these passages comes in chapter 81 with the words "When the seas are boiled over; when the souls are coupled, when the girl-child buried alive is asked what she did to deserve murder."[11] (81:6-9) This poignant passage directly attack the practice of female infanticide, not by outlawing it per se, but by pointing out how on the Day of Judgment God Himself will be there to inquire why such an abomination happened, and what justification could possibly be given.[12]

Other misdeeds are addressed in chapter 83, verses 1-6 where mercantile fraud is criticised. 89:17-19 address those who treat the poor and orphans poorly, and those who consume inheritances illegitimately.[13] This is contrasted in 90:13-16 when those who treat slaves, orphans, the poor, and strangers well are lauded. These verses pass judgment, but it was not until Muhammad reached Medina that the verses took on the tone of law.

The Madinese surahs were revealed at a time when Muhammad was no longer preaching to unbelieving pagans, but to a community of Muslims, Christians, and Jews. This change in audience is reflected by the change in style and focus of the surahs.

Where the Meccan surahs contain moral and social guidance, the Madinese surahs often take on a new tone of secular authority. Verse 4:26[14] makes this clear, that these revelations are being given by God to the Muslims as Law, not merely for guidance. Muhammad is now defining Muslim society and dictating new social norms.

Social law is largely distinguished in the surahs by its specificity. If/then statements are periodically used to outline crimes and appropriate social responses (4:15-16, 25, 89, 92, etc.), this style is mirrored in the 'legal dictates' of heaven, for in 4:31 and 4:93 the same if/then style is used to describe God's response to mankind's actions. This if/then is a classic system of legal description and can be found in the earliest Mesopotamian law codes.

In verses where a set social response to a broken dictate is not given then the if/then structure is not used and the dictate is set forth as an unequivocal command. This contrasts with verses where quantifiers are given, lessening the force of a dictate from law to guideline. Verses 4:34 and 4:36 illustrate this well. "Husbands should take good care of their wives..." vs. "Worship God, join nothing with Him..."

These guideline verses are used where it would be nearly impossible to quantify each component part of the actions desired from the faithful. While directing the singular worship of God can be accomplished succinctly, a ruling on every single circumstance in husband/wife relations is more easily summed up with the guidance to "take good care."

As indicated in verse 36, chapter 4 discusses the nature and expression of the Muslim faith at great length. Like the social law/guideline distinction there are both religious laws and religious guidelines laid down in this chapter.

Chapter four, Verses 101 and 102 are interesting in this regard for they take both forms. Verse 101 addresses the shortening of prayers in dangerous country in general. Verse 102 gives very specific guidelines for how an armed group should behave when praying while under arms in dangerous circumstances. Along with practical matters regarding the methods of worship, theological principles are also addressed in chapter four.

Verse 136 reads: "You who believe, believe in God and in His Messenger and in the Scripture He sent down to His Messenger, as well as what He sent down before." This is one of the most explicit statements in the chapter regarding religious doctrine; it is presented as an irrefutable principle of the Muslim faith. Other sections are also presented as absolute, but address the nature of God or his relationship to his believers (4:16, 24, 132, etc).[15]

The verses of Mecca and Medina broadly discuss similar topics. Morality, social order, the nature of God, the afterlife, and mankind's relationship to the Divine are all discussed at length throughout the Qur'an. However, it is the tone, style, and emphasis of the surahs that changed from Mecca to Medina.

The Meccan surahs were intended to set the groundwork, explaining the nature of God and the concept of an afterlife primarily to pagans. This was then tied to messages of social justice and correct behaviour – and it warns the people of the consequences for those who turned their backs on those messages.

In Medina, the Judgment continues not as a major theme, but as a reminder constantly tied to the other directives being revealed. In Medina, social order was largely presented as law and as binding guidelines, moral and religious directives were similarly meted out. These later surahs tend to the precise and legalistic when compared to earlier passages, as befitting the changing role of the revealed Word in Muslim society.[16]

Let's understand the basis of legislation in the Qura'an. Quran itself announces that it was revealed to reform human conditions. Islam did not erase all pre-Islamic customs and practices. Instead, it removed every facet of corruption and abolished all those customs which were harmful to the society. Like for example, Islam forbid interest on financial or monetary deals because it takes unfair advantage of the less fortunate member of the society. Fornication was forbidden due to its exploitation of women and the destruction of family bond. Use of alcohol prohibited because of the physical, psychological and spiritual damage which it inflicts on both the individual and society as a whole. Trade practices were reformed by making the basis of trade mutual consent and by disallowing all deceptive business transactions. The existing system of marriage was organised by confirming certain forms and prohibiting others. The basis of divorce was also recognised; but its pronouncements were limited and restricted. Islam with new moral and customs which served as law in its initial phase looked at everything from the perspective of human welfare. The verse which says, "It commands them to do righteousness and prohibit them from evil, and it makes allowable to them the good things and makes forbidden to them all, filth."[17]

The goal of Islamic legal is to reform and not merely control and governed. Some of the practices were inherited from earlier generations and a good example of this is Hajj which was instituted by Prophet Abraham and Ismail. Islamic principles do not contradict human reason; instead they free the human intellect from irrationality. In order to achieve its goal of reformation, it has enacted a series of legal commandments and prohibitions, which makes up the rules of conduct. Islamic laws are designed to facilitate mankind's individual and societal needs.

The Prophet PBUH discouraged unnecessary questions. He would response to repeated questions concerning whether Hajj is compulsory every year. He said, "If I said yes, it would have become compulsory. Leave me alone concerning things which I have left up to you, for certainly those before you were destroyed because of their many unnecessary questions and their arguments and disagreements with their Prophet."[18]

Some verse in Quran gives principles and not a detailed law as such. For example, the Qur'anic command for business transactions. The law in this regards is not a detailed and comprehensive law but it has set up a principle which will be suitable and relevant in all circumstances at any given period of time. The verse in the Quran says "Oh you, who believe, fulfill your contracts."[19] And another verse says, "Allah has made trade lawful and prohibited interest."[20]

In dealing with direct laws from the Quran one should also note an important point that some verses in Quran are termed as *Naskh* (Abrogation). Quran may prescribe a law suitable to people at the time of its enactment, or it may serve a particular limited purpose. However, its suitability and relevance may not be there later or its unique purpose may have been achieved in such circumstances the need for such law ceases to exist and it is no more valid. However, the *Naskh* verse if finds its relevance in contemporary issues then it will be endorsed and consider as valid.

There is great theological debate on the concept of *Naskh* and *Mansookh*. *Naskh* is an Arabic word meaning cancellation and *Mansookh* means cancelled. Quran talks about '*Naskh*' at few places, "When we substitute one revelation for another, - and Allah knows best what He reveals (in stages), - they say, "Thou art but a forger": but most of them understand not."[21] "None of Our revelations do we abrogate or cause to be forgotten, but we substitute something better or similar: Knowest thou not that Allah Hath power over all things?"[22]

Naskh-ul-hukm (meaning the verse was kept but the ruling was canceled) there are many instances in Quran, where a certain ruling was revealed in steps, each order upgrading (and sometimes canceling) previous one. For instance, one can see in these two verses Surah Al-Anfal verse number 65 and 66. The commentary by Moulana Mohammad Ali throws light on how these verses comes under abrogate verse. The commentary, on verse number 65 which says, "Oh Prophet urge the believer to fight. If there be of you twenty steadfast, they shall overcome two hundred; and if there be of you a thousand of those who disbelieve, because they are a people who do not understand", explains that it should be noted that the war to which Muslims were to be urged was the defensive war which the Muslim had to fight to save themselves and to protect the religion of Islam.[23] The Muslims were few as compared with their enemies and there was not even one Muslim to ten thousand disbelievers. Thus, there is a clear prophecy here that, notwithstanding their fewer numbers, the Muslim shall be victorious. After the battle of Badr came the battle of Uhud, in which the Muslim were less than 1 to 4 against the enemy; this was followed by battle of Ahzab, in which they were 1 to 10, yet the enemy was routed.

The following verse "Now Allah has lighted your burden and he knows that there is weakness in you. So if there be of you a hundred steadfast, they shall overcome two hundred; and if there be of you thousand, they shall overcome two thousand by Allah's permission. And Allah is with the steadfast." This verse suppose by some to abrogate the previous verse, where it is stated that twenty patient Muslim shall overcome two hundred disbelievers. This is very incorrect view according to Moulana Mohammad Ali. He explains firstly, because only an injunction could be said to be abrogate and not a statement. Secondly, because the two statements relate to two different states of the Muslims. At the time of the battle of Badr there was no Muslim army in existence. Every man available, young or old, sick or healthy had to fight to save the life of the community. They had very few arms, and they had never been trained. This is referred to in the words: "he knows that there is weakness in you." So the Muslim forces as then constituted could at most be a match for double their numbers. But a time did come when they were a match for ten times their numbers. So both the statements in the Quran proved true. But even if the words may be taken as an injunction to the Muslims to overcome twice and afterwards ten times their numbers, there is no question of abrogation. There are two commandments, one in accordance with the circumstances of the Muslim society as it was then, another in accordance with a future state when they would be well armed.[24]

Abrogation contained in it consideration for human conditions and their welfare during the era of the Prophet-hood which ended with the death of the Prophet PBUH for there can be no abrogation after his time. Legislative consideration of human welfare after the era of the Prophet PBUH can be found in the fact that Islamic laws were enacted for reasons, many of which were clearly mentioned. The Prophet Muhammad PBUH also made mention of the rationale behind his legal pronouncements. The explanation of the reasons for laws depends on the existence or non-existence of their causes. If the benefit for which the law was formulated and enacted is continuous then the law is continuous. But if it is no more valid or relevant due to changing circumstances then the law too must change and enact a new law which will be relevant. The laws related to marriage, divorce, inheritance, adultery, theft, slander etc whose effect on the society or it will promote the social stability and peace, as for things whose benefit and harm varies from place to place and from time to time then there is universal principle proclaimed in Quran which is justice, benevolence, compassion and wisdom. The law can be formulated and enacted keeping these principles in mind by the authorities and also the very crucial aspect of the law is does it will provide solution to the existing problems.

Prophet Muhammad PBUH himself practiced deduced ruling following a general Quranic principles. In case of a marriage to a woman and her maternal aunt. The Quran forbid marrying a woman and her daughter or simultaneous marriage of two sisters with the same man. The verse says, "Except for these, all other are lawful...."[25] The Prophet PBUH further informed his followers that even in the case of legal judgments with regard to disputes brought before him, he could unintentionally rule incorrectly, as some of the decisions were based on his own opinion. Umm Salaam reported that Prophet PBUH said, "I am only a human being, and you bring disputes to me. Perhaps some of you are more eloquent in their plea than others, and I judge in their favour according to what I hear from them. So whatever I rule in anyone's favour which belongs to his brother, he should not take any of it, because I have only granted him a piece of hell."[26] Such decisions based on personal reasoning represented training for companions of the Prophet PBUH in the methodology of application of the Shariah. It taught them that a judge is not held responsible if he makes a mistake in judgment due to factors beyond his control. And in order to further emphasise this important point, the Prophet PBUH also said, "There are three types of judges; one who will go to paradise and two who will go to hell. The one in paradise is the man who knows the truth and judges according to it. The man who knows the truth and is unjust in his judgment will be in hell. And the man without knowledge who makes the judgments for people will also go to hell."[27] Prophet PBUH encouraged his companions to prepare themselves to carry out rulings using reasons. The process of arriving at reasoned decisions themselves are referred to as *Ijtihad*. As has been seen that both Prophet PBUH and his companions practiced Ijtihad during this stage in the development of the Islamic law.

During this stage the Shariah consisted of laws revealed and recorded in Quran and the Sunnah. The bulk of Quranic matter consists mainly of broad, general moral directives as to what the aims and aspirations of Muslims should be, the 'ought' of the Islamic religious ethic. They relate mainly to the ideological foundation of Islam, faith and the socio-economic laws necessary for the organisation of the fledgling Muslim state.

II. The Second Stage: Establishment

This stage represents the era of the righteous Caliphs[28] and the important Sahabaah (Companions of the Prophet PBUH). It extends from Caliphate of Abu Bakr (632-634 CE) to the Islamic State which rapidly expanded during the first twenty years of this stage to include Syria, Jordan, Egypt, Iraq and Persia. Thus, Muslims were exposed to completely new social systems having diverse cultures and pattern of behaviours for which specific provisions were not found in then Shariah. Therefore do deal with the numerous new problems, the Righteous Caliphs relied heavily on decisions by consensus (Ijma) as well as *Ijtihaad*. In course of their extensive use of Ijma and Ijtihaad, these Caliphs established procedures which later became the basis for legislation in Islam that is Fiqh.

In this portion we shall examine in detail the problem solving legal apparatus developed by the Righteous Caliphs and the general approached used by individual Sahabaah in making deductions. Here in this section we will also highlight why there was no faction developed during this period of Caliphate and also what were the characteristics of Fiqh during this period.

Legal Apparatus of the Righteous Caliphs

Faced with new problems due to incoming diverse socio-cultural setup the caliphs took the following steps to resolve the issues.

1. The Caliph would initially search for specific ruling in the Qur'an.
2. If he is unable to find any rulings then he would search in Sunnah. It is a primary source of law taken from the sayings, actions and approvals of the Prophet Muhammad.
3. The third step was to look for *Qiyas* i.e. analogy. "*Qiyas* meant to seek similarity between new situations and early practices, especially those of the Prophet. The function of *Qiyas* is to discover the cause or *illah* of the revealed law so as to extend it to similar cases. Wine drinking, for example, is prohibited by explicit text. The cause for the prohibition is the intoxicating effect, hence in whatever this cause is found prohibition will become applicable."[29] *Qiyas* is "part of Islamic Law... that which subject to modification according to the need and requirements of the changing times and it is this part of the Islamic Law which endows it with wide possibilities of growth and advancement and makes it fully capable of fulfilling all the needs of an expanding human society in every age.

   There is a close relationship between *ijma'* and *Qiyas* though. *Ijtihad* is what makes Islamic jurisprudence dynamic, and *Qiyas* brought some discipline to the applied human reasoning to determine what is Islamically acceptable and what is not for things or situations that are not already covered by the other three sources. However, for the result of a *qiyas* to be broadly accepted, it also had to be validated by *ijma'*. If validated, most Muslim scholars have placed high value on *qiyas* as a methodology.
4. If he still did not find the answer in Sunnah then he would convene a meeting of the major Sahabaah (Companions) and try to generate a unanimous opinion or solutions. This is unanimity is known as *Ijma* which means consensus. *'IJMA'* means consensus,

that is, acceptance of a matter by a specified group of people. This concept implies on critical issues if there is consensus of community then it will become an integral part of the Islamic Shariah. When the great jurists agrees unanimously on an issue then it is known as *Ijma-i-haqiqi* and when the few jurists agrees with each other and other remains silent then it is called *Ijma-i-sukuti* (Silent Consensus).[30] Also it is important to note that *ijma* is merely a tertiary source and it can not be equated with the Qur'an or Sunnah. Allahmah Shaukani points out in his book *Irshad-al-fuhul* that *ijma* cannot stand by itself. It must be based on the Qur'an and *Sunnah*. Similarly Allamah Ibn Hazm also points out in his book *Kitab al- Ahkam* that *Ijma* has to be based on what can be established from the Quran and *Sunnah*.[31] Thus, *ijma* itself cannot assume central significance but it does not mean that it has no role to play. If intelligently and creatively used it can play a very significant role in modern Islamic legislation.

5. However, the difference is so great that an overwhelming majority opinion could be determined, the Caliph would make his own Ijtihad. *Ijtihad* means to derive and deduce religious opinion about some matter that is not mentioned in the sources of Islam, keeping in view the spirit and overall framework of Islam. In other words, the area of *Ijtihad* is the area in which Islam is silent and one must use one's common sense, intellect and experience to arrive at an opinion that should be in conformity with the spirit of Islam. The Ijtihad made would then become a Law.

In addition to formal meetings of the major Sahabaah which were summoned by the Caliphs for decision-making there arose many day-to-day situations where individual Sahabaah were needed to make rulings. In such cases the tend to follow three general course of actions.

In the first place, Sahabaah who were in decision-making positions made it clear that their deductions were not necessarily a divine intention. For example, when Ibn Mas'ood was questioned about the inheritance rights of a woman who had been married without a defined *Mehr*, he said, "I am giving my opinion about her. If it is correct, then it is from Allah, but if it is incorrect, then it is from me and Satan." [32]

Secondly, if they made different rulings on a problem in their individual capacities and were later informed of an authentic Hadiths on the subject, they would immediately accept it dropping all the differences.

Finally, when neither authentic proof nor unanimity could be arrived at, the companions of the Prophet PBUH used to respect the opinion of each other and would not force other Sahabaah to follow any individual opinion. The only exception to this rule was if they found people following practices, which though formerly acceptable later became prohibited. For example Mut'ah, a pre-Islamic form of temporary marriage which was allowed during the early Islamic period was forbidden by the time of Prophet's PBUH death. Some of the Sahabaah were unaware of the prohibition and thus continued to practice temporary marriage during Abu Bakr's caliphate and the first half of 'Umar's caliphate. When 'Umar became aware of the practice of Mut'ah, he forbade it and prescribed severe punishment for the offence.[33]

The Absence of Factionalism

Although the Sahabaah debated and differed on various points of law, their differences rarely reached the level of disunity and factionalism, which characterised later periods. This was due to following positive approach of the Sahabaah towards each other.

1. The Caliph's reliance on mutual consultation (Shur'aa) to arrive at ruling.
2. The ease with which a consensus could be arrived at. It was easy to hold consultative meetings since the

early Caliphs did not allow the Sahabaah to move far from the capital of the Islamic State, Madina.

3. The general reluctance of the individual Sahabaah to make legal rulings (Fataawas). Instead, they tended to re-direct puzzling questions to other Sahabaah who were better qualified to answer them.
4. The infrequent quotation of Hadith, which they used only for specific and actual problems. This was due to their fear of misquoting the Prophet PBUH who said "whoever tells a lie in my name will find his seat in the fire."[34] The fact that caliph 'Umar ibn-al-Khattab forbade excessive quotation of Ahadith and ordered Sahabaah to concentrate on the narration and the study of the Qur'an.

Characteristics of Fiqh during this Period

The historical development of Fiqh showed different characteristics trends during different period of political, socio-economic development. During the period of righteous Caliphs, the Fiqh was known to be realism; that is, it was based on actual problems rather than on hypothetical or imaginary ones. This realistic form of Fiqh was later referred to in Arabic as *al-Fiqh al-Waqi'ee* (realistic Fiqh) to distinguish it from the hypothetical Fiqh known as Ahl-ar- Ra'i which came to prominence in Kufah, Iraq, during the time of the Umayyads.

Secondly, the Righteous Caliphs as we learned above did not follow a certain procedures to achieve legal rulings, neither they nor the Sahabaah as a whole prescribed set of procedures to be followed throughout the Islamic nation nor did they make a record of the laws resulting from their legal rulings. This itself reflects in the first place that Sahabaah's respect for freedom of opinion in such matters. Such an attitude contrasts strongly with the appearance of rigidity on the part of certain later scholars. Also one should note the Sahabaah's policy of recommending for the masses the careful study of the Qur'an without the distraction of legal ruling son matter not defines therein.

The third characteristics of Fiqh in this period relate to the use of personal opinion in making legal rulings. The majority of the Sahabaah preferred to stick closely to the literal meanings of texts of the Qur'an and the Sunnah. As a general practice they avoided giving personal interpretations. However, there were other Sahabaah's who favoured the wide use of personal opinion in areas undefined either by the Qur'an or the Sunnah. But they were careful in attributing the error entirely on themselves, so as not to bring discredit to Islamic law.

The most important among the Fiqh's characteristics is during the period of the Righteous Caliphs, they were concerned with the modification of Shariah owing to one or the other factors e.g. the disappearance of the reasons of the existing laws and the changing social conditions. The changing social conditions due to tremendous influx of wealth from newly acquired territories, marriage both single and multiple became easier to contract and consequently, divorce became alarmingly more frequent. To discourage abuse of Divorce, Caliph Umar altered an aspect of law on Divorce. During Prophet PBUH period the pronouncement of three divorce at one go was considered to be merely a single divorce and it was reversible. Caliph Umar declared such pronouncements to be binding and therefore irreversible. The Madh-hab[35] during the period of the Righteous Caliph was unified and directly linked to the state as in the time of Prophet PBUH. The Madh-hab under each of the Caliphs was that of the Caliph himself since the Caliph in each has the final say in all legal decisions involving Ijtihaad. Consequently, the deduced rulings made by Caliph were never openly opposed by his successors during his lifetime. However, when the succeeding Caliph came to power, his Madh-hab would then be of his predecessor and the deduced rulings of the predecessor would be changed to conform to his opinion.

The Third Stage: Building

This stage covers the rise and fall of Umayyad dynasty. The Umayyad were in power or approximately one century extending from the death of the last Righteous Caliphs Ali ibn Taalib in 661 AD (Christian Era) and the ascendancy of the Founder of the Umayyad dynasty, so called Caliph Mu'aawiyah ibn Abu Sufiyan until the last of the Umayyad ruler around the middle of the eighth century CE.

The period was marked by great social unrest; the Ummah was divided into various sects and factions; the Caliphate was converted into a kingship. Many new practices were introduced some of which were Haraam or prohibited in Islam. The scholars refused to sit in the audiences of the caliphs and in fact fled to outlying areas to avid conflict and confusion.[36]

So far as Islamic Law and the evolution of Madh-habs are concerned, this period is noteworthy of three trends. In the first place there is a notable increase in the number of *Ijtihaads* given by scholars, since Ijma'a became more and more difficult following the exile of the scholars to the other regions which is not ruled by the Caliphate. Secondly, the narration of Hadiths became widespread and there developed an increasing tendency towards fabrication of hadiths. Finally, the third period was marked as an attempt to compile the Fiqh, i.e. jurisprudence, which was aimed at preserving the *Ijtihaad* of the Sahabaah. It was in this period too the scholars of Islamic Law first got divided into the fairly clear cut Schools of Thoughts, establishing various Madhhabs which in later period reduced to four major schools.

In the history of Fiqh and the evolution of Madh-habs, this period is of great significance. The socio-political and religious changes that took place is as follows.

Division of Ummah

The first quarter of the Century of this period witnessed a number of devastating sociopolitical blows which caused a number of sects and faction to appear. The most serious were those caused by the rebellions of the Khawaarij[37], the Shiah and the Abdullah ibn az- Zubair and his followers. The constant vying of these groups for the power resulted in general state of turmoil.

The first two factions, the Khawarij and the Shi'ah later evolved into religious sects which developed their own particular system of Fiqh. Relying on unorthodox interpretations of the Qur'an and Sunnah which suited their own socio-political views, they rejected the contributions of most of the Sahabaah and the Righteous Caliphs, declaring them to be apostates, and elevated their own leading figures to the rank of law makers.[38]

Deviation of the Umayyad Caliphs

The Umayyad Caliphs introduced a number of practices which were common in the non-Islamic states of that time, such as Byzantine, Persia and India. Many of these practices were in clear contradiction to the Fiqh of the earlier period. For example, the Central treasury, the Bayt al-maal, was turned into the personal property of the caliph and their families and taxation which was prohibited in Islam was introduced to further increase their fortune. Astrologers, magicians, courtesans were officially introduced as a form of amusement in the court of caliph. Further more the setback received to the Islamic political system was the forced acceptance of Yazeed as crown prince imposed by Caliph Mu'aawiyah in the year 679 AD, the office of caliph was converted into that of hereditary kingship. Hence the state Fiqh link was broken and a significant unifying factor of the Madh-habs was thereby lost. Due to these reasons the Islamic Scholars (Ulema) of this period avoided sitting in the audiences of the caliphs and thus the principle of Shura'a (Consultative Governance) was lost. With each successive caliph the government steadily deteriorated into a dictatorship. As a result some of the caliphs attempted to manipulated fiqh to justify their deviation. To combat this distortion and preserve authentic fiqh for later generations, scholars began to collect and compile the Fiqh of the earlier period.[39]

Dispersion of Ulema

Many scholars fled the political centres of the Umayyad state to avoid conflict and confusion as well as persecution from the various competing factions. This move results in the breakdown of the principle of Ijm'a (Unanimous agreement on points of the Islamic law). With scholars disperse in vast region, the unanimity on any issue or point of law became virtually impossible to establish. This in turn let to a significant increase in the individual Ijtihaad of scholars. These scholars attempted to deal with the multiplicity of the new problems of customs and culture in their own areas. Whenever an outstanding scholar of Fiqh arose in the area, the students and other scholars in that region would gather around him. Often in that way a number of schools of Islamic law (Madhhabs) evolved. During this stage Abu Hanifa and Sufiyan ath-Thawri became prominent in Kufa, Maalik ibn Anas in Madina, Al-Awzayi in Beirut and Al-Layth ibn Sa'ad in Egypt to mention a few.

Fabrication of Hadiths

- The narration of Hadiths increased with the increasing need for informations. Since the state had unofficially stopped relying on the Sunnah of the Prophet PBUH, scholars in their various capacities had to go in search of individual narrations of the Sunnah handed down by the Sahabaah and their students, in order to make their legal judgments. At the same time a new phenomenon developed i.e. false rendition and action began to be attributed to the Prophet PBUH for the first time. For a fabricator to be trusted he would have to relay some true Hadiths along with his fabrications. This led to the beginning of the compilation of the Hadiths and the development of the Science of Hadith Criticism, which aided local Scholars to form *Ijtehad* (legal rulings). However, when the Science of Hadiths evolved a mixture of true and false reports worked their way into the body of Islamic knowledge and was inadvertently used by some scholars in making decisions. In this was a body of incorrect Fiqh evolved, which was further bolstered by Fiqh decisions made by scholars who had rejected certain true Hadiths because they were only known to them through the Hadiths fabricators of their areas.[40]

Characteristics of Fiqh in the Umayyad Period

- Scholars and students in the Islamic Empire during this period tended to divide into two major groups. One group of scholars leaned towards limiting their deductions to available texts, while the other group favoured the extensive use of deduction reasoning and Ijtihaad.
- The first group avoided making legal rulings on an issue if clearly defined texts from Hadiths or the Qur'an related to the issue were not available. Their position were based on the obvious meaning of the Quranic verses,

  "Do not follow what you have no knowledge"[41]
- The laws whose purpose was identified in the holy Qur'an were used in *Qiyas* (anological deduction)[42] where as those left undefined were not. Because of this position, the scholars of this school of thought were called *Ahl al-Hadiths*. The centre of the Ahl al-Hadiths scholars was Madina and the Fiqh of the Madina School was, for the most part, practical and based on real problems.

The Other group of scholars felt that all of the various laws revealed in Holy Qur'an had identifiable reasons behind them, whether these reasons were identified by Qura'an or not. In cases where reasons for law had not been specifically defined, these scholars used their powers of reasoning to arrive at possible reasons. Then they applied that law to other circumstances, which had similar causes. Their approach was based on the practice of some of the major Sahabaah who had deduced reasons for some of them became to be known as *Ahl ar-ra'i* (reasoning people). The centre of Ahl ar-ra'i scholars was Kufah in Iraq. The Fiqh of Kufa developed along hypothetical lines. Problems were invented and variation of existing situation guessed at, then imaginary solutions were worked out and recorded. In their discussion they often used the phrase "what if it were like this?"[43]

Reason for differences

The different approaches of the *Ahl al-Hadiths* and *Ahl al-ra'i* scholars maybe traced to certain political factors combined with the differing socio-cultural backgrounds of the two areas in which their schools of thought flourished. From the time of the last Righteous Caliph Ali ibn Abu Talib, the capital if Islamic state first shifted to Iraq and then to Syria. Thus, the Hijaaz[44] was spared from much of the turbulence and influx of foreign cultures and ideas which took place at the Centre of the state. Life in the Hijaaz continued to be simple and easy going to its isolation. Hijaaz was also the home of the Prophet PBUH and birth place of the Islamic state. Consequently, there was an abundance of Hadiths in this region as well as a wealth of legal rulings made by the first three Caliphs, Abu Bakr, Umar and Uthmaan. On the other hand Iraq was a new and strange land for Muslims. When capital of the Islamic state was established there, it became a virtual melting pot of various cultures and gave rise to great number of situations and events which were outside the experience of Muslim scholars of that time. Further more, because of the number of Sahabaah who settled there was small. Hadiths were not nearly as available as in Hijaaz. Indeed Iraq became the birth place of fabricated Hadiths as well as breeding ground for most of the deviant sects. Not being able to rely on the validity of quoted Hadiths, the Scholars of Iraq decided to rely on Hadiths, to a lesser extent then the Scholars of Hijaaz. The few Hadiths which these

Iraqi Scholars considered accurate were only accepted after verifying and fulfilling the strict conditions. Ultimately the result of this development was that the Iraqi schools of thoughts and its scholars depended more on reason and logic than on the narrated Sunnah of the Prophet PBUH.[45]

Compilation of Fiqh

During the period of Four Righteous Caliphs (632-661 AD) there was no compilation of Fataawas (legal rulings) which had been made by Sahaabah. The Muslim state was rapidly expanding and everything was in the state of flux. The practice of narration of Hadiths has just started and the early band of Muslims who formed the core of the state had just begun the awesome task of guiding the young Muslim nation. Thus, there was neither the time nor opportunity for undertaking a compilation of the various rulings and opinions held by the Sahaabah. Further more, the Sahaabah themselves tended to view their efforts at Ijtihaad not as infallible truth binding on the entire Muslim nation, but merely as opinions applicable to their particular time and situation.

It was during the Umayyad period that the very first attempts at a compilation of legal rulings occurred. With the change of the governmental structure from Caliphate to Monarchy during this period rulings were increasingly being made which went against and contradicted the rulings of the Sahaabah. Those who had studied under the Sahabaah in the various centres of Islamic learning realised that if serious efforts were not made to preserve and secure the earlier rulings, later generations of Muslim would be unable to benefit from the contributions of the Sahabaahs. Accordingly, early scholars of the Hijaaz collected the various rulings of 'Abdullah ibn Abbaas, 'Abdullah ibn 'Umar and 'Aa'esha bint Abu Bakr. Similarly, the scholars of Iraq collected the rulings of 'Abdullah ibn Mas'oud and those of 'Ali ibn Abu Talib. Unfortunately none of these early collections have survived in their original form. They are only now known by the references made to them in the books of the next generation of scholars.[46] However, the large number of rulings contained in the original collections has been preserved by way of narration in the books of Hadiths, in history books, as well as in later books of Fiqh.

THE FOURTH STAGE: FLOWERING

This stage extends from approximately 750 BC to 950 AD and covers the rise of the 'Abbaasid Dynasty founded by the Caliph Abul-'Abbaas (reign 750-754)[47]. It was during this period that Fiqh took shape as an independent Islamic Science; Islamic scholarship was encouraged and actively supported by Caliph. It got flourished as discussion and debate on various controversial issues became widespread. *Madh-habs* or school of thoughts got multiplied and various compilation of Hadiths and Fiqh were made. Further the Arabic translation of scientific, philosophical and theological works were exerted influence on Islamic thoughts. By the end of this period the Fiqh got divided in to two sections: i.e. Fundamental principles (Usool) and secondary principles of scientific, philosophical and theological works (Furoo'). The source of Ismalic law were identified and differences developed between the major *Madh-habs* separating them from each other.[48]

The Development of Fiqh

In the development of Fiqh during this period, there were two major trends relating to the evolution of the *Madh-habs*. The first occurred during the period of the Great Imams, founder of the major *Madh-habs* and their major students. Although these *Madh-habs* were fast becoming distinct entities, they continued the tradition of flexibility in making and accepting legal rulings which had characterised the earlier periods. The second trend covered the period following the death of the major scholars of the *Madh-habs*. It represents the beginning of that rigidity in making and accepting legal rulings which is the main characteristics of Madh-habs and consequently of Fiqh, in succeeding generations.

Period of the Great Imams

The development of Fiqh in the period of the Great Imams (750-850 AD) and their major students was affected by the following factors.

A. State's Support for Scholars

The early 'Abbassid Caliph made a show of great respect for Islamic law and its scholars. The reason for this lay in the fact that they owed their office to their claim that they were seeking a return to a Caliphate based on Shariah and its legitimate interpretation. Consequently, the 'Abbaasid Caliphs of this period all took pride in sending their children to study under the major scholars of the time and what is more, some of the Caliph became scholars of Islamic law in their own rights. For example, Caliph Haroon Rashid (786-809 AD). Furthermore these Caliphs made a practice of consulting the most outstanding Islamic scholars on most matters of fiqh. A classic example is that of Imam Maalik whom Caliph Al-Mansoor commissioned to compile an authoritative book of the Sunnah of the Prophet PBUH. On its completion, the Caliph consulted Imam Maalik about allowing him to make it the State Constitution which would have made the *Madh-hab* of Imam Maalik binding on all Muslims. However, Imaam refused to have it done, since he was aware that his compilation including only those Hadiths of the Prophet PBUH that were available in Hijaaz where Imam Maalik had taught and founded his Madh-habs. He felt strongly that no single Madh-habs should be binding on all Muslims in view of the fact that any single *Madh-habs* would exclude the many other Hadiths narrated by Sahaabah who had traveled to other parts of the state.[49] This is the clear example of the flexibility in accepting and adopting other Imam's work and this very flexibility which characterised the founder of the *Madh-habs*. The factor of state support and patronisation of Fiqh scholars contributed largely to the flourishing of the many *Madh-habs* which had arisen in the later part of the Umayyad period.

However, one can not ignore the fact that although the scholars and judges were allowed a greater measure of freedom of opinion, they were often subjected to severe punishments if their rulings ran counter to political policy. For example, Imam Maalik was jailed, beaten and tortured for giving a Fatwa that challenged an official decree of the 'Abbasids Caliph. According to this decree, the people were made to take an oath that if they broke their oath of allegiance to the Caliphs they would be automatically divorced from their wives. Imam Maalik's fatwa ruled that divorce under compulsion was null and void.

B. Increase in Centres of Learning

Though the State of North Africa and Spain[50] had split off from the 'Abbasid empire, the territories of the 'Abbasid state were expanded to include all of Persia, India and Southern Russia and the capital was not moved to Baghdad. Consequently, the centres of learning and *Madh-habs* multiplied.[51]

Scholars and students from the various centres of learning began journeying back and forth in search of knowledge about the conclusion reached by their contemporaries in other parts of the Muslim states. A good example is the journey of Muhammad ibn-al Hasan, a prominent student of Abu Hanifa Founder of *Hanafi Madh-habs*, from Iraq to Madina in order to study under Imam Maalik, founder of *Maaliki Madh-habs* and to memorise his book of Hadiths, *al-Muwatta*. Likewise, Imam ash-Shafi'ee, founder of Shafi'ee Madh-habs journeyed first to Hijaz[52] to study under Imam Maalik, then to Iraq in order to study under Muhammad ibn-Hasan, and finally to Egypt to study under Imam al-Layth ibn Sa'd, founder of the Laythee Madh-habs. These journey resulted firstly in the reconciliation of some of the major differences which had aroused among scholars and ultimately resulted in the combination of some of the schools of Islamic legal thoughts. For example, Imam ash-Shafi'ee included the Fiqh of Hijaaz with that of Iraq and Egypt and formed a new school of law, the Shafi'ee Madh-habs. This is again a noteworthy example of the flexibility of the early Imam's in their approach to Fiqh.

C. The Spread of Debate and Discussions

Whenever scholars or their students met, they would exchange thoughts on various Islamic issues which aroused in their particular areas. If there was a major difference of opinion about a particular solution they would debate back and forth until they reach to a common conclusion or various options were accepted. These legal debates also took place by exchanging mails as in case of the debate between Imam Maalik and Imam al-Layth about the customs in Madina.[53] The huge increase in the number of debating sessions, whether by mails or face to face meetings between the founders and students of various *Madh-habs* resulted in the clarification of certain important issues and repealing of mistaken rulings or judgments among scholars of Islamic Law.[54]

In the initial stage of development of the Madh-habs there was a marked lack of rigidity or dogmatism on the part of scholars and their students. That is, issues were objectively analysed and conclusion arrived at on the basis of the validity of the proofs presented. In fact, Imam Abu Hanifa and Imam Shafi'ee were on record as stating that if a Hadiths was known to be accurate, then that should be considered as their *Madh-hab*. A noteworthy example concerns the law relating to the drinking of *khamr* and other intoxicants. Imam Abu Hanifa, founder of Hanafi Madh-habs, maintained that the Islamic prohibition of Khamr covered only the product of fermented grape juice (the literal meaning of *khamr* and did not extend to intoxicants in general). According to this ruling, intoxicating drinks made from other sources were allowable so long as the consumer did not become drunk. However, Abu Hanifa's three main students (Abu Yousuf, Muhammad ibn al-Hasan and Zufar) later rejected the ruling of their teacher since they encountered a reliable Hadiths of the Prophet

PBUH clearly indicating that all intoxicants were to be included in the meaning of *khamr*.[55]

This free exchange of ideas and willingness to change even the rulings of the founding fathers of the *Madh-habs* vividly illustrates the absence of that rigidity and sectarianism which characterised the methodology of later scholars of the *Madh-habs*.

Period of the Minor Scholars

The development of Fiqh during the period of the minor scholars of the Madh-habs (850-950 AD) that is the second generation of students was affected by the following factors:

A. Compilation of Fiqh

In order to make legal rulings and establish principles, previous scholars were obliged to spend a great deal of time and effort hunting in various parts of the Islamic State for Hadiths and *Athars* (sayings and acts of the Sahaabah and their students). In this period, the Sunnah of the Prophet PBUH was systematically collected and compiled in books of Hadith, thereby leaving scholars free to concentrate on the comprehension and application of Hadith. Fiqh was also compiled on a wide scale and in a systematic fashion during this period. Some scholars personally compiled their own rulings, while others, such as Imam Abu Hanifa and Imam Ahmad ibn Hambal, dictated various problems and their solutions to their students, who subsequently compiled them. Imam Maalik's al-Muwatta is a collection of Hadiths and opinions of the Sahaabah along with his personal rulings and Imam ash-Shafi'ee book of Fiqh entitled al-Umm contains his legal rulings supported by their proofs.[56]

Types of Compilation

1. The early books of Fiqh were usually a mixture of legal rulings, Hadiths, opinion of the Sahaabah. Al-Muwatta of Imam Maalik is a classical example of this stage.

2. Some books of Fiqh were about the basic principles of Fiqh, Hadiths being mentioned only in order to prove the correctness of the author's deductions. *Kitab al-Kharaaj* by Imam Abu Yusouf[57] and al-Umm by Imam ash-Shafi'ee are both good examples of this type of writing.
3. Other books on Fiqh concentrated on the application of Fiqh principles but little references to Hadiths. These books were arranged in chapters according to the issues under discussion. The six books of Imam Muhammad ibn al-Hasan[58] and al-Mudawwanah by Imam Ibn al-Qasim[59] are examples of this type of writings.

At first, the compilation of proofs for each legal ruling on various issues included the texts of Hadiths along with their chains of narrators. Gradually concern for the chains of narrators decreased, and scholars merely quoted the text of the appropriate Hadiths along with a reference to the books of Hadiths in which it could be found. With the de-emphasising of the importance of Hadiths, or by neglecting to mention their sources and their levels of authenticity. Thus, the opinions of the *Madh-habs* were gradually given precedence over one of the primary sources of Islamic Law, namely the Sunnah. In this evolution lays the beginning of the rigid approach which later became the hallmark of the *Madh-habs*. However, later in this period, some prominent scholars reversed this trend, somewhat, by re-introducing the practice of quoting the sources and commenting on the accuracy of the Hadiths.

B. Court Debate

There were also court debates during this period which were held for the interest and amusement of the caliphs and members of the royal court. Some scholars like magicians, singers, dancers and jesters, had become a permanent fixture of the royal court.[60] They competed among themselves for the favours of the Caliphs, and they invented issues solely for the purpose of debate. As a result, hypothetical Fiqh took on new dimensions as it evolved from sublime origins in the era of the Sahaabah and the early scholars, to the ridiculous product of court debates.

Court debate also spawned competitiveness and dogmatism since the loser of a debate not only lost monetary reward from the Caliph but also personal prestige. Further more, because of loss of personal prestige also entailed loss of prestige on the part of one's *Madh-habs*, the principle of defending one's *Madh-habs*, right or wrong, came to be considered virtue. As a result, *Madh-hab* sectarianism became rampant among the court scholars.

C. Compilation of Hadiths

During compilation of Hadith there arose an opposing trend among specialists in Hadiths compilation and criticism, where by issues of Fiqh were tackled without dependence on the traditional rulings of the earlier scholars by basing their positions on authentic Hadiths wherever available, rather that slavishly following earlier rulings merely because they had been made by prominent scholars. Focusing on Hadiths to resolve the problems of Fiqh, great scholars of Hadiths like Imam al-Bukhari (810-870 AD) and Imam Muslim (817-875 AD) went to great pains to collect from all possible sources of authentic Hadiths of Prophet PBUH and the *Athars* of the Sahaabah. These they arranged in chapters according to the format established by the Fiqh scholars. The initiator of this trend was the last of the major Imam, Ahmad ibn Hambal, who compiled the most extensive work of Hadiths called al-Musnad.[61] Both Imam al-Bukhari and Imam Muslim were among his students.

D. The Organisation of Fiqh

Through translation of the great books of sciences and philosophy from Greece, Rome, Persia and India,[62] Islamic scholars gained insight into new systems of reasoning, deduction and inference. This new knowledge influenced their approach to Fiqh which they proceeded to organise into *Usool* (fundamentals) and secondary *Furoo'* (Principles).

In Time *Tafseer* (explanation of the Qur'an), Hadiths and *Nahw* (grammer) developed under these influences into specialised branches of learning. The position of major scholars of Fiqh, were recorded and the primary sources of Islamic law were identified and classified in order of their importance.[63]

The Sources of Islamic Law

By the end of this period, the following sources of Islamic law in the order stated became widely accepted by most of the scholars.

1. The Holy Qur'an

The Qur'an was the first source of law and its passages were accepted unanimously as being authentic. However, there were some differences of opinion in interpretation of some of its passages.

2. The Sunnah

The hadiths of the Holy Prophet PBUH is the next most important source. However, scholars for their acceptance and application set various conditions.

3. Opinion of the Sahabaah

The opinion of the Sahaabah either as a group or individual was considered the third most important source of law. This source was divided into two parts according to the positions taken by the Sahaabah.

(a) If they were united on an opinion it was referred to as *Ijma'a.*

(b) If they had different opinions on a single issue, each opinion was referred to as a Ra'i (personal opinion).

4. Qiyaas

Ijtihaad based on evidence found either in the Qur'an, the Sunnah or *Ijma'a* was next in order of importance. The method of reasoning used was a form of a analogical deduction called *Qiyaas*. An example of Qiyaas is the prohibition of marijuana based on the Prophet's statement: "Every intoxicant is *Khamr* and every form of *Khamr* is Haram."[64] Since Marijuana has intoxicating effect it can be classified as *Khamr* and thus *Haram* (Prohibited).

5. Istihsaan (Legal Preference)

This principle involves the preference of an opinion based on a circumstantial need than over an opinion based on Qiyaas. This principle, referred to by various names, scholars of most schools or thought used i.e. *istislaah*. An application of Istihsaan is seen in the treatment of a contract for the manufacture and sale of an item. According to Qiyaas based on the Prophet's statement, "whoever sells food should not do so until he has in his own possession",[65] contract of this type are invalid, since the item is nonexistent at the time of the contract. However since such contracts have been universally accepted by people and the need for such contract is obvious, the ruling by Qiyaas was dropped and the contracts were allowed, based on the principle of preference (Istihsaan).

6. 'Urf or Custom

Local customs were accepted as a source of law in a given region as long as they did not contradict any of the principles of Islamic law. For example, local marriage customs concerning dowry' payment. The dowry (Mahr) according to Islamic law must be agreed upon as part of the marriage contract but it has no set time to be paid. It was the custom of Egyptian as well as others that a portion of it called the *Muqaddam* i.e. must be paid before marriage and *Mu'akhkhar* is only required to be paid in the case of death or divorce, according to whichever occur first.[66]

With the above classification one can derive that although the process of organisation and classification was, for the most part, a positive development, nevertheless, when coupled with the prevailing trends towards factionalism, it served to further widen the gaps between the *Madh-habs*. Thus, we find the slight variations in the terminology given to the same principle become a source of friction and opposition. For example, the Maliki *Madh-habs* has considered the Hanafi principle of Istihasaan unacceptable and yet applied the same principle under the name of *Massalih Mursalah* (Public interest). While the Shafi'i Madh-habs rejected both these terms and applied a similar principle calling it *Istis-haab*.[67]

THE MADH-HABS: SCHOOLS OF ISLAMIC LEGAL THOUGHT

In the previous topic we have seen the evolution of the *Madh-habs* within the historical context of the overall development of Fiqh. During the era of Prophethood, the foundations of Fiqh were laid down in the Prophet Mohammed's *Ijtihad* (reasoning rulings) as well as those of his Sahaabah (followers). In the following stage, that of the Righteous Caliphs, the Fiqh principle of *Ijma'a* (decision by unanimity) evolved and *Ijtihad* became an independent principle of Fiqh under the name *Qiyas*. The Madh-habs during this period was in reality that of each of the Righteous Caliphs, since the final say in legal matters rested with them. However, all legal decisions were subjected to alteration on the basis of recorded statements or practices of the Prophet PBUH that is, Hadiths. There was no room for rigidity of factionalism.

In the earlier period of Umayyad dynasty we saw the division of Fiqh scholars into two main Madh-hab with respect to Ijtihad: *Ahl ar-Ra'i* and *Ahl al-Hadiths*. These two Madh-habs evolved into a number of new Madh-habs during the shift from Caliphate to Monarchy. Since the scholars and their students were dispersed throughout the Umayyad state, their personal Ijtihad increased in order to solve local issues. However, during the Umayyad periods and that of the early 'Abbasids, students of Fiqh freely and frequently changed teachers and exchanged legal opinions. In effect, therefore, the flexibility of the previous was maintained.[68]

During the Abbasid period Fiqh was formalised and systematised. The number of *Madh-habs* decreased and the differences between them became emphasised due to the state's preference for some *Madh-hab* over other and the rise of *Madh-hab* rivalry promoted by court debates. And the destruction of the Abbasids Caliphate and the decline of Ijtihad and culminated in its disappearance. The number of Madh-habs decreased to four which evolved into completely distinct and often became an antagonistic entities. The difference between them became insurmountable in the minds of their adherents and elements of fanaticism and sectarianism strived in *Madh-habs*. Since the applicability of Sharia'ah in different context, time and places was largely depended upon the principle of Ijtihad, the loss of this important principle spelled the inevitable stagnation and decline of Fiqh.

Let's see the major Madh-habs chronologically with the respect to their founders, formation and fundamental principles.

The Hanafi Madh-habs: Founder Imam Abu Hanifa (703-767 AD)

This Madh-hab was named after its founding scholars, Abu Hanifa, whose actual name was Nu'man ibn Thabit. He was born in the year 702 AF, Kufah in Iraq. His father was a silk merchant of Persian origin, who accepted Islam during the reign of the Righteous Caliph. Abu Hanifa began his earlier studies in the field of philosophy and dialectics known as 'Ilm al-Kalam, but after mastering its various disciplines, he left it and went into an in-depth study of Fiqh and Hadiths. He chose as his main teacher, Hammad ibn Zayd, who was among the greatest scholars of Hadiths in his time. Abu Hanifa studied under him for eighteen years. During this time he became qualified to teach but remained Hammad's student until latter died in the year 742 AD. After Hammad's death Abu Hanifa took up the position of teacher at the age of forty and became the most outstanding scholar in Kufa. As such, he appeared to be valuable prize to the Umayyad caliphs of that time. They offered him the position of Qazi (judge) of Kufah. But he refused the post inspite of being physically beaten for his refusal by the Ameer of Kufa, Yazeed ibn 'Umar. Similarly, during the rule of the 'Abbassids, he also refused royal appointment, and was consequently imprisoned in Baghdad by the Caliph Abu Ja'far al-Mansoor (745-775 AD). He remained imprisoned until his death in 767 AD. Abu Hanifa was considered among the minor Taa'bi'un (student of the Sahaabah), because he had met few of the Sahaabah and had related some Hadiths from them.[69]

Imam Abu Hanifa based his teaching method on the principle of Shoorah (group discussion). He would present a legal problem to his students for debate and discussion and tell them to records its solution whenever they arrived at a unified position. Because of this interactive approach to making legal rulings, we could say that the Hanafi *Madh-hab* was as much a product of Abu Hanifa's student's effort as it was a product of his own efforts. They would also debate on hypothetical problems and work out solutions, based on the principle of preparing for a problem before its occurrence. Because of their leaning towards hypothetical Fiqh which often introduce an issue with the question, "what if so and so happened?" they became to be known as *Ahl A-Ra'i* (The Opinion people).[70]

The early jurists of this *Madh-habs* deduced Islamic laws from the following sources, which are listed in the order of their importance:

1. **The Holy Qur'an**

   They considered the Qur'an to be the primary unquestionable source of Islamic law. In fact, it was used to determine the accuracy of the other sources. Accordingly any other sources that contradicted the Qur'an were considered inaccurate.

2. **The Sunnah**

   The Sunnah was consulted as the second most important source of Islamic law, but with some qualification as to its use. They stipulated that it was not sufficient that a Hadiths be accurate *Sahi*, but it had to be also widely known *Mash-hoor*, if it was to be used as a legal proof. This condition was laid down as a safeguard against false Hadiths which were cropping up frequently in that region where only few notable Sahaabah had settled.

3. **Ijmaa' of Sahaabah**

   Third in importance as a source of Islamic law was the unanimous opinion of the Sahaabah on any point of law not specified in the Qur'an or the Sunnah. That is, Ijmaa' of the Sahabaah, was given precedence over the personal opinion of Abu Hanifa and his students in their deduction of Islamic law. The Hanafi *Madh-habs* also recognised the Ijmaa' of Muslim scholars in any age as valid and binding on Muslims.

4. **Individual opinion of the Sahaabah**

   If there were different opinions among the Sahaabah on a particular point of law and no Ijmaa' was subsequently formed, Abu Hanifa would choose the opinion which appeared most appropriate to the case in question. In establishing this as a vital principle of his *Madh-habs*, Abu Hanifa again gains more weight to the opinions of the Sahaabah than to his own.[71] However, he did apply his own reasoning in a limited sense by choosing one of their various opinions.

5. ***Qiyas* (Analogical deduction)**

   Abu Hanifa felt no obligation to accept the deductions of the students of the Sahaabah (Ta'abi'un) in areas where no clear proof was available from any of the above mentioned sources. He considered himself the equal of the Taabi'un and would make his own Ijtihad based on the principles of *Qiyas* which he and his students established.

6. **Istihsan (Preference)**

   Istihsan, in short, preference of one proof over another

proof because it appears more suitable, even though the preferred proof may be technically weaker than the other one. This may involve the preference of Hadiths which is specific over a general one, or it may even involve the preference of a more suitable law over the one deduced by Qiyas.

7. **'Urf (Local custom)**

   Local customs were given legal weight in areas where there were no binding Islamic customs were available. It was through the application of this principle that various customs found in the diverse culture within the Islamic world entered the legal system and mistakenly classified as Islamic.[72]

THE AWZAA'EE MADH-HABS: FOUNDER IMAM AL-AWZAA'EE (708-774 AD)

This *Madh-habs* is named after the Syrian scholars 'Abdur Rehman ibn al-Awzaa'ee who was born in Ba'labek in the year 708 AD. He became as one of the major scholars of Hadiths of eight century AD and was opposed to excessive use of Qiyas and other forms of reasoning in cases where clear texts from the Qur'an or Sunnah were available. Imam Awzaa'ee spent most of his life in Beirut, eventually dying there in year 774 AD, but his *Madh-hab* became widespread in Syria, Jordan, Palestine and Lebanon as well as Spain.

This Madh-hab remained the main school of thought in Syria until the tenth century CE, when Abu Zar'ah Muhammad ibn Uthman of the Shafi'i Madh-hab was appointed judge of Damascus. Abu Zar'ah began the practice of giving a prize of one hundred dinars to any student who memorised the book, *Mukhtasar al-Muzanee*, a basic book of Shafi'i Fiqh. Naturally, this practice caused the Shafi'i Madh-hab to spread rapidly in Syria and the number of Awzaa'ee followers continued to dwindle until eleventh century when none were to be found.[73] However, his contribution to the science of Fiqh was recorded and remains to this day in most of the books of comparative Fiqh.

THE MALIKI MADH-HAB: FOUNDER IMAM MALIK (717-801 AD)

The founding scholars of this *Madh-habs*, Malik ibn Anas ibn 'Aamir, was born in Madina in the year 717 AD. His grandfather, Aamir was among the major Sahaabah of Madina. Malik studied Hadiths under az-Zuhri who was the greatest Hadiths scholar of his time as well as under the great Hadiths narrator, Naari', the freed slave of Shabaah 'Abdullah ibn 'Umar. Malik's only journey outside Madina were for Haj, and thus he largely limited himself to the knowledge available in Madina.

Imam Malik was severely beaten in the year 764 AD by the order of the Amir of Madina, because he made a legal ruling that forced divorced is invalid and is not acceptable in Islam. This ruling of Imam Malik confronted the Abbasid ruler's practice of adding a clause in the Oath of Allegiance to the ruler that however broke the oath was automatically divorced. Imam Malik was tied and beaten until his arms became severely damaged to such a degree that he became disable and could not clasp his hand on chest during *Salaat* or prayer and thus he began the practice of praying with his hands at his sides according to some report. Imam Malik continued to teach Hadiths in Madina over a period of forty years and he managed to compile a book containing hadiths of the Prophet PBUH and Athars of Sahaabah and their successors which he named Al-Muwatta' (the Beaten Path). He began his compilation of Hadiths at the request of the 'Abbasid Caliph, Abu Ja'far al-Mansoor, (754-775 CE) who wanted comprehensive code of law based on the Prophet's Sunnah which could be applied uniformly throughout his realm. But, on its completion, Imam Malik refused to have it forced on the people pointing out that the Sahaabah had scattered throughout the Islamic empire and had taken with them other parts of the Sunnah which also had to be considered in any laws imposed throughout the state. Caliph Haroon Rashid (768-809 AD) also made the same request to the Imam, but he was also turned down. Imam Malik died in the city of his birth in the year 801 AD at the venerable age of 83.[74]

Imam Malik's method of teaching was based on the narration of Hadiths and the discussion of their meanings in the context of problems of that day. He would either narrate to his student Hadiths and *Athars* (statement of Sahaabah) on various topics of Islamic law then discuss their implications, or he would inquire about problems which had arisen in the areas from where his students came, then narrate appropriate Hadiths and *Athars* which could be used to solve them.

After Imam Malik completed al-Muwatta', he used to narrate it to his students as the sum total of his *Madh-habs*, but would add or subtract from it slightly, whenever new information reached him. He used to strictly avoid speculation and hypothetical Fiqh and thus his school and its followers were referred to as '*Ahl al-Hadiths*' (people of the hadiths).

Sources of Law used by the Maliki Madh-habs

1. **The Qur'an**

   Like the other entire Imam's Malik considered the Qur'an to be the primary source of Islamic law and utilised it without laying any pre-conditions for its applications.

2. **The Sunnah**

   The Sunnah was used by Imam Malik as the second most important source of Islamic law, but, like Abu Hanifa, he put some restrictions on some of its use. If a Hadith were contradicted by the customary practice of the Madinites, he rejected it. He did not, however, insist that a Hadith be *Mash-hoor* (well known) before it could be applied as Abu Hanifa did. Instead he used any Hadiths that was narrated to him as long as none of the narrators were known liars or extremely weak memorizers.

3. ***Aadaat* (Practices) of the Madinites**

   Imam Malik reasoned that since many of the Madinites

were direct descendants of the Sahaabah and Madina was were Prophet PBUH spent the last ten years of his life, practices common to all Madinites must have been allowed, if not encouraged by the Prophet PBUH himself. Thus, Imam Malik regarded common Madinites practices as a form of highly authentic Sunnah narrated in deeds rather than words.[75]

4. **Ijma'a of the Sahaabaah**

Imam Malik like Imam Abu Hanifa considered the Ijma'a of the Sahaabah, as well as that of later scholars as the third most important source of Islamic law.

5. **Individual Opinion of the Sahaabah**

Imam Malik gave full weight to the opinions of the Sahaabah whether they were conflicting or in agreement and included them in his book of hadith, *al-Muwatta*. However, the consensus of Sahaabah was given precedence over individual opinions of the Sahaabah.

6. **Qiyaas**

Imam Malik used to apply his own deductive reasoning on matters not covered by the previously mentioned sources. However, he was very cautious about doing so because of the subjectivity of such forms of reasoning.

7. **Customs of the Madinites**

Imam Malik also gave some importance to the isolated practices found among a few people of Madina so long as they were not in contradiction to known hadiths. He reasoned that such customs, though occurring only in isolated instances, must also have been handed down from earlier generations and sanctioned by the Sahabaah or even the Prophet PBUH himself. Imam Malik considered the various customs and social habits of people throughout the Muslim world as possible source of secondary laws.[76]

8. ***Istislaah* (Welfare)**

The principle of *Istihsaan* developed by Abu Hanifa was also applied by Imam Malik and his student except that they called it by the name *Istislaah* which means seeking that which is more suitable. It deals with things which mean seeking that which is more suitable. It deals with things which are fro human welfare but have not been specifically considered by the Shariah. An example of Istislaah is found in Caliph 'Ali's ruling that a whole group of people who took part in a murder were guilty even though only one of the group had actually committed the act of murder. Another example is the rights of a Muslim leader to collect taxes from the rich other than Zakat if the interest of the state demands it, where as in Shariah only Zakat has been specified. Imam Malik also applied the principle of Istislaah to deduce laws more in keeping with needs which arose from current situations than those deduced by Qiyaas.[77]

Main students of the Mailik *Madh-habs*

The most notable students of Imam Malik were al-Qasim and Ibn Wahab.

Abu 'Abdur-Rahmaan ibn al-Qasim (745-813 AD)

Al-Qasim was born in Egypt but travelled to Madina where he studied under his teacher and mentor for a period of more that twenty years. He wrote an extensive book on the Fiqh of the Madh-habs, eclipsing even al-Muwatta of Malik himself and called it Mudawwanah.[78]

Abu Abdillaah ibn Wahab (742-819 AD)

Ibn Wahab also travelled from Egypt to Madina in order to study under Imam Malik. He distinguished himself in the deduction of laws to such a degree that Malik gave him the title of al-Mufti which means the official expounder of Islamic law. Ibn Wahab was offered an appointment as judge of

Egypt, but turned it down in order to maintain his integrity as an independent scholar. Imam Malik had other famous students from other Madh-habs. Some of them modified their own Madh-habs based on what they learnt from Malik, for example, Muhammad ash-Shaybani who was among the foremost students of Abu Hanifa. There were others who developed their own Madh-habs by combining Malik's teachings with that of others, for example Muhammad ibn Idris ash-Shafi'I who studied for many years under Imam Malik as well as under Abu Hanifa's student Muhammad as-Shaybani.

THE ZAYDI MADH-HAB: FOUNDER IMAM ZAYD (700-740 AD)

This Madh-habs traces its origin to one of Ali ibn Abu Taalib's great grandsons through his son al-Husain. Imam Zayd's father, Ali Zayn-ul Abidin, was well known for his great legal knowledge and his narration of hadiths. Born in Al-Madina in the year 700 AD, Zayd ibn Ali soon became one of the foremost scholars of the Alawi family. He narrated Hadiths from all of his relatives including his older brother, Muhammad al-Baaqir.[79] Zayd expanded his knowledge by travelling to the other major centres of learning his knowledge by travelling to the other major centres of learning in Iraq, Kufah, Basrah and Wasit, where he sat and exchanged views with his contemporaries like Abu Hanifa and Sufiyan ath-thawree.

The Umayyad caliph, Hishaam ibn 'Abdul Malik (reign 724-473 AD) never missed an opportunity to degrade and humiliate the 'Alawi family and Zayd ibn Ali was often singled out for abuse. He was not allowed to leave the city of Madina without the permission of its governor and his requests for permission were often turned down repeatedly. Eventually, Zayd became the first of Ali's descendants to fight the caliphate from the Umayyads after the catastrophe in Karbala. He travelled secretly to Kufa where he was joined by his Shi'tte of Iraq, Wasit and other places. He planned and prepared for the battle with Umayyads. A number of people advised him not trust the Kufans, as it was their betrayal of Imam Hussain which led to his untimely death, but Zayd didn't paid heed. While preparation for war was complete a dispute arose among his new followers when they found out that Zayd didn't consider the first two Caliph's Abu Bakr and Umar to be apostates who stole the Caliphate from his grandfather. The majority of his followers broke away from him and declared his nephew, Ja'far as-Siddique to be the Imam of the time instead of Zayd. Hishaam's army took advantage of this confusion and made a surprise attack on the Kufa. Only four hundred followers rallied with Imam Zayd and he was killed in the battle.[80]

Formation of the Zaydi Madh-habs

Imam Zayd was a scholars concerned mainly with the narration of Hadiths and recitation of the Qur'an. He taught in circles of learning in the cities of Madina, Basra, and Wasit and thus had a large number of students. The method used by Zaydwas that of narrating Hadiths and teaching art of Qur'anic recitation. If legal question was raised, he would solve them or choose an opinion of one of his contemporaries like the jurist 'Abdur Rahman ibn Abu Laila. The rulings of the Madh-habs were not dictated nor recorded by Zayd himself but by his students.

Source of Law used by the Zaydi Madh-habs

The jurists of the Madh-habs evolved the following sources from Imam Zayd's ruling as the basis from which they deduced Islamic laws.

1. **The Qur'an**

   The holy Qur'an was considered the primary source of Islamic law. The existing copy of the Qur'an was considered to be complete without any of the deletions by many extremist Shi'ite sects.

2. The Sunnah

The sayings, actions and approvals of the Prophet PBUH were considered the second most important source of Islamic law. The Sunnah was not restricted to narrations of the Alawi family or their followers, but included all reliable narration.

3. Aqwaal 'Ali

Rulings and Statements of Ali ibn Abu Taalib which were not merely his personal opinions were considered by Imam Zayd to be part of the Sunnah. That is, in Ali' did not say or imply that it was his opinion, then Zayd assumed that it was from the Prophet PBUH. However, Zayd did not accept everything attributed to Ali and sometimes made rulings contrary to what were claimed to be Ali's rulings.

4. *Ijma* of the Sahaabah

Zayd recongnised the *Ijmaa'* of the Sahaabah as a source of Islamic law. Hence, although he felt that his grandfather was better suited for the leadership than Caliph Abu Bakr, 'Umar and 'Uthman, the unanimous acceptance of their caliphate by the Sahaabah made it, in his opinion, legally binding.

5. *Qiyas* (Analogy)

According to the jurists of this Madh-hab, both the principles of Istihsaan and that of Istislaah involved a form of analogical deduction. Consequently, they considered them a part of what was known as *Qiyan* in the other Madh-hab.

6. *'Aql*

Human intellect was considered as a source of Islamic law where none of the previous sources was applicable. As a youth, Imam Zayd had met and studied under Waasil ibn 'Ataa, founder of the Mu'atazilite school of thought. The Mu'atazilites were the first to propound the principle of 'Aql; whatever, the intellect considered good was good and whatever it considered bad was bad. However, according to the Mua'tazilah, 'Aql came directly after the Qur'an and Sunnah, and thus they rejected Qiyaas, as well as the opinions of the Sahaabah, whereas Imam Zayd placed the principle of 'Aql last and recognised *Qiyas*.

The Laythee Madh-habs: The Founder: Imam al-Layth (716-791 AD)

This Madh-habs was named after al-Layth ibn Sa'd who was born in Egypt of Persian parentage in the year 716 AD. After an extensive study of all the then known areas of Islamic learning al-Layth became the major scholar of Egypt. He was contemporary to both Imam Abu Hanifa and Imam Malik. In fact, he carried on a debate with Imam Malik by mails on various points of Islamic law, one of which was Malik's inclusion of Madinite Custom as an independent source of law.

Reasons for the Madh-habs Disappearence

Imam Layth Madh-habs disappeared shortly after his death in 791 CE for the following reasons. He neither, compiled, dictated nor instructed his followers to record his legal opinions and their proofs according to his interpretations of the Qur'an, Sunnah and legal positions of the Sahaabah. Thus, very little mention of his Madh-habs beyond a few references in the early books of comparative Fiqh. Also the number of students under al-Layth was small and since none of them became outstanding jurists; they were not in an influential position to popularise his Madh-hab. Ash-Shafi'i one of the most outstanding Fiqh scholar settled in Egypt immediately after al-Layth's death and his Madh-hab quickly displaced of al-Layth.[81]

It is interesting to note that Imam ash-Shafi'i who had studied extensively under Imam Malik and under al-Layth's students was reported to have observed that al-Layth was greater jurists than Malik but his students neglected him.[82]

The Thawree Madh-habs: The Founder: Imam ath-Thawree (719-777 AD)

Imam Sufiyan ath-Thawree was born in Kufa in the year 719 AD and after an extensive study of Hadiths and Fiqh became the main Fiqh scholar of the Hadiths school in Kufa. He held similar views to those of his contemporary, Abu Hanifa, however he opposed the latter's use of *Qiyas* and *Istihsaan*.

There occurred a series of confrontations between Imam Sufiyan and officials of the Abbasid state due to his outspoken nature and his refusal to support state policies which contradicted the Shariah. Caliph al-Mansoor (ruled from 759-744 AD) sent a letter to the Imam ath-Thawree requesting him to accept the post of Qazi of Kufa on condition that he will not make any judgment or ruling in opposition to the state policy. On receipt of the letter, Sufiyan tore it up and threw it into the Tigris river in disgust, but, as a result he was forced to give up his teaching and flee for his life. He remained in hiding until he died in the year 777 AD.

Reasons for the Madh-habs Disappearance

The two main factors are as follows:

(a) The Imam spent the greater part of his life in hiding and thus was unable to attract a large number of students who might subsequently spread his opinions in the circle of learning.

(b) Although he did carry out some fairly extensive compilation of Hadiths and their interpretations, he requested in his will that his main student, Ammar ibn Saif, erase all his writings and burn whatever could not be erased. "Ammar dutifully destroyed his teachers writing but many of the Imams idea were recorded by the students of the other Imam, so they have survived till today but not in an organised form.[83]

The Shafi'ii Madh-habs: The Founder: Imam Ash-Shafi'ii (769-820 AD)

The full name of the scholar after whom this school of legal thought has been named was Muhammad ibn Idrees ash-Shafi'ii. He was born in town of Gaza on the Mediterranean coast of what was then known as Shaam in the year 796 AD, but travelled to Madina in his youth to study Fiqh and Hadiths under Imam Malik. He succeeded in memorising the whole of Malik's book, al-Muwatta and recited it to him from memory, word perfect.

Ash-Shafi'ii remained under Malik until the latter died in 801 AD. Then he went to Yemen and taught there. He remained there until he was accused of Shi'ite leanings in the year 805 AD and brought as a prisoner before the Abbasid Caliph Haroon ar-Rasheed (ruled from 786-809 AD). Fortunately he was bale to prove correctness of his belief and was subsequently released. Ash-Shafi'ii remained in Iraq and studied for a while under Imam Muhammad ibn-Hasan, the famous student of Abu Hanifa. Later he travelled to Egypt in order to study under Imam al-Layth, but by the time he reached there the Imam had passed away. However, he was able to study the Madh-habs of Al-Layth from al-Layth's students. Ash Shafi'ii remained in Egypt until his death in the year 820 AD during the rule of the Caliph al-Mamoon (ruled from 812-832 AD).[84]

Formation of Shafi'ii Madh-habs

Imam Ash Shafi'ii combined the Fiqh of Hijaz (Maliki thought) with that of Iraq, (Hanafi thought) and created a new Madh-habs which he dictated to his students in the form of a book called al-Hujjah (the Evidence). This dictation took place in Iraq in the year 810 AD and a number of his students memorised his book and narrated it to others. This book and period of his scholarship are usually referred to as al-Madh-habs al-Qadeem (the old school of thoughts) to differentiate it from the second period of his scholarship which occurred after he reached Egypt. In Egypt he absorbed the Fiqh of

Imam al-Layth ibn Sa'd and dictated *al-Madh-habs al jadeed* (the new school of thoughts) to his students in the form of another book which he named al-Umm (he essence). Because of his exposure to a completely new set of Hadiths and legal reasoning, in *al-Madh-habs al jaded*, he reversed many of the legal positions which we had held while in Iraq. Imam ash-Shafi'ii holds the distinction of being the first Imam to systematise the fundamental principles of Fiqh which he recorded in his book called *ar-Risalah*.[85]

Source of Law used by Shafi'ii Madh-habs

1. **The Qur'an**

   Ash-Shafi'ii did not differ from the previously mentioned Imams, in their uncompromising stand in relation to the primacy of the Qur'an among the source of Islamic law. He relied on it completely as those before him adding only the new insight which he gained from a deep study of its meaning.

2. **The Sunnah**

   Imam Ash-Shafi'ii laid down only one condition for the acceptance of Hadiths, namely that they be authentic (Sahih). He rejected all the other conditions set by Imam Abu Hanifa and Imam Malik. He was also noted for his great contributions to the science of Hadiths criticism.

3. **Ijma'a**

   Although Ash-Shafi'ii had serious doubts about the possibility of the Ijma'a in a number of cases, he conceded that in the few cases where it was known to have occurred, it should be regarded as the third most important source of Islamic law.

4. **Individual opinion of the Sahaabah**

   Approval was given by Imam Shafi'ii to the individual opinions of the Sahaabah on condition that they were not at variance with each other. If there were conflicting opinions among the Sahaabah on a legal point, he like Abu Hanifa, would choose whichever opinion was the closest to the source and leave the rest.

5. **Qiyaas (Analogy)**

   Qiyaas was in the Imam's opinion a valid method for deducing further laws from the previous sources. However, he placed it last in order of importance, considering his personal opinions inferior to proofs based on the opinions of the companions.

6. **Istis-haab (Linking)**

   Both the principle Istihsan used by Abu Hanifa and Istislaah used by Maalik were rejected by Ash-Shafi'ii and considered a form of Bid'ah (innovation), since, in his opinion, they were based mostly on human reasoning in areas where revealed laws already existed. However, in dealing with similar issues Ash Shafi'ii was obliged to use a principle similar to Istihsaan and Istislaah which he called *istis-haab.* Istis-haab literally means seeking a link, but legally it refers to the process of deducing Fiqh laws by linking a later set of circumstances with an earlier set. It is based on the assumption that the Fiqh laws applicable to certain conditions remain valid so long as it is not certain that these conditions have altered. If, for example, on account of the long absence of someone, it is doubtful whether he is alive or dead, the by Istis-haab all rules must remain in force that would hold if one knew for certain that he was still alive.[86]

Main students of Shafi'ii Madh-hab:

Al-Muzani (791-876 AD)

Al-Muzanee's full name was Imaa'eelibn Yahya al-Muzani. He was the constant companion of Imam Ash Shafi'ii throughout his stay in Egypt. Al-Muzani was noted for writing a book which comprehensively gathered the Fiqh of

Ash-Shafi'ii. Later condensed under the title Mukhtasal al-Muzani, it became the most widely read Fiqh book of the Shafi'ii Madh-habs.

Ar-Rabi' Al-Maraadi (790-873 AD)

Ar-Rabi' was noted as the main narrator of Ash Shafi'ii's book *al-Umm*. He wrote it down during Imam Ash Shafi'ii's lifetime along with *Ar-Rasaalah* and other books.

Yousuf ibn Yahyaa al-Buwaytee

Yousuf ibn Yahyaa succeeded Ash Shafi'ii as the main teacher of the Madh-hab. He was imprisoned and tortured to death in Baghdad because he rejected the officially sanctioned Mua'tazilite philosophy on the creation of the Qur'an.[87]

The Hambali Madh-habs: The Founder: Imam Ahmad (778-855 AD)

The scholar to whom this Madh-hab is attributed is Ahmad ibn Hambal ash-Shaybani, who was born in Baghdad in the year 778 AD. He became one of the great memorisers and narrators of hadiths of his time. Concentrating on the study of Hadiths, Ahmad studied Fiqh and science of Hadiths under Imam Abu Yusuf, the famous student of Imam Abu Hanifa, as well as under Imam Ash Shafi'ii himself. Imam Ahmad went through a series of persecution under the caliphs of his time due to their adoption of Mua'atazilite philosophy. He was jailed and beaten for two years by order of Caliph al-Ma'moon rule (813-842 AD), because of his rejection of the philosophical concept that the Qur'an was created. Later set free, he continued teachings in Baghdad until al-Wathiq became caliph rule (842-846 AD) and renewed the persecution. There upon, Imam Ahmad stopped teaching and went into hiding for five years until caliph al-Mutawakkil (847-862 AD) took over. Caliph al-Mutawakkil ended the inquisition permanently by expelling the Mua'tazilite scholars and officially rejecting their philosophy. Imam Ahmad continued to teach in Baghdad until he died in the year 855 AD.

Imam Ahmad's greatest concern was the collection, narration and interpretation of Hadiths. His teaching method consisted of dictating Hadiths from his vast collection known as *al-Musnad*, which contained over 30,000 Ahadith as well as the various opinions of the Sahaabah concerning their interpretation. He would then apply the Hadith or rulings to various existing problems. If he could not find suitable hadiths or opinion to solve a problem he would offer his own opinion while forbidding his students to record any of his own solutions. As a result, his Madh-habs was recorded, not by his students but by their students.[88]

Source of law used by the Hambali Madh-habs

1. **The Quran**

   There was no difference between the way Ahmad ibn Hambal approached Quran and that of those who preceded him. In other words, the Quran was given precedence over all use under all circumstances.

2. **The Sunnah**

   Likewise, the Sunnah of the Prophet PBUH occupied the number two position among the fundamental principles used by the founder of this school in the deduction of laws. His only stipulation was that it be Ma'arfu, i.e. attributed directly to the Prophet PBUH.

3. **Ijma'a of the Sahaabah**

   Imam Ahmad recognised the consensus of opinion of the Sahaabah and placed it in the third position among the fundamental principles. However, he discredited the claims of Ijma'a in post-Sahaabah's era. He termed it as being inaccurate due to the vast number of scholars and their wide diffusion throughout the Muslim empire. In his opinion Ijma'a after the era of the Sahaabah was impossible.

4. **Individual opinions of the Sahaabah**

   If a problem arose in an area where the Sahaabah had expressed conflicting opinions, Imam Ahmad like

Imam Malik would give credence to all the various individual opinions. Because of this, there developed within the Madh-habs many instances of multiple rulings for individual issues.

5. **Hadiths *Da'eef* (weak Hadiths)**

   For a ruling on a case where none of the previous four principles offered a ready solution, the Imam used to prefer to use a weak Hadiths rather than applying his own deductive reasoning (qiyas). However, this was on fact that one of its narrators was classified as a *Faasiq* (Disobedient),[89] as *Kadh-haab* (liar).

6. **Qiyaas**

   As a last resort, that is when no other major principle could be directly applied, Imam Ahmad would reluctantly apply the principle of Qiyas and deduce a solution based on one or more of the previous principles.[90]

Main students of the Imam Ahmad Hambal:

Imam Ahmad's main students were his own two sons, Saalih (died 873 AD) and Abdullah (died 903 AD). Imam Bukhari and Imam Muslim, compilers of the most outstanding collections of Hadiths, were the great scholars who studied under Imam Ahmad.

The Dhaahiri Madh-hab: The Founder: Imam Dawood (815-883 AD)

The founder of this School of Thought, Dawood ibn 'Ali, was born in Kufah in the year 815 AD. His early Fiqh studies were under Imam Ash Shafi'ii' students, but he later inclined towards the study of Hadiths and joined the circle of Imam Ahmad ibn Hambal. He continued to study under Ahmad until he was expelled from Ahmad's classes because he voiced the opinion that Quran was *Muhdat* (newly created). After his expulsion, he took an independent path of reasoning based on the obvious and literal meanings *Dhaahir* of the text of the Quran and the Sunnah. Because of this approach, his Madh-hab was called the Dhaahiri Madh-hab and he became known as Dawood adh- Dhaahiri.[91]

Source of law used by the Imam Dawood

1. **The Quran and Sunnah**

   Like all of the other Ayimma (plural of Imam), Dawood considered the Quran to be the foremost source of Islamic law followed by the Sunnah. However, only literal interpretations of their texts were considered by him as valid, which means they were only applied in the particular circumstances which they described.

2. **Ijma'a of the Sahaabah**

   Imam Dawood gave credence to the Ijma'a of the Sahabah. He reasoned that their unanimity would only have been on points of law revealed to the Prophet PBUH and known to the Sahaabah, but not narrated as Hadiths for some reason or the other. Therefore, Ijma'a of the Sahaabah was not considered by him as resulting from reasoning (Qiyas).

3. **Qiyas**

   Since Imam Dawood limited the application of the Qur'an and the Sunnah to their literal meaning, he automatically denied validity of rulings based on any form of reasoned opinion, including Qiyas. However, the principle of Mafhoom (understood meaning) which he applied to the Quran and Sunnah in place of Qiyas turned out to be virtually indistinguishable from Qiyas (analogical deduction).

Dhaahiri Madh-hab

Due to the limited scope of the Dhaahiri Madh-hab and the absence of outstanding scholar to pass on its principles and rulings, it did not last very long. In fact, it did not get a foothold in any regions in the Muslim empire during Imam Dawood's lifetime and even after his death.

In later times, all scholars who denied the validity of Qiyas were labeled as Dhaahiri, even though they had not actually studied under Imam Dawood or his students, or even read their works.

The most noted student of the Dhaahiri Madh-hab was a brilliant eleventh century AD Spanish scholar named 'Ali ibn Ahmad ibn Hazm al-Andalusi (died 1070 AD). Ibn Hazm revived this Madh-hab and defended it in the numerous outstanding works which he wrote in various fields of Islamic Study; for example, *Ihkaam al-Ahkaam* in the field of Usool al-Fiqh, *al-Faisal* in Theology and *al-Muhalla* in Fiqh. Due to Ibn Hazm's tireless efforts, the Madh-hab took hold in Islamic Spain where it flourished and from there it spread to some areas of North Africa and elsewhere. It remained prevalent in Spain until the Islamic State began to crumble there in the early 1400's. With the disappearance of Muslim states of Andalus, the Madh-habs also disappeared, leaving behind only a number of scholarly writings, most of which were done by Ibn Hazm himself.[92]

The Jariri Madh-hab: The Founder: Imam at- Tabari (839-923 AD)

This Madh-hab was founded by Muhammad ibn Jarir ibn Yazid at-Tabari who was born in the province of Tabaristan in the year 839 AD. He acquired a high degree of proficiency in the field of Hadith, Fiqh and History. As a travelling jurist, he studied the system of Imam Abu Hanifa, Imam Malik, Imam Ash-Shafi'ii and others. For the first ten years after his return from Egypt he strictly followed the Shafi'ii Madh-hab. At the end of that period he founded the school of his own. Whose followers called themselves Jariri after his father's name but his Madh-hab could not survive either.

Ibn Jarir was most noted for his outstanding Tafsir of the Quran which he called Jaami'al Bayan, which also popularly known as Tafsir at-Tabari. Of equal importance and fame was his history of the world called Taarikh as Rasul was-Muluk, commonly known as Taarikh at-Tabari.[93]

Main Reasons for Conflicting Rulings

We have seen that although the Imams of the our major Madh-habs were all agreed on the primacy of the four fundamental principles of Islamic law i.e. Quran, Sunnah, Ijma'a and Qiyas, certain differences have occurred still exist among the rulings of their Madh-habs. These differences arose for various reasons, the chief ones being related to the following aspects:

- Interpretation of word meanings and grammatical constructions.
- History of Hadiths and its narrators. Its availability, authenticity, conditions for acceptance and interpretation of textual conflict.
- Admissibility of certain traditions like Ijma'a, *aadaat* Arab customs, Istihsaan and opinion of Sahaabah.
- Methods of Qiyas.

1. Meanings of the Word.

The interpretational differences which occurred over the meanings of words, has three basic forms:

(a) Shared literal meanings

There are few words which occur in both the Quran and the Sunnah with more than one literal meanings; for e.g. the word Qur (plural Quru or Aqra), which means menses as well as the time of purity between menses. Thus, scholars of Fiqh were divided into two camps concerning the interpretation of the Quranic verse, "Divorced women should wait three Quru."[94]

The particular interpretation chosen makes an important differences when considering the case of a divorced woman who has started her third menses. According to those who considered Qur' to be the period of purity, the divorce becomes finalised as soon as her menses have started, while according to those who viewed Qur' as the actual menses, it is not finalised until her third menses have ended.

Imam Malik, Imam Ash Shafi'ii and Imam Ahmad ruled that Qur' meant to be the period of purity. Only Imam Abu Hanifa ruled that Qur' means the actual menses.[95]

To further understand the stand of Imam Abu Hanifa let us see the Hadiths narrated by Ayesha who said "Umm Habibah had irregular menses and she asked the Prophet PBUH about it. He told her to stop praying during the days of her Qur's."[96] Ayeesha also reported to have said, "I told Barirah to observe a waiting period *iddah* of three menses."[97] These narration clearly indicates that the intended meanings of Qur' is the menses itself.

(b) Literal and Figurative meanings

There are also some words in the Quran and the Sunnah which have both literal and figurative meanings. For example, the word Lams (touch) is literally used to indicate touching by the hand or coming in contact of two objects, and figuratively to indicate sexual intercourse. Thus, the jurists were of three different opinions concerning the meaning of the Quranic verse; "...or you touched (Laamastum) women and can not find water, then make Tayammum from clean earth."[98]

This verse occurs in the context of the factor which breaks the state of Ablution.

(c) Grammatical Meanings

There were also certain grammatical constructions in Arabic, which were ambiguous. For example, the word *elaa* (to) could simply mean "up to but not including", as in the case of this Quranic verse,

"And complete the fast up to (elaa) the night."[99]

The fast is continued upto Maghrib (sunset), the beginning of the night, but does not include the night itself. There is no dispute about this interpretation. However, *elaa* (to) also means "upto and including", as in the case of the Quranic verse, "And we will drive the guilty up to (elaa) Hell like a weary herd."[100]

2. Narrations of Hadiths

The cause of legal differences, which developed among jurists over the narration and application of Hadiths, can be understood with the following points.

(a) Availabilty of Hadiths

There were numerous cases where certain narrations of Hadiths, did not reach some of the scholars, due to the fact that the Sahaabah who narrated them had settled in various regions throughout the Islamic empire, and the major Madh-habs were founded in different parts of the empire, before the comprehensive compilation of hadiths were made. To be more specific the Madh-hab of Imam Abu Hanifa (702-767 AD), Imam Malik (717-855 AD), Imam Ash-Shafi'ii and Imam Ahmad Hambal (778-855 AD) were founded between the middle of the eighth century AD and the early part of the ninth century. Where as the most authentic and comprehensive compilations of Hadiths (the Siha Sitta, The Authentic Six) were not available until the later part of the ninth century and the early decade of the tenth.

(b) Weak narration of Hadiths

There were cases where some jurists based their rulings on Hadiths which were in fact Da'eef (weak and unreliable). They were unaware of the unreliability of those Hadiths or also because they took the position that a weak hadiths was to be preferred to their Qiyas.

Since the development of science of Hadiths it is being found that there are various traditions which is said to come under the Da'eef hadiths. There few types of Da'eef Hadiths which is mentioned below.

Types of the Da'eef Ahadith

(a) *The Mu'allaq Traditions:* These are those Traditions in which one or two transmitters are omitted in the beginning of the Isnad.

(b) *The Maqtu Traditions:* These are those traditions which are reported by a Tabi'i, a man of second category after the Prophet.

(c) *The Munqati Traditions:* These are the broken traditions.

(d) *The Mursal Traditions:* These are the incomplete traditions in the Isnad of which a companion (Sahabi) is omitted, e.g. A Tabi'i says, the Prophet said....

(e) *The Musahhaf Traditions:* These are the traditions which have a mistake in words or letters of the Isnad or the Matn e.g. Hasan is written as Hashan.

(f) *The Shadh Traditions:* These are the traditions with a reliable chain of reporters but their meanings are contrary to other similarly attested traditions narrated by the majority of the contemporary transmitters.

(g) *The Maudu Traditions:* These are the fabricated and untrue Traditions."[101]

(c) Condition for the Acceptance of Hadiths

Other differences among jurists in the area of the Sunnah arose from various conditions they placed on its acceptability. For example, Imam Abu Hanifa stipulated that Hadiths had to be *Mash-hoor* (Well known) before being regarded as admissible evidence, whereas Imam Milk stipulated that a Hadiths must not contradict the customs of the Madinites in order to be admissible. On other hand, Imam Ahmad considered *Mursal.*[102] Hadiths as acceptable as proof while Imam Ash-Shafi'ii accepted only Mursal hadiths of Sa'eed ibn al-Mussayib which most Hadiths scholars believed it to be authentic.[103]

(d) Resolutions of Textual conflict in Hadiths

The founders of the Madh-habs and their students took two main approaches in resolving apparent contradictions between the literal meanings of some of the recorded narrations of hadiths. Some jurists chose the path of *tarjih* which means giving preference to some hadiths while rejecting other on the same topic. *Tarjih* is a legal concept that comes into play when there exists two or more apparently contradictory items of legal evidence that cannot be reconciled in any other way as provided by legal theory. So if this is the case, one opinion or evidence will be given preference or precedence over the other, based on the conditions stipulated by legal scholars. This process is called *tarjih*.[104] On the other hand, some of the other jurists chose the path of *Jama'* which involved combining of such hadiths using it in a general sense.

3. Admissibility of Certain Principles

There were some among the Imams who developed a number of controversial principles on which they based some of their rulings. As a result, both the rulings and the principles became source of differences among jurists. For example, the majority of the jurist recognised the validity of Ijma'a among the generations after the Sahaabah but Imam Ash-Shafi'ii questioned its occurrence while Imam Ahmad rejected it outright. Similarly the majority of the jurists rejected Imam Mailk's reliance on the custom of Madinites as source of legislation. And Imam Abu Hanifa's principle of Istihsaan and Malik's Istislaah were both disallowed by Imam Ash-Shafi'ii as being too independent of Quran, the Sunnah and Ijma'a. That is to say, they relied too much in his opinion on human reasoning. On the other hand Imam Ash-Shafi'ii felt that the opinion of the Sahaabah had to be accepted on legal matters, while others felt that it was only reasoning on their part which was not binding later generations.[105]

4. Methods of Qiyas

The various approaches which jurists took in their application of Qiyas were perhaps the largest source of differences among them. Some narrowed down the scope of Qiyas by setting a number of preconditions for its use, while others expanded its scope. Because this principle was based on opinion to a greater extent than any of the others, there were no hard and fast rules with which to contain it and thus a wide range of differences developed.

THE FIFTH STAGE: CONSOLIDATION

This stage covers the period between the year 950 AD and the sacking of Baghdad (1259 AD) and represents the decline of the 'Abbasid dynasty until its eventual collapse. Competitive debates called *Munazarat* continued to flourish under the patronage of the Abbasid caliphs and some of these debates were actually recorded in books. In time, the spirit of rivalry largely generated by these debates spread to the masses, and Madh-hab factionalism became widespread. There was a drastic reduction in the number of Madh-habs and the structure and operation of the four schools that survived became highly systematised. Scholars within a Madh-habs were obliged to base their *ijtihad* solely on the fundamental principles (Usool) of their particular Madh-hab. During this period the compilation of Fiqh was further formalised and further deepened the Madh-habs rivalry.

Four School of Thoughts or Madh-habs

During this stage, the number of major Madh-habs (Schools of Islamic Thoughts) dwindled to four; three major and one minor. In other words the Madh-habs of great Imam like al-Awz'ii, Sufiyan ath-Thawri, Ibn Ali Layla, Abu Thawr and al-Layth ibn Sa'ad had all disappeared leaving only the Madh-habs of Imam Abu Hanifa, Imam Malik, Imam Ash-Shafi'ii and Imam Ahmad Hambal. In course of time, these schools of Islamic legal thoughts became so predominant that the common people soon forgot that any other schools ever existed. Each of these schools soon took on dynamism of its own and their respective Madh-habs.[106]

During this stage the scholars of each Madh-habs analysed all the rulings of their Madh-hab's founding scholars, deduced the fundamental principles behind their rulings and codified them. They also made limited Ijtihads on issues which the founders had not come across. However, this area soon became exhausted due to the widespread use of the hypothetical Fiqh. Ultimately independent Ijtihad was discarded in favour of Ijtihad based upon the established principles of a particular Madh-habs which also known as *Ijtihad Madh-habi*, as this new form of reasoning came to be known, was based on deduction of laws for new issues according to the scholars of this period. They even sometimes differed with the founders of their Madh-habs with respect to the fundamental principles.[107]

The Scholars of the Madh-habs also made use of the principle of Tarjih which involved preferring and favouring certain opinions held by scholars within a given Madh-habs. Difference of opinion on one issue within a school had arisen when the founding scholars as well as their students changed their earlier opinions. Both version were recorded and passed on to later generation as different opinions of the Madh-habs. Differences of opinion also arise from different interpretation of statements made by earlier scholars of the Madh-habs. In each Madh-habs, the scholars during this period of consolidation sifted out weak and fabricated statements which had been attributed to the founders of their respective Madh-habs. They also classified the narrations of opinions of the founder according to their accuracy. This process of authentication and classification was referred to as *Tashrih*.[108]

This detailed systematic treatment of Fiqh within each of the Madh-habs greatly facilitated the process of arriving at legal rulings within a Madh-hab. However, as in the case of the systematic treatment of the sources of Islamic law in the previous stage, the very fine distinctions elaborated on by the scholars of this period further contributed to Madh-hab factionalism. During this segment of the 'Abbasid rule, a format for writing Fiqh books evolved. This format became a standard, which has remained in practice until today. The various issues were grouped under main headings and the main headings under different chapters. Each of which represented a major topics from Shari'ah.[109]

The authors would begin with the four pillars after *Imaan* (faith), since Imaan was dealt within books of Islamic theology. After treating the laws and issues concerning *Taharat* (Hygiene) and *Salaah* (prayer). *Sawm* (Fasting), *Zakat* (Tax) and *Haj* (pilgrimage), then they would proceed on a *Nikah* (marriage) and *talaq* (Divorce), then *Bay* (Business Transaction) and then *Aadaab* (etiquettes). In dealing with any of these issues, and author from any one Madh-habs would mention the different proofs used by all of the Madh-habs position, while refuting the arguments of the other Madh-habs.[110]

THE SIXTH STAGE: STAGNATION AND DECLINE

This stage covers approximately six centuries starting with the sacking of Baghdad in 1258 and the execution of the last Abbasid Caliph, al-Musta'sim and ending around the middle of the nineteenth century of the Christian era. This period also represents the rise of the Ottoman Empire, founded in 1299 CE by the Turkish leader 'Uthman I, until its decline under the attack of European colonialism.

The prevailing characteristics of this period were that of Taqlid (the blind following of a Madh-hab) and factionalism. This degenerative trend resulted in the curbing of all forms of *Ijtihad* and the evolution of Madh-habs into totally separate entities closely resembling sects. The compilation of Fiqh during this period was limited to commenting on previous works and was directed towards promotion of individual Madh-habs. Thus, the dynamism of Fiqh was lost and many of the laws became increasingly outmoded and inapplicable in their existing forms. In order to fill this legislative gap, European law codes were gradually introduced in place of some of the Islamic laws. Eventually with the advance of European colonialism and the breaking up of the Muslim empire, European laws replaced Islamic laws. Certain reformers sought to stem the tide of stagnation and decline, calling for a return to the original purity of Islam and its laws. However, factionalism has continued to the present day, in spite of an increase in Institutional teaching of comparative fiqh.[111]

Taqlid proved to be antagonistic to the religious values given in Quran. Quran provides moral guidelines to human beings. It enables human beings to live a meaningful and purposeful life. A life without reason and void of intellectual content cannot be said to be a purposeful or meaningful life. Religion, as pointed out, is a constant quest for truth and moral uprightness and this quest is not possible without active intellect. In any quest for truth intellect plays very important role. Ignorance or lack of intellect leads to moral degeneration. Qur'an describes ignorance as darkness and knowledge 'ilm as light and poses the question can darkness be equated with light? Also, it teaches Muslims a prayer rabbe zidni 'ilman i.e. O Sustainer, increase me in knowledge (20-114). Now acquisition of knowledge is not possible without the help of reason. Knowledge and reason go together. It is reason which produces knowledge. Thus, the Qur'an accords highest priority to i'man on one hand, and to reason and knowledge, on the other. One, in fact, compliments the other. According to Qur'an i'man cannot be complete without the active role of reason.[112] Hence to accept *Taqlid* then would mean depriving ourselves to fulfill our Iman which is the most important aspect of Islam.

Emergence of *Taqlid*

Taqlid in Islam refers to accepting and following the verdicts of scholars of *fiqh* in their exposition and interpretation of Islamic law, without demanding from them an in-depth explanation of the processes required to arrive at such a verdict.[113] It implies that the duty of ordinary Muslims is to trustingly accept the authority of scholars in this matter and act upon their verdict.

Though there are several ayat in the Quran that forbid the taqlid of others in matters of religion (5:104-5, 17:36, 21:52-54 43:22-24).[114] However, this prohibition is interpreted to refer only to the fundamentals of religion (*usul ad-din*) and not to details of law and ritual practices (subsidiary elements of religion or *furu 'ad-din*) these can only be learned through extensive study, and those who have not carried out this study can follow the guidance of those who have. In orthodox Sunni Islam, it is generally regarded as impermissible for a person who has not mastered all the details of fiqh to derive their own rulings on matters of law.

During this period the scholars left all forms of *Ijtihad* and unanimously issued legal rulings, which was intended to close the door of *Ijtihad* permanently. They reasoned that all possible issues had already been raised and addressed and therefore there was no need for further *Ijtihad*. With that step, a new concept of Madh-hab arose, namely that one of the four Madh-habs had to be followed for one's Islam to be valid. This concept became firmly embedded among the masses as well as the scholars of Fiqh. Thus, the religion of Islam itself became restricted within the confines of the four existing Madh-habs; Hanafi, Shafi'ii, Maliki and Hambali. These Schools of law came to be considered divinely ordained manifestation of Islam. All of them supposed to be completely correct, equal and representative of true Islam, yet there were innumerable differences among them. In fact, there were scholars in this period who interpreted some hadiths in such a way as to prove that the Prophet PBUH himself had predicted the appearance of Imam and their Madh-habs. Consequently, any attempt to go beyond these canonical Madh-habs was considered heretical and anyone who refused to follow one of these Madh-habs was classified an apostle. The ultra conservative scholars of this period even went so far as to rule that whoever was caught transferring from Madh-hab to another was liable to punishment at the discretion of the local judge. A ruling was also made, in the Hanafi Madh-habs prohibiting the marriage of a Hanafi to a Shafi'ii. And even the second most important pillar of Islam *Salaah* (Offering Namaz) was not spared the effects of Madh-hab fanaticism. The followers of the various Madh-habs began to refuse to pray behind the Imam from other

Madh-habs. This resulted in the building of separate prayer niches in the Mosque. There were people in the community who belong to different Madh-habs and hence this separation in the Mosque. Mosque of this type can still be seen in places like Syria, where Sunni Muslims follow either the Hanafi or Shafi'ii Madh-hab. Even the most holy Mosque al-Haram (Ka'ba) of Mecca which represents the unity of Muslims and the religion of Islam, was not spared. Separate prayer niches were set up around the Ka'ba; one for an Imam from each of the schools. And when the time for prayer came, an Imam from one of the Madh-habs would lead a congregation of followers and so on. It is interesting to note that separate places of prayer for each of the Madh-habs remained around Ka'ba until the first quarter of the twentieth century when King Abdul Aziz ibn Saud and his army conquered Mecca on October 1924; he united all the worshippers behind a single Imam regardless of his or their Madh-habs.[115]

Reason for *Taqlid*

Taqlid (blind following) has to be distinguished from the followings based on reasons. The principle of following the rulings of our predecessors is a normal methodology. In fact, it is by closely following earlier interpretations of Islam that the message of Islam remains uncorrupted through time. For, those early interpretations were founded on the Prophet's PBUH divine inspiration and his divinely guided life style. The best generation was during the period of Prophet PBUH and his companions but since Muslims of earlier generation, with the exception of the Prophet PBUH were not infalliable, even those earlier interpretations should not be followed blindly without regard to certain basic principles of reason which enable us to distinguish between right and wrong. In this book the term *Taqlid* (blind following) is used to refer to the actions to those who slavishly follow a single Madh-hab regardless of errors that they see. As for the common people who do not have the knowledge to make independent decisions in doubtful situations, it is for them to follow whatever knowledge is available to them, keep their minds open and rely on open-minded scholars as much as possible.[116]

Taqlid was the result of a number of factors, internal and external to the Madh-habs, which affected the development of Fiqh and the attitude of scholars. There were many factors and causes which resulted in stagnation of the Fiqh science. Or we can say these factors led to the stagnation stage.

(1) The School of Fiqh was completely formed and the minute details were worked out. The laws for what had occurred as well as what might occur, were already deduced and recorded due to the extensive development of speculative Fiqh. This left no room for *Ijtihad* and originality of the law as a result the scholars were entirely dependent on the earlier work of the scholars from different Madh-habs without making any effort for new consensus.

(2) The Abbasid caliphate, which had come to power under the banner of restoring Islamic law to its former place, lost its power to the king's ministers many of whom were Shi'ites and the empire eventually broke up. The new rules by proxy were more interested in private power struggles than in either religious scholarship or government according to Islamic laws.

(3) The crumbling of the Abbasid empire into mini-states was accompanied by each state following the Madh-habs, Spain the Maliki Madh-hab and Turkey and India The Hanafi Madh-hab. Each state began the practice of choosing its governors administrator and judges only from those who followed its official Madh-habs. Consequently, scholars who wanted to become judges (Qazi) in the courts of these states had to follow the official Madh-habs.

(4) Some unqualified individuals began to claim the right to make *Ijtihad* in order to twist the religion to suit their wishes. Consequently, many incompetent scholars began making rulings which misguided the

> masses on a number of issues. This led to fabrication of Hadiths and fiqh leading to ambiguous and confronting rulings. The reputed scholars to check such practice tried to close the door of Ijtihad in order to protect Shariah from being tampered with.[117]

The same factor which led to *Taqlid* also caused scholars to confine their creative activity to merely editing and revising previous works. The Fiqh books of earlier scholars were condensed and abridgements of them were made. These abridgements were later shortened in order to make them easy to memorise. The comprehensive works of the earlier scholars were condensed further to make summaries. It became a virtual riddles to the student of that period. The following generation of scholars began to write explanation of these summaries. And then later scholars wrote commentaries on the explanations.

During this period some books on the fundamentals of Fiqh (usul al-fiqh) were written. In these works the correct method of making *Ijtihad* was outlined and the conditions which were laid down by these scholars were so strict that they excluded not only the scholars of their times but also many of the earlier scholars who had made *Ijtihad*.[118]

There were also a few books, which were written, on comparative Fiqh during this period. As in the previous period, the opinions of the Madh-habs and their proofs were collected and criticised in these books. The authors then defined the opinion as most authentic, of those scholars who belong to their own particular Madh-habs. Towards the end of this period, an attempt was made to codify Islamic law under the auspices of the Ottoman Caliph. A panel of seven top ranking scholars of fiqh was formed and entrusted this job. It was completed in 1876 AD and enforced as law by the Sultan throughout the Ottoman Empire under the title *Majallah al-Ahkam al-Aadilah* (The Just Code).[119] However, even this seemingly noble attempt was affected by Madh-habs fanaticism. All of the scholars on the committee were appointed from the Hanafi Madh-hab. Consequently, while drafting the Code the contribution to Fiqh Madh-habs were completely ignored.

In course of time the European imperialism beginning with Java, which fell to the Dutch in 1684, absorbed Muslim East Asian States. After Transylvania and Hungary fell from Ottoman hands to Austria in 1699 and the defeat of Ottomans by Russia in Russo-Turkish war of 1768-74, the European territories of the Ottoman Empire were soon lost, one after another.[120] This process culminated in the total dissolution of the Ottoman Empire during the First World War and its division into colonies and protectorates. As a result European Law codes replaced Islamic laws throughout the Muslim world.

Although European colonialism was officially ended some years ago, Islamic law has remained disuse in all Muslim countries with exception of Saudi Arabia which has codified Islamic law according to the Hambali Madh-hab, Pakistan to a large degree according to the Hanafi Madh-hab and Iran which has recently done so according to the Ja'fari Madh-hab.[121]

The Imams and *Taqlid*

During the early stage of evolution of Fiqh scholars from different regions and times evolved principles of Fiqh as well as specific law of Fiqh in order to resolve various new issues as they arose. The correctness of their interpretations was proportional to their innate capabilities and to the type and quantity of evidence available to them at the time of making rulings. Some were faced with the additional factor of cultural differences and many were deprived of the assistance or consultation owing to their distance from their colleagues and consequently difficulties in communication. Hence the difference of opinion from region to region. Historically therefore appearance of more than one Madh-habs was inevitable. Further more as the numbers of Madh-habs increased and communication and other factors exercised their influence, difference and contradictions too were a natural outcome. However, so long as scholars managed to keep the goal with truth foremost in their mind and were not led astray by sectarianism, fanaticism or a desire for personal glory and reward, the essential spirit of Islam was preserved in their Madh-habs. In such circumstances, scholars were in no way reluctant to abandon their individual opinions in favour of rulings by others which were clearly shown to be nearer the intended meaning deducible from the Qur'an and the Sunnah. In other words there was continuing search for truth until the negative factors became prominent in the lives of some of the scholars. Then indeed the blind following of the Madh-hab (Taqlid) coupled with ban on Ijtihad led to the widespread promotion of sectarianism among the masses and the general decline in the search for truth among many scholars. Thereafter, the four surviving Madh-habs, with different sometimes with contradictory rulings, assumed the character of infallibility and spurious Hadiths arose to bolster this anti-Islamic trait. As a counter to this decline, various reform movements through the ages have called for unification of the Madh-habs or in some cases rejection of the need for any Madh-hab.[122]

From the historical development of Fiqh and the evolution of the Madh-habs described here we have seen that there was a period during which natural differences among the various Madh-habs became extremely exaggerated to the point of sectarianism, so much so that scholars of that time discarded Ijtihad and imposed upon the Muslims the Taqlid of one of the four major Madh-habs. However, Imam's to whom the four schools are attributed were themselves totally against the enthronement of these differences and fought vehemently against Taqlid either among their own followers or among the masses in general. Yet today till today many people feel that if an authentic hadiths should be discarded because accepting it would mean declaring that the Imam of one's Madh-hab was mistaken in his rulings which in their opinion are an act of disrespect or even blasphemy. Little do they realise that their preference of their Imam's opinion over Prophet PBUH statement itself is in total opposition to the stand taken by their Imams.[123]

Imam Abu Hanifa and *Taqlid*

Imam Abu Hanifa used to discourage his students from recording his opinions, since they were often based on Qiyas (analogical deduction). However, he made an exception of those opinions which were thoroughly debated and agreed upon by all his students. His student, Abu Yusuf reported that the Imam once told him, "Woe is on you Yaqub. Do not write down all you hear from me for surely I may hold an opinion today and leave it tomorrow, hold another tomorrow and leave it the day after." This prohibition by Imam kept his student from blindly imitating his view and helped to develop in them a respect for their own opinions as well as that of others.

Imam Abu Hanifa also made many strong statements concerning the blind following of his opinions and those of his students. In fact, he strictly forbade anyone from following their opinions or making legal rulings based on them unless such a person was familiar with the proofs which he and his students had used and from where they has deduced them. Imam Abu Hanifa's students Zufar reported that Imam said "It is forbidden for anyone who does not know my proofs to make a ruling according to my statements, for verily we are only humans we may say something today and reject it tomorrow."[124]

Imam Abu Hanifa was always aware of his limitations. His student Muhammad ibn al-Hasan, reported that he said, "If I have made rulings which contradicts Allah's book of the messenger's Hadiths, reject my rulings." It is also recorded that he pointed out the fact that the principle to follow, if one wanted to follow his Madh-habs as he intended it to be followed. Imam ibn Abdul Barr reported that Imam Abu Hanifa said, "If a Hadiths is found to be *Sahih* (authentic), it is my Madh-hab."[125]

Imam Malik and *Taqlid*

Imam Malik never hesitated to change his rulings, even if he had already uttered them in public, if proof which contradicts his ruling comes to him from reliable source. One of his main students, Ibn Wahab confirmed this attitude of the Imam saying, "I once heard some one asked Imam Malik about washing between the toes as during Wudoo (Ablution), to which he replied people do not have to do it. I waited until most of the people left the study circle and informed him that there is a Hadith concerning it. He asked what it was? I said that al-Layth ibn Sa'd, ibn luhayah and Amr ibn Al-Harith all related from al-Mustawarid ibn Shidaad al-Quraish that he saw Allah's messenger PBUH rubs between his toes with his little finger", Malik said "that is good hadith which I ever heard before." He later, when people asked him about washing between the toes, he used to insist that it must be washed." This narration is clear proof that Imam Malik's Madh-hab like Abu Hanifa was that of the sound Hadiths should be given precedence over Imam's opinion.[126]

Imam Malik also emphasised the fact that he was subject to error and that the only rulings of his which should be used were those which did not come in conflict with the Qur'an and Hadith. Ibn 'Abdul Barr reported that Malik once said, "verily I am only a man, I err and am at times correct ; so thoroughly investigate my opinions, then take whatever agrees with the Quran and Sunnah, and rejects whatever contradicts them."[127] This statement clearly proves that Quran and Hadiths were given preference over all else by this great scholar who never intended that his opinion should be rigidly followed.

When Abbasid Caliph Abu Ja'afar al Mansoor and Haroon al-Rashid requested that Malik allow them to make his collection of Hadiths called al-Muwatta, the official authority in the state on Sunnah, he refused on both occasions, pointing out that the Sahaabah had scattered throughout the land and had left behind many hadiths which is not there in his collection. Thus, Malik turned down the opportunity to have his Madh-hab made the official Madh-hab of the Islamic state and in doing so, he set an example those others might have been wise to follow.

Imam Ash-Shafi'ii and *Taqlid*

Imam Ash-Shafi'ii like his teacher Malik pointed out in no uncertain terms that it was not possible for anyone at that time to be aware of all the Hadiths which were narrated from the Prophet PBUH or to remember all Hadiths which he had encountered; therefore they were bound to make some wrong judgments. This means that the only firm and reliable method, which could be unutilised under all circumstances to decide what was correct and what was not, was the Sunnah of Prophet PBUH. The Hadiths scholar al-Haakim collected a statement of Ash-Shafi'ii in which he said, "There is no one among us who has not had a Sunnah of Prophet elude him or have one slip his mind; so no matter what rulings I have made or fundamental principles I have proposed, there will be in them things contrary to rulings of the Messenger's Sunnah. Therefore, the correct ruling is according to what Allah's messenger said, and that is my ruling."[128]

The Imam also stressed a very important point concerning personal opinion versus the Sunnah. He said. "The Muslims were of a unanimous opinion that one who comes across an authentic Sunnah of Allah's messenger is not allowed to disregard it in favour of someone else's opinion". This point strikes at the very heart of *Taqlid* which has one of its pillars the rejection of the Sunnah for the opinion of the Madh-hab.

Al-Haakim also collected opinions from Imam Ash-Shafi'ii the same statement made by Imam Abu Hanifa concerning the relationship between his Madh-hab and authentic hadiths, "If a Hadith is found to be *Sahih* (authentic) it is my Madh-Hab."[129] Such was the uncompromising stand of this great Imam who, while in Baghdad, wrote a book called *al-Hujjah* as a summary of his Madh-hab, only to turn around and write a new book called *al-Umm*, representing the new Madh-hab which he formed after journeying to Egypt and acquiring new knowledge from the Madh-hab of Imam al-Layth ibn Sa'd.

Imam Ahmad ibn Hambal and *Taqlid*

Imam Ahmad carried on the tradition of his teacher, Imam Ash-Shafi'ii as well as that of the earlier Imam by trying to instill in his students a high respect for the sources of Islam and a disdain for rigid imitation of scholars opinions. But, because Talid had begun to take root among some of the followers of the earlier Imam, Imam Hambal took even more drastic action. Whereas Abu Hanifa discouraged his students from recording all of his opinions, Imam Ahmad forbade them from recording any of his opinions at all. Thus, his Madh-hab was not compiled in written form until the era of his students.

Imam Ahmad Hambal was very explicit in his warnings against *taqlid* as is evident in the following saying of his recorded by Ibn Qayyim, "Do not blindly follow my rulings, those of Malik, ash-Shafi'ii, al-Awza'ii or Ath-Thawri, take your rulings from where took theirs." Similarly in another of his statements recorded by Ibn Abdul Barr. He said, "The opinion of al-Awza'ii, Malik and Abu Hanifa are simply opinions and to me they are all equal, but the real criterion for right or wrong is in the Hadiths."[130]

The Imam's preference for Hadith over opinion was so great that he used to prefer a weak Hadiths over a deduced ruling. His respect for the Sunnah of the Prophet PBUH which he himself collected in a major work of over 30,000 Hadiths called al-Musnad Al-Kabir, was so great that he also gave severe warnings to those who would dare disregard a Hadith of the Prophet PBUH. Ibn Jawzi reported that Imam Ahmad Said, "whoever rejects an authentic Hadiths of Allah's messenger PBUH is on the verge of destruction." The holy Prophet PBUH had given the following order to his companions and Muslims in general, "convey what you have heard from me, even if it is only a verse (from the Quran)."[131] In order that divine guidance would be available to all generations of Muslim until the Last Day. Because of that, Imam Ahmad fought vigilantly against anything which could possibly interfere with the conveyance of divine guidance to his generation as well as those to come.[132]

Nevertheless, the prohibition of *Taqlid* does not mean that everyone must return to the sources before doing anything and it does not mean that all the work of the earlier scholars should be rejected or neglected, for that would be impractical and in most cases impossible. It does, however, mean that those who have sufficient knowledge of the various branches of Islamic sciences should not hesitate to look at the sources as well as the opinions of all the scholars, regardless of their Madh-hab. A scholar should have an inclusive and open minded approach in his search for knowledge otherwise his rulings likely to be biased and sectarian. Let us not forget that even in searching through the sources he is obliged to rely on the great works of the earlier scholars, or deduced his ruling from one of their deductions. In doing so will be following one of the earlier Imams directly or indirectly. However, this form of following is not to be considered *Taqlid,* which we have shown was forbidden categorically by the Imams. This form is called *Ittibaa* wherein reliable Hadiths take precedence over all opinions.

It is obvious that the great majority of Muslims will not be able to return to the sources, due to their lack of knowledge, and they will therefore be obliged to apply *Ittibaa* only to the degree of their ability. Many can achieve awareness of the relevant Hadiths by asking questions concerning the basis for rulings given to them and reading the books of Hadiths. No true scholars should be offended by such questions if asked to them. Similarly if the masses are forced to seek explanations and proofs along with the various rulings, and books which are not biased or sectarian.

Period of Reformers

In spite of the general decay of the Islamic legal science

as described above, there existed from time to time throughout this period few outstanding scholars who oppose *Taqlid* and dared to raise the banner of Ijtihad. They called for return to the roots of the religion, to the true sources of Islamic law and to rely on these foundations above all else.

Ahmad ibn Taymiyah (1263-1328 AD) was not foremost among the reformers of this period. Because of his challenge of the status quo, many of his contemporaries declared him an apostate and authorities imprisoned him repeatedly. Ibn Taymiyah however was the greatest scholar of his time. Initially he studied Fiqh according to the Hambali Madh-hab, but did not restrict himself to it. He studied the source of Islamic law in depth and mastered all Islamic sciences which were known at that time. Furthermore he examined the writings of various sects which had broken off from Islam, studied the religious books of Christians, the Jews and their various sects and wrote extensive critiques on all of them. Ibn Taymiyah also took part in the Jihad against the Mongols who occupied the Eastern and Northern provinces of the former Abbasid state and the Mongols were the great antagonists of Ijtihad and a return to pure source of Islam which he had raised. This banner of Ijtihad was carried out by the next generation of great scholars like Ibn Qayyim, a great scholar of the field of Fiqh and Hadiths criticism and Ibn Kathir, a master of *tafsir* (Commentary), History and Hadiths.

Muhammad ibn 'Ali ash-Shawkani (1757-1853 AD) born near the town of Shawkan in Yemen, was also among the reformers. Ash-Shawkani studied Fiqh according to the Zaidi Madh-hab[133] and became one of its outstanding scholars. He then did an in-depth study of the Hadiths of his time. At this point he freed himself form the boundaries of each Madh-habs and began making independent *Ijtihad.* He wrote a number of works in Fiqh and its fundamental in which issues studied from the point of view of all the Madh-habs were concluded with solution based solely on the most accurate proofs and the most convincing arguments. Imam ash-Shawkani took the position that Taqleed was Haram and wrote number of books on the topic, for example, *Al-Qawl al-Mufid fi Hukm at-Taqlid*. Consequently, he also came under attack from most of the scholars.

Another noteworthy reformer was the great scholar Ahmad ibn 'Abdur Raheem better know, as Shah Wali Allah Dihlavi (1703-1762 AD). He was born in the Indian sub-continent where *Taqlid* was, perhaps more rampant. After he had mastered the various Islamic sciences, he called for the re-opening of the door of Ijtihad and the reunification of the schools of Fiqh. In this effort to re-examine Islamic principles and to find out on what authority the legal schools based their regulations, Shah Wali Allah rejuvenate the study of Hadiths. Although he did not go so far to reject the existing Fiqh schools, nevertheless he taught that everyone was free to choose a particular decision different from that taken by the school to which he belonged himself if he was convinced that the case was better confirmed by the Hadiths.[134]

However, the over all state of degeneration and stagnation has continued until today, despite the efforts of modern thinkers like Jamal ad-din al-Afghani (1839-1897 AD) who traveled throughout the Muslim world calling for reform. Another reformist scholar was Muhammad Abduh (1849-1905 AD), he was among Afghani's most famous students. Under the influence of Afghani and Ibn Muhammad 'Abduh, its supporters were systematically attacked. But, due to Muhammad Abduh's leaning towards extreme modernism, his legal rulings and interpretation gave birth modern commentaries. The Egyptian theologian and nationalist Muhammad Abduh ibn Hasan Khayr Allah (1849-1905) was a founder of modernist reform in Islamic religion, of the Arabic literary renaissance of the last hundred years, and of Egyptian nationalism.

Abduh's writings were considerable. Among his religious books special mention should be made of *Risalat al-Tawhid* (1897); Epistle on the Unity [of God], a work summarising his theological views); *Al-Islam wa-al-Nasraniyah maal-Ilm wa-al-Madaniyah* (1902; Islam and Christianity in Relation to Science and Civilisation); and *Al-Islam wa-al-Radd ala Muntaqidih* (1909; Islam and a Rebuttal to Its Critics).

In the area of language and literature Abduh wrote extensive commentaries on several classical Arabic literary works and coedited a 17-volume work on Arabic philology; in the mundane field his *Taqrir fi Islah al-Mahakim al-Shariyah* (1900; Report on the Reform of the Shariyah Courts) should be noted.

Most ambitious of all Abduh's works was his *Tafsir al-Quran al-Hakim* (1927-1935; Commentary on the Koran). The huge project was never completed, but the 12 volumes that appeared are the most important expression of modernist views of the scripture of Islam.[135]

Other scholars of the twentieth century, such as Hasan al-Bannaa (1949), founder of the Ikhwan Muslimun movement, Sayyed Abu Ala Maududi (1903-1979), founder of Jama'at Islami movement and more recently the great Hadiths scholar of our era Nasir ad-dinal-Albani have picked up the banner of Islamic Revival and have called for the unification of Madh-habs. But to this date, majority of scholars remain firmly bound to sectarian Islam. With very few exceptions present day Islamic institutions of learning are actively propagating a sectarian view of Islam.

It is also a fact that comparative Fiqh is now being given a prominent place in the syllabus of these institutions and the study of Hadith has become more popular than it was earlier. Each university adheres to the official State Madh-hab of the Islamic law syllabus known as *Usul al-Din*. This is done to fulfill the local governments need for judges who conform to the Madh-hab used in the civil system of the state. For example, the University of Al-Azhar in Egypt, the most venerated institution in the Muslim world, is the only university in which all the major Madh-habs are taught. However, the all the Madh-habs has their own departments having professor and students belonging to that particular Madh-habs. Also whenever the conflicting opinion is encountered in the course of these studies, the teacher in the sectarian institution rejects it without any proper reasoning. Similarly, if a strong Hadiths which appears contrary to the position taken by the Madh-habs is met while reading the books of Hadiths, the teacher either re-interprets it to support his Madh-habs or he deftly explains it away. And if neither of the two is possible, a series of weak Hadiths are quoted in support of the Madh-hab's position.[136]

Difference among the Ummah

In the preceding discussions we have traced the historical development of Madh-habs, schools of Islamic legal thought, and to show their overall contributions to the progressive enrichment and unifying character of Fiqh within the Muslim world. It has been amply demonstrated that the liberal thinking which characterised the early Imam and their Madh-habs from the time of the Prophet PBUH down through the ages, has been ironically replaced by a certain rigidity and dogmatism. Since the late thirteenth century, not only have the Madh-habs become the spawning ground for sectarianism, but Fiqh has lost its original vitality which was enshrined in the principle of Ijtihad and thus it has not been able to keep pace with changing circumstances. As a result, Madh-hab sectarianism and inflexibility of Fiqh, the traditional purity, unity and dynamism of Islam have been threatened throughout the Muslim world.

At the outset it has become very important to examine the phenomenon of differences and disagreement in the light of the positions of early scholars and their students. He will also endeavour to reinforce the fact that while differences of opinion are inevitable, but unreasoning and factionalism have no place in the religion of Islam. In treating the historical development and evolution of the Madh-habs and the concurrent growth of Fiqh into a full fledged Islamic science, we have seen that the great Imam and founders of the

Madh-habs generally adopted the stand that Madh-hab singly or in their totality were not infallible and the following of any one Madh-hab was not obligatory for Muslims. But the pervasive influence of *Taqlid* has resulted in a belief that the four Madh-habs are divinely ordained therefore infallible. So much rigidity ingrained now that a Muslim should not change his or her Madh-habs and it is wrong to pick and choose ruling across Madh-habs. The one who dares to openly to deny the infallibility of the Madh-habs are accursed as innovator and apostate.

In the year1924-25, the followers of Muhammad ibn Abdul Wahab (1703-1787) zealously destroyed all structures built over graves of the Sahaabah and other revered persons in the cemeteries of the Holy cities of Mecca and Madina. The so called Wahabi were also opposed to *Tawassul* (seeking intercession from dead), which had become the widespread practice among the Muslim masses and also among the scholars. Since *Tawassul* and the attachment to the monument and shrines had long been ingrained in the Muslim world, the destructive act of the Wahabis in 1924-25 appeared to be innovative and extremist; hence the application of the epithet apostate and innovator came into use. It should be noted that ibn Abdul Wahab, founder of the Wahabi movement, followed the Fiqh of the Hambali Madh-hab and that his present day followers continue to do so. The Wahabis believes that by opposing the *Tawassul* and destroying the monuments and shrines, they were attacking anti-Islamic practice.[137]

Similarly the term Ahl-e-Hadiths was title of respect and praise given to the scholars in the past who like Imam Malik, devoted much time and effort to the specialised study of Hadiths. Towards the end of the nineteenth century this title was adopted by a reform movement in India and Pakistan which called for a return to the Quran and the Hadiths as the basis of Fiqh and which opposed the dogmatic adherence to Madh-habs. However, present day Madh-hab fanaticism and sectarianism have distorted the meaning of the term

Ahl-e-Hadiths to apply to one who fanatically opposes the following of any of the Madh-habs.[138]

The irony is that, in light of our insight into the historical evolution of Madh-habs and concurrent development of Fiqh, the true deviants from the teachings of Islam are not the so-called Wahabi and Ahl-e-hadiths but those people who would rigidly insist on every Muslim following one or another of the four Madh-habs and on their believing blindly in the infallibility of all four Madh-habs, despite certain glaring contradictions in their rulings on points of Islamic law. The author of *Taqlid* and *Ijtihad* writes that it was realised from the exposition of the Wujub of Taqlid that adoption of different verdicts leads to anarchy. It is therefore imperative to make Taqlid of Madh-habs which has been so formulated and arranged in regard to principles (Usul) and details that answer to all questions could be obtained thereby obviating the need to refer to an external source. This all-embracing quality by an act of Allah is found existing in only the four Madh-hab. It is therefore imperative to adopt one of four Madh-habs.[139]

Some of them claimed that the Madh-habs were divinely ordained and the prophet himself prophesied their coming. Most of them rest their case mainly on the evidence of the following Hadiths:

(a) "Differences among my Sahaabah are a mercy for you."[140]

(b) "My Sahaabah are like stars. You will be guided by whichever of them you follow."[141]

However, before these Hadiths can be accepted as evidence for sectarianism, they must be clearly shown to be authentic. A verification of these Hadiths has indeed been made by eminent scholars and their conclusions are recorded here after. As for the Hadiths in which the Prophet PBUH was supposed to have foretold the coming of the Imams and their Madh-habs, the authentic ones are all generally worded with no specific mention of either the names of the Imam or their

Madh-habs, while those Hadiths that are specifically worded are all fabricated.[142]

With regards to Hadith, one can say it has no chain of narration connecting it to anyone, much less to the prophet PBUH; nor is it to be found in any of the books of Hadiths. It is therefore incorrect to refer to it as authentic Hadith. Although such Hadiths are found in the books of Hadith, they have all proven to be unauthentic. Thus, the Hadiths used as evidence for the glorification and perpetuation of differences among Madh-habs, is totally unacceptable from the point of view of authenticity. Not only these Hadiths are unauthentic but they are in direct contradiction to Holy Quran. Their meanings are in obvious conflict with the Quran itself. Throughout the Quran's one hundred and fourteen chapters it has been cursed and forbidden the religious disagreement and has ordered unity and integrity of all Ummah. It has been explicitly forbidden in the following verse which says, "Do not dispute among yourselves and cause your own failure and loss of power"[143] and in another verse Quran says "Do not be like those among the idolaters who split up their religion into sects, each group happy with what they had."[144]

Differences among the Sahaabah (Companions of Prophet PBUH)

The differences of opinion which occurred among the Sahaabah were for the most part natural and unavoidable. A large portion of it was due to their different reasoning abilities which reflected in their various interpretations of Quranic verses and Hadiths. There were other causes which led to differences during their time which later disappeared. For example, the wide distribution of Hadiths made it impossible for any individual Sahaabah to be aware of them all and thus wrong decisions were bound to be made where information was lacking. Obviously, they cannot be blamed for there or similar mistakes, which were not intentional. Furthermore, it is clear that they readily corrected their wrong rulings or decisions in the search for truth which excludes these conflicting rulings from the category of accursed disagreements. In this connection, the Prophet PBUH had said, "If a judge strives to his utmost and make correct ruling, he receives two rewards, but if he strive and err he still receives one".[145] Based on this Hadiths, the Sahaabah are considered absolved from blame for conflicting rulings. However, any discrepancies apparent in their different rulings are not to be glorified and perpetuated.

The earlier scholars were well aware of the causes of differences among the Sahaabah and the tendency for people who want to perpetuate them. They made definitive statements on matter in an effort to emancipate dogmatism and sectarianism based on conflicting rulings of the Sahaabah. Although the Sahaabah differed in the application of some principles, they used to go to extremes to preserve an appearance of unity and avoid things which would divide their ranks. But, among later scholars and followers who blindly and dogmatically clung to the inherited Madh-habs, we find the complete opposite. Conservative sectarians among later scholars at times carried their difference even beyond that extreme, making rulings which hampered the brotherhood and unity of Islam.

References

1. Islamic Encyclopedia.
2. See the notes on *Usul al Fiqh* prepared by the professors of the shari'ah Faculty, Al Azhar University; for the academic year 1382/ 1963, p. 22.
3. *Al Nasikh wa al Mansukh*: This is the study of those verses of the Qur'an whose content have abrogated a legal meaning another verse, or in a Hadith, which is therefore called *al Mansukh*. This branch of *al Usul* also studies whether or not the contents of a Hadith may abrogate legal meanings in the Qur'an, and in other Hadith.
4. Taha Jabir Al 'Alwani , USUL AL FIQH: Methodology for Research and Knowledge in Islamic Jurisprudence, Research Moncgraph, pub: International Institute of Islamic thoughts.
5. *Ibid.*

6. *Ibid.*
7. *Ibid.*
8. The Holy Quran, Surah: Al-Baqarah, Chap. 2, Verse: 219.
9. The Quran, Surah: An-Noor, Chap. 24, Verse : 6-9.
10. Chapter and Verses from the Holy Quran.
11. Holy Quran, Chapter: 81, Verse: 6-9.
12. Andrew Pedry, The Dominant Themes in the Meccan and Medinan Surahs of the Qur'an by Article, www.suit101.com.
13. Holy Quran chapter : 89, Verse: 17-19.
14. The Holy Quran. Chapter : 4, Verse: 26.
15. The Holy Quran Chapter: 4, Verse: 16, 24, 132.
16. Sells, Michael, "Approaching the Qur'an: The Early Revelations". White Cloud, 2007.
17. The Holy Quran, Surah: 7, verse: 157, commentary by Muhammad Asad.
18. Tarikh at-Tashri al-Islami pp. 20-21, Abu Ameenah Philips, Evolution of Fiqh, International Islamic Publication House, Riyadh, 1990, p. 29.
19. The Holy Qur'an, Chap. 5, Verse: 1.
20. *Ibid;* Chap. 2, Verse: 275.
21. The Holy Quran, Chap. 16, Verse: 101.
22. *Ibid:* Chap. 2, verse: 106.
23. Moulana Mohammad Ali, The Holy Quran, sixth edition, Lahore, 1973, p. 378.
24. *Ibid:* p. 379.
25. The Holy Quran, Surah: Nisa, Chap. 4, Verse: 24.
26. Collected by Abu Dawoo, Sunnan Abu Dawood (Eng. Trans.), Vol. 3, p. 1016, no: 3576.
27. Reported by Buraydah and collected by Abu Dawood (Sunan Abu Dawood (Eng. Trans), Vol. 3, p. 682, No. 3051.
28. The Righteous Caliph Abu Bakr, 'Umar, Uthmaan and 'Ali, were four of the closest companions of the Prophet (PBUH), who presided over the Muslim State after the Prophet's death.
29. Muhammad Muslehuddin. Philosophy of Islamic Law and Orientalists [Kazi Publications, 1985]. p. 135.
30. Tashri' Process of law making in Islam, The Qur'an, Women and Modern Society, Dr. Asghar Ali Engineer, Sterling Publisher, New Delhi, 1999, p. 25.
31. *Ibid,* p. 26.

32. Collected by At- Tirmidhi, an- Nassaa'ee and Abu Dawood (Sunan Abu Dawood (English Translation), Vol. 2, p. 567, No. 2111) and authenticated by Sahih Sunan Abu Dawood, Vol. 2, pp. 397-8, No. 1858. Sa'eed reported that Umar used to say that the Deyah (compensation for accidental murder) is given to male paternal relatives of the husband, until addahhak ibn Sufiyan said to him, "Allah's messenger PBUH wrote to me to give Ashyam ad-Dibabee's wife from her husband's Deyah." So Umar withdrew his opinion.
33. Abdul Hamid Siddiqi, Shahi Muslim, (Lahore: SH. Muhammad Ashraf, 1976) Vol. 2, pp. 610-1.
34. Collected by Al Bukhari (Sahih Al-Bukhari (English), Vol. 4, p. 442, no.667) and Abu Dawood (Sunan Abu Dawood (English), Vol. 3, p. 1036. 3643.
35. Presently known to be the four schools of thoughts Hanafi, Shafi, Maliki and Hambali.

    So far as the Fiqh is concerned during Calpih's period there continued to be one general approach that is one Madh-hab. However the different practices of Sahabaah as Ibn'Umar in Madina and Abdullah ibn Mas'ood in Kufah, Iraq, in the use of personal opinion could be seen as the beginning of a division of Islamic scholars into different Madh-habs.
36. Muhammad Shalabi, Al- Madhkal fee at-Ta'reef bil fiqh al-Islami, Beirut: Daar an-Nahdah al-Arabeeyah, 1969, pp. 121-122 (English Translaion by Abu Amina B. Philip).
37. The Kharijites [Kharidjites, in Arabic Khawarij, singular Khariji, meaning "those that seceded"] were members of the earliest sect in Islam that left the followers of Ali [cousin and son-in-law of Muhammad]. The third Caliph, Uthman, was killed by mutineers in 656 AD, and a struggle for succession ensued between Ali, and Mu'awiya, governor of Damascus. The Kharijites left the followers of Ali [the Shia] because of Shia willingness to allow human arbitration of Ali's dispute with Mu'awiya in 657, rather than divine judgment. The Kharijites believed that the Imam should be elected for his moral qualities. The Kharijites considered that Ali made a mistake in looking for a compromise with Mu'awiya. For this reason they are not considered as properly Shiite by some commentators. Ali defeated their rebellion, but the Kharijites survived and an adherent of the movement murdered Ali in 661.

    Kharijites rejected primogeniture succession of the Quraysh, the tribe of Muhammad, and assert that leadership of Islam, the caliphate, should be designated by an imam elected by the community from candidates who possess spiritual and personal qualities.

The Kharijite theology was a radical fundamentalism, with uncompromised observance of the Quran in defiance of corrupt authorities. Kharijites considered moderate Muslims to be "hypocrites" and "unbelievers" who could be killed with impunity. The Kharijites Islamic sect in late 7th and early 8th century AD was concentrated in today's southern Iraq. Kharijite uprisings continued under the Umayyads in Iraq, Iran, and Arabia. The apogee of Kharijites influence came between 690 and 730, when their main city, Basra, emerged as a centre of Islamic learning. Finally, under the Abbasids, Kharijism was suppressed in Iraq.

38. *Ibid.,* p. 123.
39. *Ibid.,* p. 124.
40. *Ibid.,* p. 124.
41. Surah: 17- Al-Israa, Verse : 36. The Holy Qur'an.
42. Arriving at conclusion by logical reasoning based on similarities.
43. www.islamicweb.com/beliefs/fiqh/alalwani_usulalfiqh
44. Western coast of Arabian Peninsula including Mecca and Madina.
45. Muhammad Shalabi, Al- Madhkal fee at-Ta'reef bil fiqh al-Islami, Beirut: Daar an-Nahdah al-Arabeeyah, 1969, pp. 126-127 (English Translation by Abu Amina B. Philip).
46. Abu Ameenah Philips, Evolution of Fiqh, International Islamic Publication House, Riyadh, 1990, pp. 58.
47. The 'Abbaasids were descendants of al-Abbaas, the uncle of the Prophet Muhammad PBUH.
48. Muhammad Shalabi, Al- Madhkal fee at-Ta'reef bil fiqh al-Islami, Beirut: Daar an-Nahdah al-Arabeeyah, 1969, p. 128 (English Translaion by Abu Amina B. Philip).
49. Muhammad Rahimmuddin, Translation of Muwatta Imam Malik, New Delhi, Kitab Bhavan; first ed. 1981, preface p. v.
50. An Umayyad Prince, 'Abdur Rahmaan ibn Mu'aawiyah dramatically escaping death at the hands of 'Abbasids, succeeded in reaching Spain where he laid the foundation of the Umayyad dynasty of Cordova in 756 AD.
51. www.wsu.edu/~dee/ISLAM/ABASSID
52. The western coast of the Arabian Peninsula which includes the cities of Mecca and Madina.
53. Imam al-Layth opposed Imam Maalik's inclusion of the customs of Madinites as a source of legal rulings.
54. Muhammad Shalabi, Al- Madhkal fee at-Ta'reef bil fiqh al-Islami, Beirut: Daar an-Nahdah al-Arabeeyah, 1969, p. 130 (English Translation by Abu Amina B. Philip).

55. Abu Ameenah Philips, Evolution of Fiqh, International Islamic Publication House, Riyadh, 1990, pp. 64.
56. *Ibid.,* p. 65.
57. One of the main student of Imam Abu Hanifa.
58. One of the main student of Imam Abu Hanifa.
59. The main student of Imam Maalik.
60. Hassan Ibrahim Hassan, Islam: A Religious, Political, Social and Economic Study, (Iraq: University of Baghdad, 1967) pp. 356.
61. The Hadiths in his work were arranged alphabetically according to the names of the narrators among the Sahaabah.
62. Most of the translation occurred during the first half of this period (750-830 AD) but its effect was mostly felt in the latter half of the period.
63. Muhammad Shalabi, Al- Madhkal fee at-Ta'reef bil fiqh al-Islami, Beirut: Daar an-Nahdah al-Arabeeyah, 1969, pp. 133 (English Translaion by Abu Amina B. Philip).
64. Collected by Muslim (Sahih Muslim (English Trans), Vol. 3, p. 1108, no. 4963) and Abu Daawud (Sunan Abu Dawood (English Trans), Vol. 3, p. 1043, No. 3672).
65. Collected by Imam Maalik (Muwatta Imam Malik (English Trans), p. 296, no. 1324).
66. Muhammad Mustafa Shalabee, Usool al Fiqh al-Islami (Beirut, Lebanon: Daar al-Nahdah al-Arabiya, Second edition. 1978) p. 314. (English Translaion by Abu Amina B. Philip)
67. *Ibid.,* p. 315.
68. *Ibid.,* p. 315.
69. *Ibid.,* p. 316.
70. *Ibid.,* p. 316.
71. Muhammad Yusuf Musa, Taarikh al-fiqh al-Islami, Cairo, Dar al-kitab al-Arabi, 1955, Vol. 3, p. 62 ((English Translaion by Abu Amina B. Philip).

72-73. Muhammad Shalabi, Al- Madhkal fee at-Ta'reef bil fiqh al-Islami, Beirut: Daar an-Nahdah al-Arabeeyah, 1969, pp. 175-183 (English Translation by Abu Amina B. Philip).

74. *Ibid.,* pp. 205-6.
75. *Ibid.,* pp. 184-187.
76. Muhammad Abu Zahrah, Taareekh al-Madhaahib al-Islamiya, (Cairo: Dar al-Fikr al-'Arabi, Vol. 2, pp. 216, 217. (English Translation by Abu Amina B. Philip)
77. *Ibid.,* p. 217.

78. *Ibid.,* p. 217.
79. Bozena Gajanee Strzyzewska, tareekh at-Tashree' al-Islami, (Beirut, Lebonana: Daar al-Aafaaque al-Jadeedah, 1st ed. 1980), p. 168.
80. The fifth of the twelve Imams odorised by the Shi'ite Twelver sect.
81. Muhammad Abu Zahrah, Taareekh al-Madhaahib al-Islamiya, (Cairo: Dar al-Fikr al-'Arabi, Vol. 2, pp. 749-793. (English Translation by Abu Amina B. Philip)
82. Muhammad Shalabi, Al- Madhkal fee at-Ta'reef bil fiqh al-Islami, Beirut: Daar an-Nahdah al-Arabeeyah, 1969, pp. 205 (English Translation by Abu Amina B. Philip).
83. *Ibid.,* p. 205.
84. *Ibid.,* pp. 206- 207.
85. Among these students was Ahmed ibn Hambal, founder of the Hambali Madh-habs and Abu Thawr founder of the Abu Thawr Madh-habs.
86. Abu Ameenah Philips, Evolution of Fiqh, International Islamic Publication House, Riyadh, 1990, p. 89.
87. *Ibid.,* p. 91.
88. Bozena Gajanee Strzyzewska, Tareekh at-Tashree' al-Islami, (Beirut, Lebonan : Daar al-Aafaque al-Jadeedah, 1st ed. 1980), pp. 175-176, (English Translation by Abu Amina B. Philip).
89. *Ibid.,* p. 176.
90. *"Faasiq"* is the subject or the nominative form from the root *"Fa-Seen-Qaaf"* (فسق). The basic verb derived from the referred root means "he disobeyed". From a purely literal perspective, the subject or the nominative form of this verb (i.e. *Faasiq*) would mean "the one who disobeys". Nevertheless, it should be kept in mind that in the classical Arabic language, the attributive noun or the nominative noun, when used as an attribute, is used to imply a degree of severity and perpetuation. In other words, the verb "فسق" (he disobeyed) can be used for a trivial incident of not following the directives of an authority, but the noun "فاسق" would generally be used to imply a more permanent attitude of disobedience in a person. www.understanding-islam.com.
91. Muhammad Shalabi, Al- Madhkal fee at-Ta'reef bil fiqh al-Islami, Beirut: Daar an-Nahdah al-Arabeeyah, 1969, pp. 202-203 (English Translation by Abu Amina B. Philip).
92. Bozena Gajanee Strzyzewska, Tareekh at-Tashree' al-Islami, (Beirut, Lebonan : Daar al-Aafaque al-Jadeedah, 1st ed.1980), pp.181-182, (English Translation by Abu Amina B. Philip).

93. *Ibid.,* p. 182.
94. Bozena Gajanee Strzyzewska, Tareekh at-Tashree' al-Islami, (Beirut, Lebonan : Daar al-Aafaque al-Jadeedah, 1st ed.1980), pp.182, 183 (English Translation by Abu Amina B. Philip).
95. The Holy Quran, Chap – 2 , Surah: Al-Baqarah , Verse: 228.
96. Abdullah Abdul Muhsin at-tarki, Asbaab Ikhtilaaf al-Fuqaha, Riyad, Matba'ah as-Sa'adah,1st ed.1974, p. 190. Translation by Abu Amina B. Philip.
97. Collected by An Nasa'ee and Abu Dawood, Sunan Abu Dawood, (Eng,Trans.), (Lahore: SH. Muhammad Ashraf, 1984) Vol. 1, p. 71, No. 285. This Hadiths is also collected in Sahi Muslim.
98. Collected by Ibn Maajah and authenticated by al-Albani in Irwa al-Ghaleel, Vol. 7, p. 200, No. 2120.
99. Holy Quran, Chap:4, Surah Al-Nisa, Verse: 43 and Chap. 5 Surah Maida, Verse: 6.
100. *Ibid.,* 2:187, Surah al-Baqarah; Verse:187.
101. *Ibid.,* 19: 86, Surah Maryam; Verse: 86.
102. www.darultavhid.com
103. *Mursal* means the Hadiths reported by one of the Students of the Sahaabah without mentioning the name of the Sahaabi (Companion) from whom he heard.
104. Abu Ameenah Philips, Evolution of Fiqh, International Islamic Publication House, Riyadh, 1990, pp. 105.
105. Source: Islam and Christian-Muslim Relations, Vol. 15, No. 2, pp. 237-256, April 2004, Ermin Sinovic, The Majority Principle in Islamic Legal and Political Thought.
106. Asbaab Ikhtilaaf al-Fuqahaa, pp.126-138. Abu Ameenah Philips, Evolution of Fiqh, International Islamic Publication House, Riyadh, 1990, p. 107.
107. Abu Ameenah Philips, Evolution of Fiqh, International Islamic Publication House, Riyadh, 1990, p. 109.
108. *Ibid.,* p. 110.
109. Dr. Asghar Ali Engineer's lecture notes, 2005.
110. Abu Ameenah Philips, Evolution of Fiqh, International Islamic Publication House, Riyadh, 1990, p. 110.
111. *Ibid.,* p. 110.
112. *Ibid.,* p. 112.
113. Dr. Asghar Ali Engineer, Religion, Faith and Reason, Islam and Madern Age, January 2001.
114. www.wikipedia.org.

115. Holy Quran: 5:104-5, 17:36, 21:52-54 43:22-24.
116. www.understandingislam.com
117. Abu Ameenah Philips, Evolution of Fiqh, International Islamic Publication House, Riyadh, 1990, pp. 114.
118. *Ibid.,* p. 115.
119. *Ibid.,* p. 116
120. Anwar Ahmed Qadri, Islamic Jurisprudence in the Modern World, Lahore, Pakistan Ashraf, First Edition 1963, p. 65.
121. *Ibid.,* p. 85.
122. The Fiqh Madh-hab of the Ithna Ashari (The Twelvers) Shi'ites sect.
123. Abu Ameenah Philips, Evolution of Fiqh, International Islamic Publication House, Riyadh, 1990, p. 123.
124. *Ibid.*
125. *Ibid.,* p. 126.
126. *Ibid.*
127. Ibn Abee Hatim, al-Jarh wat-Ta'deel, Majlis Daa'irah al-Ma'arif al-Uthmaniyah, Hyderabad, India, 1952, forward, pp. 31-33.
128. *Ibid.,* p. 127.
129. *Ibid.,* p. 128.
130. *Ibid.,* p. 128.
131. *Ibid.,* p. 129.
132. Narrated by Abdullah ibn 'Amr ibn al-Aas and collected by al-Bikhari (Sahih Al-Bukhari, (Arabic-English), Vol. 4, p. 442, no. 667).
133. Abu Ameenah Philips, Evolution of Fiqh, International Islamic Publication House, Riyadh, 1990, pp. 130.
134. One of the major Shi'ite Madh-habs of Fiqh.
135. Abu Ameenah Philips, Evolution of Fiqh, International Islamic Publication House, Riyadh, 1990, pp. 119.
136. www.yourdictionary.com
137. Abu Ameenah Philips, Evolution of Fiqh, International Islamic Publication House, Riyadh, 1990, p. 130.
138. www.islamchest.com
139. *Ibid.,* p. 136.
140. Moulana Muhammad Maseehullah Sherwani, Taqlid and Ijtihad, Pot Elizabeth, South Africa, Pub. Majlisul Ulama of South Africa, p. 13.
141. Allegedly reported by Jabir and collected by Al-Bayhaqi.

142. Allegedly reported by Ibn 'Umar and collected by Ibn Battah in al-Albanah 'Asaakri' quoted in 'silsilah al- Ahadiths ad-Da'eef was al-Mawdu'ah, (Beirut; al-Maktab al-Islami, 3rd ed; 1972, Vol. 1, p:82. www.hadith.com

143. For example al-Kahteeb collected a Hadith attributed to the Prophet PBUH through Abu Hurayrah in which he was supposed to have said "There will be among my Ummah a man called Abu Hanifa, he will be lamp of my Ummah." Al-Khateeb and al-Hakim declared it *Mawdu* (forged), among the fabrications of Muhammad ibn Sa'eed al Marwazi, (Muhammad ibn Ali ash-Shawkani, al-Fawaa'id al-Majmoo'ah,) (Beirut; al-Maktab al-Islami, 2nd ed, 1972), p. 320, no: 1226. Al-Khateeb collected another report through Anas in which Prophet PBUH was quoted as saying "There will come after me a man called an-Numaan ibn Thabit, petnamed Abu Hanifa, Allah's religion and my Sunnah will be revived by him." It has in its chain of narrators Ahmad al-Juwaybari, a known fabricator of Hadiths and Muhammad ibn Yazid, whose narration are classified *matruk* (unacceptable) by Hadiths scholars. (Ali ibn 'Iraq, Tanzih ash-Shariah al Mafru'ah (Beirut: Dar al Kutub al "Ilmiyah, 1979), Vol. 2, p. 30, No. 10. www.islamic-awareness.org

144. Surah Al Anfal: Chap. 8, Verse: 46.

145. Surah Ar-Rum: Chap. 11, Verse: 118-119.

146. Narrated by 'Abdullah ibn'Amr ibn al'Aas and collected by al-Bukhari (Sahih Bukhari, (Arabic English), Vol. 4,p. 442, no.667) and Sahih Muslim (English Trans.), Vol. 3, p. 930, No. 4251.

2

Analysis of the Interviews

There have been numerous reforms introduced pertaining to Muslim family law in all the Muslim countries and also in the countries where Muslims are in minorities as well. In India this has been a major issue since post-partition period which resulted in communal politics and inter-religious conflicts mainly between Hindus and Muslims. The Muslim leadership doggedly resists any reform in certain aspects and the Hindu communal leadership would not accept anything short of complete abolition of personal law especially Muslim law which is tagged as backward and anti-constitutional. As a result the Muslim women face problems and in some cases pretty serious ones.

All major Muslim intellectuals, writers and legal experts agree that reform is not impossible. In fact Dissolution of Muslim Marriage Act 1939 is one of the best examples of reforms made in pre-partition period by the Ulama. Also one of the technique of drafting law namely *siyasa shariah* which allows flexibility. There is a strong need to address the issue having considered the contemporary context of Muslims and especially Muslim woman who is aware of her rights in Quran. Codification will definitely curtail the arbitrary practice of Shariah or customary law which is also termed as Shariah.

In this research on Codification of Muslim Personal Law we intended to cover the groups for our interviews, who are directly associated with Muslim Personal Law issues. The survey used face to face interview methodology. The team got 200 samples of interview of Ulama (Religious Clerics) belonging to both Sunni and Shia sect, among Sunnis Ulama were from Hanafi, Shafi, Ahl-e-Hadiths, Jamat-e-Islami, Deobandi and Barealvi factions, and Lawyer and Social Activists. Interviews were conducted in Deoband, Saharanpur, Meerut, Bareily, Azamgarh, Mubarakpur, Mau, Kopaganj, Khairabad, Bilaria Ganj, Banaras, Lucknow, Moradabad, Basti, Aligarh, Delhi and Mumbai. The Lawyers and Activists were mainly from Mumbai, Delhi, Lucknow, Benaras, Deoband, Saharanpur, Aligarh, and Azamgarh. The institutions of Islamic teachings, the team approached for the interviews of Mufti and Ulama, were Darul-Uloom, Nadwatul Uloom, Mazahir Uloom, Jamiat-ur-Rashaad, Jamia Ashrafia, Darul Musannifin, Jamia Salafia, Jamait al-Banaat, Aligarh University, All India Muslim Personal Law Board, Unity Degree College, and National Minority of Youth Front.

The questionnaire consisted of eighteen questions on the need for codification and certain reforms we want to bring in so to make it more gender just and as per the Quranic principles. The following table will throw light on the responses of the Ulama, Lawyers and Activists.

Table 1

Q.1 Do you think Shariah is flexible enough to respond to changed situation in modern context?

Table 1

Response	***Ulama***	***Social Activists***	***Lawyers***
Yes	95%	100%	98%
No	5%		2%
Uncertain			

The first question in the questionnaire deals with the very crucial and basic understanding of the Muslim community of whether Shariah can be changed or not. It is a well known belief among the Muslim community that Shariah is wholly divine and hence to think about change or reform means interfering in divine work which amounts to committing sin. The Ulema (clerics) too encourage such myth and are not willing to educate the community. The Activists gave unanimous 100 per cent response that Shariah can be reformed and change. 98 per cent Lawyers also agreed and sighted that we have good example of reform in the 1939 Act of Dissolution of Muslim Marriage. This question when asked to Ulema we got surprisingly a very good percentage of affirmative response which supports change and reform in Shariah law or according to them Fiqh needs to be change than Shariah rather. Shariah, in their understanding, is synonymous to principles and values given in Quran. 95 per cent of Ulema said that there are fixed principles of framing law and in every period *Ijtihad* took place. Anything which negates justice and Quran, such law needs to be changed. Ulema say *Ahkaam* (Obligatory commands in Quran) can't be change. It is also highlighted that Shariah is partially divine which can't be change like the *Ahkaamat* and the part of Shariah which is human can be changed and reformed according to present context and circumstances. In some places customs or *urf* has become part of Shariah which can be changed and needs to be reformed by the Ulema and legal experts in Islamic law.

There are several legal concepts in Islamic jurisprudence and its principles that can be brought into discussion concerning the majority principle. *Ijma'* is considered a source of law in Islamic legal theory. Its place is immediately after the textual sources, namely the Qur'an and Sunna. Different Muslim scholars have defined it in various ways. The first is offered by al-Ghazali who defined *ijma'* as 'an agreement of the *umma* of Muhammad (PBUH) in particular on any given religious matter'. The second, which is commonly accepted, states that *ijma'* is 'an agreement of the scholars of the

Muslim *umma* of a particular age on a certain issue'. The difference is that al-Ghazali's definition requires the unanimous agreement of the whole *umma,* whereas the second definition demands unanimity only on the part of Muslim scholars. In Prophet's (PBUH) tradition, Hadith indicates that it is preferable to reach decisions in matters of common concern on a consensual basis. The Shariah underwent conceptual changes. Cantwell Smith, noted scholar of Islam, through his diligent research comes to the significant conclusion that in the early centuries of Islam the concept of *shara'i-ahkaam* (injunction) was moral rather than legal.

Ijma created more diverse opinions and never there was unanimity among the *Fuqaha* (Jurist) of the classical period and hence Shariah is human intervention and the four Schools of Thoughts Hanafi, Shafi, Hanbali and Maliki proves that jurisprudence differs. Therefore, technique of *Ijtihad* (reasoning) was adopted in the formulation of Shariah law. *Ijtihad* is a continous process of development. *Mujtahid* is the person who exercised *Ijtihad*, recongnises and makes known the legal meaning of the Quranic rule or Sunnah (Prophets Traditions). It would appear that Shariah is flexible and changeable. The history of the Schools of Muslim Law is a story of diversification of Islamic jurisprudence which has been comprehensively discussed in the chapter on Evolution of Islamic law.

Q.2. Does Islam gives equal rights to women?

Table 1.1

Response	*Ulama*	*Social Activists*	*Lawyer*
Yes	62%	100%	72%
No	38%		13%
Uncertain			15%

Table 1.1 deals with the question whether Islam gives equal rights to women. Sixty-two per cent Ulema surprisingly opines equality of both the sexes. A couple of Ulema even went to the extent of saying women in fact have more rights

than men in Islam. Lawyer seems to be more gender unjust with 72 per cent only agrees to gender parity. 100 per cent activists trust that Islam does not discriminate and is extremely gender just. Those Ulema and Lawyers who disagrees believe that somewhere men have more rights because he is a maintainer. They even argue saying men are biologically stronger than women and therefore had to perform more duties and hence he is been given superiority over women, that what as per their understanding even Quran says. They quote from Quran the verse from Surah 4: verse 34 which says men are superior to women'. The word *Qawwaam* ironically has been interpreted by these Ulema as Master, Protector or the one who is superior. However, its true meaning in the Dictionary of Quran, *Mufradatul Quran* written by Imam Raghib explains *Qawwaam* derives from the root word *Qama* which means to stand up. To stand up means is to maintain. The verse completes with the saying the God has given ability to be better than the other. It is no where mentioned that men are better than women. Whoever looks after the family and kin will be *Qawwaam* and in this proves that Women can also be *Qawwaam*. I would like to highlight some specific instances in Quran on gender equality. "Allah does not allow the deeds of any person, male or female, to be lost" (Surah: 3, Verse: 195; 4:124; 16:97; 33:73; 40: 40; 57: 12). "The punishment and liability to punishment of male and female is not distinct" (Surah 2, Verse: 178; 5:38; 24:2; 24:4 to 10). "In the performance of duty of enjoining good and forbidding what is wrong, there is no difference between male and female" (Surah: 9; Verse: 71). "Like the male, a female is also an individual with right to earn money or property and having full power of disposition over the same" (Surah: 4; Verse: 32). Everyone should be content with whatever be the sex of the child born to him/her. He bestows female upon whom He will, and bestow male upon whom He will." (Surah: 42, Verse: 49). She is free to contract like male and her consent for her *Nikah* or marriage is also essential (Surah: 4: Verse: 3; 4: 19). The only measure of superiority of one over the other is the extent to which one is more pious and God-fearing (Surah: 49; Verse: 13). Islam thus placed man and woman on the same footing in economic independence, property rights, right to contract and legal processes.

Table 2: Polygamy

Q.3. Do you think Polygamy- Desirable?

Table: 2

Response	*Ulama*	*Social Activists*	*Lawyers*
Yes	85%	5%	79%
No	15%	95%	21%
Uncertain			

In Table 2, the question is Polygamy whether it is desirable or should it be allowed under stringent conditions. 85 per cent of Ulema says that Polygamy is desirable and hence should not be restricted or banned. Only 5 per cent activists agree that Polygamy should be allowed but under strict conditions. 95 per cent activists demands ban. 79 per cent lawyers too hold the similar view that of the Ulema that more than one marriage is desirable. In table 2.2 when asked that stringent condition should be laid down to allow second marriage, only 37 per cent Ulama agrees and 63 per cent of them dismiss any condition for second marriage. 82 per cent Lawyers and 34 per cent of activists demands for strict conditions. Various reasons are sighted by the Ulema and some lawyers that if we banned polygamy or restrict it then there will be a major increase in prostitution and keeping mistresses. One cannot justify any unjust practice by projecting a fear of another grave exploitative practice. In Quran nowhere directly or indirectly such reason is given. Such responses on the contrary demean the most Permissible act of Nikah which enshrines moral protection of the spouses. Islam as per the injunction given in Quran permits polygamy only in emergency situation of war or where the male-female ratio is not appropriate due to other natural calamities or disasters. Marriage as an institution is encouraged by Islam because family life not only ensures survival of the human race but also guarantees social stability and a dignified existence for both woman and man. According to the Quranic philosophy, there is nothing wrong with sex if it is used for procreation within the marital framework and not merely enjoyment and pleasure. The Quran specifically forbids sexual relations for fornicating and receiving paramour cannot impart dignity to women. It would not only reduce sex to merely physical pleasure but would also lead to a much greater exploitation of women. According to the Quran, husband and wife is each other's garment (Surah: 2; Verse: 187). Thus, marriage is not merely for sexual urge; it has higher end and exalted motives and is a relationship of love and mutual respect. Quran if we study carefully neither encourage neither polygamy nor permits concubinage. Let us see what Quran says on this matter. From the Quran, chapter 4: 3, says "And if you fear that you cannot do justice to orphans, marry such women as seem good to you, two, or three, of four; but if you fear you will not do justice, then marry only one or that which your right hands possess. This is more proper that you may not do injustice."

> This verse expressly though permits marriage with more than one woman. But this verse can not be read in isolation. It has to be understood with the conjunction with the preceding verse, i.e. verse: 1 and 2 of chapter 4. The first verse explains the creation of man and woman from the same source and thus emphasises equality of the sexes. The second verse exhorts Muslim to give orphans their property and not to exchange their good property with the bad property of their ward. The third verse relating to polygamy also begins with the word "And if your fear you cannot do justice to orphans...." Polygamy here is concerned with doing justice to orphans. Thus, it can be seen that the emphasis in these verses is not on marrying more than one woman but on doing justice to the orphans. The context of these verses is very important to understand this injunction. Those days guardians often

used to misappropriate their wards properties and sometimes did so by marrying them without even paying the dower money. The Quran wanted to check this malpractice. The eminent commentators of Quran agree that these verses were revealed immediately after the battle of Uhud and were meant to provide guidance to Muslims after that cataclysmic event. In this battle 70 out of 700 men were slain and this carnage sharply reduced the number of Muslim males. Many Muslim women were widowed and girls orphaned. They had to be taken care of and in prevalent social condition this could be best done by allowing Muslim men to marry widows and orphans, up to four in number, strictly on condition that they did justice to all of them and if they were not capable of doing so then they should not marry more than one woman.

This injunction is a clear pointer to the fact that monogamy is the rule in the Islamic law and only as an exception it was considered necessary and it is subject to harsh restrictions and conditions. Thus, it is crystal clear from the above explanation that Polygamy is not at all Islamic law and if Ulema and those who think it is permissible without the element of justice then this negates Quranic principle completely.

Table 2.1: Stringent conditions are necessary for taking more than one wife

Response	*Ulama*	*Social Activists*	*Lawyers*
Yes	37%	34%	82%
No	63%		18%
Uncertain/Banned		66%	

Table: 2.1 is a question whether stringent conditions are necessary for taking more than one wife? Only 37 per cent of Ulema agree for Polygamy on strict and valid conditions. 63 per cent doesn't agree to regulate polygamy by implementing strict conditions. They fear this will lead to immoral activities and prostitution will flourish. However

82 per cent Lawyers stressed on strict condition to approve polygamous marriage. Among activists 34 per cent agrees for strict and stringent conditions and the remaining 66 per cent demands for ban on Polygamy. Moulana Zafeeruddin Nadvi illustrates the genuine need of more than wife in the following paragraph, in his book Modesty and Chastity in Islam. "If a man's need is genuine and he is sure that in case of a abstention from the second marriage, he is likely to be involved in sin, the simple permission becomes a law for him so that he protect his chastity which is otherwise threatened. But such needs are not common to everyday life. The wife may be sterile and the natural desire for progeny may compel the husband to seek an alternative; she may come to suffer from an incurable disease and the sexual desire of the husband and also the need for nursing of the ailing wife demands immediately that he should marry a second wife. And there are so many emergencies that can arise and force one to take advantage of the Quranic permission of more than one wife.

Islam did not approve of unhindered polygamy. It regulates the right by making it subject to the norm of justice, equal or rather satisfying treatment to each wife and kindness to all of them. It is also necessary that the husband who marries more than one wife should be possessed of means to bear the expenses equally of each wife. It would not be justice to add to the family a wife whom he cannot provide her maintenance or to feed and maintain he has to curtail the expenses of other wife and member of his family. This is what is meant by Imam Shafi'i who interprets the word *al la ta'ulu* in the verse as you should not marry more than one wife if you fear that you will be adding to the number of your dependents. The Quran explicitly commands men to do justice between the wives and to avoid injustice.

The renowned commentator Mohammad Asad makes the following comment on the verse 129 from chapter 4: "This refers to cases where a man has more than one wife- a waiver which is conditional upon his determination and ability to treat them with equal fairness as laid down in verse 3 of this surah (chapter 4). Since a man who is fully conscious of his moral responsibility might feel that he is committing a sin if he loves one of his wives more than the other (or others), the verse provides 'judicial enlightenment' on this point by making it clear that feelings are beyond a human being's control; in other words, that the require equality of treatment relates only to outward behaviour towards practical dealings with one's wives. However, in view of the fact that a man's behaviour towards another person is, in the long run, almost inevitably influenced by what he feels about that person, the above passage – read in conjunction with verse 3, and especially its concluding sentence – imposes a moral restriction on plural marriage.

Ironically, Ulema and Lawyers though agrees to equal treatment of all the wives and say it is must but also accepts that to be equal in emotional sense with all the wives is not possible and it is not in husband's control.

Table: 2.2 - First wife's permission is necessary

Response	*Ulama*	*Social Activists*	*Lawyers*
Yes	4%	34%	59%
No	96%		41%
Uncertain/Banned		66%	

Table: 2.2: explains the response of the Ulema, Lawyers and Activists on the issue whether first wife's permission is necessary for taking another wife. 96 per cent of the Ulema says it is not require at all and husband only need to inform his first wife and only 4 per cent of Ulema said it is must and husband should inform and seek permission from the first wife. 59 per cent Lawyers says that permission is must but remaining 41 per cent conforms to the view of Ulama. Activists again only 34 per cent who doesn't demand ban on Polygamy says first wife's permission is mandatory and the Qazi should make sure that the permission is not given under any threat or pressure.

Table 2.3: Do you think Qazi should enquire into reasons for which second, third or fourth wife is taken?

Response	*Ulama*	*Social Activists*	*Lawyers*
Yes	7%	98%	8%
No	93%	2%	89%
Uncertain/Banned			3%

Table 2.3: The question in table 2.3 deals with whether Qazi should enquire into reasons for which second, third or fourth wife is taken? Only 7 per cent Ulema says in affirmative that Qazi should enquire the reason before performing the Nikah. That means 97 per cent Ulema unfortunately responded that Qazi's duty is to conduct the marriage ceremony and he is not suppose to enquire the reason. It is between the couple. A small percentage of Ulema say that Qazi can only enquire the number of marriage done by the groom. Whether one, two, three or four and not exceeding four. Around 8 per cent of lawyers also feel that Qazi's duty is to conduct Nikah and he cannot enquire. But the activists whom we interviewed say it is Qazi's important duty to enquire the valid reason and whether the man is capable to maintain more than one wife. 98 per cent of Activists urged that Qazi should enquire without fail and if found that reasons are not valid then should strictly discourage such marriage.

Table 2.4: Do you think no reason is needed to take other wife?

Response	*Ulama*	*Social Activists*	*Lawyers*
Yes	81%		82%
No	19%	34%	18%
Uncertain/Banned		66%	

Table 2.4: Question raised here is whether reason is needed to take another wife? To this 81 per cent Ulema says no reason is required because man is polygamous by nature and it is his natural tendency that he needs multiple partners. 82 per cent ironically Lawyers too agrees that no reason is

require, man should only be able to maintain the wives. Activists who agrees to restrict polygamy 34 per cent of them says a valid reason is needed and it is not by nature man should have more wives but one should abide to Quranic injunction with whom they can marry and in what terms. The reason Quran sights in its verses which we discussed in Table 2 which deal with the issue of Polygamy. Further one can clearly point out that Quran's intention is not to promote polygamy on the contrary it warns in its verse 129 of chapter 4, the impossibility of maintaining equality between the wives and consequently the futility of marrying more than one wife. Thus, no where it indicates that a man by nature is monogamous and Quran ridicule any form of injustice committed on first wife.

Justice Aftab quotes Maulana Omar Ahmad Osmani, very authentically that verse: 3 of chapter 4 applies only to orphan girls and widows and does not allow plurality of wives from amongst other women. The relevant words of the translation of the verse are: "And if ye fear that ye will not deal fairly by the orphans, marry of the women who seem good to you, two or three or four..." 'The women' is the translation of *an nisaa* while 'orphans' is the translation of the words *al yatama*. The argument is that the definite article *al* in *al nisaa* must refer to *yatama* i.e. Orphans otherwise the word *nisaa* would have been sufficient to convey the sense of generality of women. Maulana Osmani further quotes *Ahkam ul Quran* by Jassas in support that the *yatama* does not mean orphans only but also includes widow and divorcees. Women covered by either category abounded in the then Muslim society. The meaning of the verse is that man can marry upto four wives from among those helpless orphans and widows provided they are capable of maintaining justice and equality between them. The permission to marry more than one is limited to emergency referred to above and is in no way general in nature. The argument or the reason sighted by the Ulema is not in conformity with the Quranic values and hence confronts Quran and its spirit of justice.

Unfortunately such practice in Islam which is meant for social stability during emergency situation has been encouraged as a common practice and presently it is promoted as right of man to have more wives and the *niyaah* (intention) of marriage is love, respect, equal rights and maintenance. The intention of *Nikah* is not to fulfill one's physical need only as justified by our learned Ulema that restriction on polygamy will increase prostitution. Let me quote here few definitions as what *Nikah* means or the objective of *Nikah* (marriage) in Islamic laws which are codified Family laws in other Muslim countries. In Algeria Ahwal-e-Shaksiyah define Nikah as 'Moral protection of the spouses'. Indonesian Family law explains it as a 'Foundation of Family', legal definition in Iraq and Syria is 'Life in Partnership'. Moroccan Law explains Nikah as 'Discharge of Family Liabilities' where as Somalia and Yemen Family Law defines as 'Equal Rights and Duties of the Spouses'. The purpose of highlighting all these legal definitions of Nikah is to bring to the notice that Marriage is not meant for venting one's sexual desires as our Ulema and some lawyers claims that some men have more sexual urge and one wife may not able to handle and hence there should be more than one wife and mostly men are polygamous so Polygamy should be not be regulated. If at all Polygamy is permitted then there should be valid reasons like in many Islamic countries a husband needs to seek permission from the court to allow second marriage. The court will investigates and verify and has stipulated conditions for the second marriage. The man may receive permission from a court to contract a second marriage only if his wife cannot carry out her conjugal duties, or his wife is crippled or terminally ill, or his wife cannot bear him child, the present wife has given him the permission, husband's ability to support all his wives and children is certain and his ability to be fair to all his wives and children is certain. So there has to be solid valid reason for second marriage and in exceptional cases.

Table 2.5: Do you think capability of husband to do equal justice is necessary for taking another wife?

Response	*Ulama*	*Social Activists*	*Lawyers*
Yes	90%	34%	92%
No			
Uncertain/Banned	10%	66%	8%

Table 2.5 deals with very important question pertaining to polygamy that is capability of husband to do equal justice. 90 per cent Ulema firmly believe in equal justice though but in material terms only and they accept the fact that to love equally is not in man's control and it is very natural that emotionally he will be inclined towards one wife. 34 per cent Activist supports that if polygamous marriage happen then it his husband's utmost duty to maintain all the wives and children equally without doing injustice to other. 92 per cent Lawyers too firmly agrees to the condition of maintaining wives with justice and equality. In material terms he has to maintain all the wives equally. From chapter 4, verse 2 and verse 3 the injunction on Polygamy can be understood in the context of the ill treatment meted out to the orphans by the Arabs. After the death of the father his brother or uncles and such other near relatives used to take into possession the property of the children of the deceased, and did not return it to them even after they attained majority. They used to misappropriate their good cattle and give in exchange lean and useless cattle from their own herd. Sometimes they would mixed the property of the orphans with their own properties and misappropriate the same. They would marry the female orphans without payment of dower according to their status and were not particular about discharging their liabilities towards them.

The third verse relating to polygamy also begins with the words: "And if ye fears that you will not deal fairly by the orphans, marry of the women, who seems good to you, two or three or four, and if ye fear that ye cannot do justice then one or that your right hand possess. Thus it is more likely that ye will not do injustice."

This verse enjoins upon the guardians to deal fairly with the female orphans under their guardianship. Marry them only if you can deal with them fairly. This permission is subject to the condition of treating all the wives equally. If one is not capable maintaining more than wife then one can marry only one. This way one would not commit injustice.

According to Maulana Omar Ahmad Osmani verse three of the chapter four namely, *Nisa*, holds that general rule is monogamy while polygamy is an exception limited to the above mentioned circumstances. According to Maulana Omar also, the exception is the war emergency in which plurality of only orphans and widows is permitted.

Maintaining them again is very crucial in Islamic law. Laws are strict when it comes to absolute equality among the wives. The equality applies among things to the time passed in the society of each wife, and food, clothes and lodging supplied to them. The condition imposed to pass equal time with each wife so that none of them may feel lonely or neglected and not necessarily for sexual intimacy.

Table 2.6: Do you think justice means sharing equal time and giving equal maintenance to all wives is enough for doing justice or equal love is also necessary for justice being done?

Response	*Ulama*	*Social Activists*	*Lawyers*
Yes	86%	34%	96%
No	14%		4%
Uncertain/Banned		66%	

The question asked in Table 2.6 received ambiguous answer where Ulama and Lawyers could take one final stand. Like 86 per cent Ulama says that justice does includes equal love but this is an impossible task for a husband to fulfill. 96 per cent Lawyers too insists on equal love but they too agrees to the fact that it is not in human control to love all the wives equally. 34 per cent Activist dominantly said equal love and respect has to be the main condition when it comes to equal treatment of all the wives. Any unjust treatment should not be tolerated and law should be such that husbands should be penalised for such behaviour. Here Ulama and Lawyers very well accept the fact that emotions are not in husband's control, he tends to incline emotionally more with one of his wives.

Thus, it is very clear from the above fact that Polygamy demands justice and being human one is not capable of being just completely. The verse 129 of chapter 4 which is reproduced here is 'Ye will not be able to deal equally between wives, however much ye wish (to do so), as in suspense. If Ye do good and keep from evil, Lo! Allah is ever forgiving, Merciful.'[1] The verse command equality between the wives but only to the extent it is possible. Thus, equality is possible in respect of the amount of maintenance, the time of seclusion with each wife etc. But in matter of emotions equality is impossible. The verse, therefore, refers to an evident truth that how-so-ever you desire you will not be able to maintain equality. The verse further cautions that not to incline to one wife only and leaving the other in suspense. Thus, it is clear by this verse that justice cannot ignore love which is an important factor in any marital relation and hence it is impossible to maintain wives equally. Therefore, the condition of equality to go for polygamous marriage cannot be fulfilled from the above mentioned verse from Holy Quran.

Table: 3 – Divorce

Do you think triple divorce in one sitting is permissible?

Response	*Ulama*	*Social Activists*	*Lawyers*
Yes	97%	-	69%
No	3%	100%-	31%
Uncertain/Banned			

Table 3: The Table 3 has the response to the most un- Islamic practice which is very popular among the Muslims i.e. *Talaq-e-Biddah,* the form of divorce prevalent during pre-Islamic period and hence termed as sinful by the Prophet PBUH. However, the Muslim community understands and

believes that this is the only form of divorce in Shariah. The Ulema to our surprise claimed triple divorce to be *biddah* and sinful but vehemently declares that if someone adopts this method to divorce one's wife then it will be considered as valid. The divorce will be accepted. Ulama explain that one should adopt these forms of divorce like *talaq-e-raja'ee, talaq-e-bayna* and *talaq-e-mughallaza*. However, Ulama have made least efforts to educate Muslims on these forms of divorce law in Shariah. They support *talaq-e-bid'at* and least show any support to ban such un-Islamic practice. Our second target group i.e. social activists unanimously oppose triple divorce and demand for its complete banned and any violation should be punishable. 100 per cent of the activists condemn and demands abolition of triple oral divorce. Whereas only 31 per cent lawyers do not agrees to such divorce. The remaining 69 per cent accepts because Ulama endorse their support to such form of divorce and fatwa from Darul Ifta supports triple divorce. Lawyers confessed that being Lawyer does not entitle them to be the expert of *Fiqh* (Islamic Jurisprudence) and Muslims would only like to consult Ulama than any lawyer on Shariah issue.

At present in Ulama accepts Oral triple Divorce whether in presence or absence of two witnesses is valid even if it goes against Quranic form of Divorce. *Bid'at* means an innovation or something new, a novelty or something unprecedented. Imam Raghib said in Mufradatul Quran that *albida'a* means to admit an innovation in the religion which may not be traceable to any utterance or action of the Prophet PBUH nor is proved from the earlier established principles of Shariah. It is related that all *Bid'at* and each *Bid'at* or new thing is a deviation from truth and each deviation is in fire. Therefore, nomenclature *talaq-e-bid'at* cannot be applied to something which has the sanction of the Prophet PBUH or which was made effective by him. Also one needs to think, Hazrat Omar, the second Caliph, about his right to substitute a Quranic or Sunnah injunction by different rule. Also our religious scholars never admit that Hazrat Omar after a period strictly made a rule to punish those who practice *Talaq-e-Biddah* for violating Quranic injunction.

This form of Divorce is completely banned in all Muslim countries and it is declared as a sin which is punishable by the state.

Table 3.1: Can divorce be valid in state of anger and in drunken state?

Response	*Ulama*	*Social Activists*	*Lawyers*
Yes	99%	-	69%
No	1%	100%	31%
Uncertain/Banned			

Table 3.1: 99 per cent Ulama without any apprehension says husbands often divorce wives in state of anger and never in love. Divorce is an angry reaction of a human being they believe. It doesn't matter one looses rational thinking in anger and later repent for the decision. Divorce takes place. Also they replied in affirmative in state of drunkenness too the divorce occurs. Ulama strictly says it's a punishment for the drunkard husband. But our Ulama how come ignores the plight of the wife and if there are children then who is punished for whose crime? Also intention counts and when one is in state of anger may repent later when he realises his mistake. But Ulama insist that to utter the word *Talaq* intentionally or unintentionally the divorce takes place.

Table 3.2: Can triple divorce be given through – Telephone, E-mail and SMS?

Response	*Ulama*	*Social Activists*	*Lawyers*
Yes	99%	-	76%
No	1%	100%	21%
Uncertain/Banned			3%

Table 3.2: Oral pronouncement of Divorce or by e-mail, SMS or by telephone is permissible and allowed by 99 per cent of Ulama except 1 per cent of Muftis disapproves such method

of divorcing. 76 per cent Lawyers to blindly accepts that because they have to consult Ulama. Though there is recent judgment by the Supreme Court which disapproves divorce by such method and orders the parties to follow Quranic form of Divorce i.e Talaq-e-Ahsan. The procedure of Talaq in the Quran ensures that the divorce is not arbitrary since arbitrariness is checked by making the procedure of divorce spread over a period of three months during which he has the right to revoke the divorce. 100 per cent of the activist voiced their condemnation and demand for complete ban on such practice.

Table 3.3: Is divorce valid without two witnesses as required by the Holy Quran in Surah: 65, Verse: 2?

Response	*Ulama*	*Social Activists*	*Lawyers*
Yes	98%	-	68%
No	2%	100%	32%

Table 3.3: Here the question raised was whether two witnesses require during pronouncement of divorce as commanded in Holy Quran in Surah: 65, Verse:2. The reply of the Ulama proves that they outrightly negate Quranic injunctions. 98 per cent of Ulama asserts that no witness is require and some Ulama went to the extent of saying that there is no such verse in Quran. Only 2 per cent of Ulama agrees that there has to be two witnesses while following the divorce procedure. 68 per cent of Lawyers too ironically says that no witness is require where as 100 per cent activist vehemently responded that it is unjust not to have witnesses and in Islam both for Nikah and Talaq two witnesses is require. Let us see what Quranic verse says- "And when they have [nearly] fulfilled their term, either retain them (wife) according to acceptable terms or part with them (wife) according to acceptable terms. And bring to witness two just men from among you and establish the testimony for [the acceptance of] Allah. That is instructed to whoever should believe in Allah and the Last day. And whoever fears Allah - He will make for him a way out."

Also let us have look at this narration of Hadiths found in the collection compiled by Abu Dawud. The Hadiths quotes, Ibn 'Abbas who says that this implies calling to witness two men both at divorce and at reconciliation. (Ibn Jarir). Hadrat `Imran bin Husain was asked: "A man divorced his wife and then took her back, but he neither called anybody to witness pronouncement of the divorce nor resumption of the relation." He replied: "You pronounced the divorce against the Sunnah and you took your wife back against the Sunnah. You should call to witness men both at divorce and at resumption of relation, and you should not commit this mistake again." (Abu Da'ud, Iba Majah). If a man pronounces divorce against the approved method as explained above or fails to reckon the waiting-period accurately and also fails to call the men to witness the divorce, reconciliation, or separation then such irregular form of divorce does not take place at all. This is what all the Imam of four schools of thoughts also unanimously agrees. Here the opinion of Ulama not only goes against the giants of Islamic jurisprudence but also counters the just and fair procedure ordained in Quran.

Table 3.4: Is Arbitration as mentioned in the Holy Quran (Surah: 4, Verse: 35) necessary before divorce?

Response	*Ulama*	*Social Activists*	*Lawyers*
Yes	97%	100%	95%
No	3%	-	
Uncertain/Banned			5%

Table 3.4: In the above table we have discussed that Quran has given a clear procedure to seek separation between husband and wife. In Table 3.4 when asked whether Arbitration process as mentioned in the Surah4, Verse 35 as must before making final pronouncement of divorce, 97 per cent Ulama agrees that there should be an effort for reconciliation from both the sides, 100 per cent Activist stress that without the Arbitration procedure divorce should not be held valid and among lawyers 95 per cent is of the opinion that this is

the correct way to adopt and 5 per cent without giving a second thought is unable to agree that divorce must need arbitration according to Shariah Law. Let us see what the verse 35 of chap 4 says- "And if ye fear a breach between them twain (the man and the wife) appoint an arbiter from his folk and an arbiter from her folk. If they desire amendment Allah will make them of one mind." This verse lays down the procedure to be adopted when a case for divorce arises. It is not for the husband to put away his wife; it is the business of the judge to decide the case. The judge is require to appoint two arbiters, one belonging to the wife's family and the other to the husbands. These two arbiters will find out the facts bit their objective must be to effect a reconciliation between the parties. If all attempts and hopes of reconciliation fail, a divorce is allowed, but the final decision for divorce rests with the judge who is legally entitled to pronounce a divorce.

Table 3.5: Do you think divorce should be pronounced preferably only once at a time during period of *Tuhar*

Response	***Ulama***	***Social Activists***	***Lawyers***
Yes	99%	100%	75%
No	1%	-	5%
Uncertain/Banned			20%

Table 3.5 poses very important question and about which mainly Muslims are unaware of. Here the questions asked is whether divorce should be pronounced once at a time and during the period of *Tuhar*, period without menses. Except 1 per cent of Ulama, 99 per cent affirms that divorce should only be said during *Tuhar* period. 20 per cent of the lawyer is not aware of such requirement for divorce and among them 75 per cent agrees to this condition of *Tuhar*. 100 per cent Activist are by now educated and hence they opine that *Tuhar* condition is must. *Talaq-e-Sunnah* which is unanimously the most approved form of divorce among the Muslim law in various countries has following conditions: (a) he pronounced the formula of divorce once, in a single sentence; (b) he must

do so when the woman is in a state of purity (*tuhar*) and there is no bar to sexual intercourse; (c) he must abstain from the exercise of conjugal rights after pronouncing the formula, for the space of three *Tuhar*. This latter class is intended to demonstrate that the resolve, on the husband's part, to separate from the wife is not a passing whim, but is the result of a settled determination. On the lapse of the term of three *Tuhar*, the separation takes effect as irrevocable divorce. In the *Hasan* form, the husband is required to pronounce the formula three times during three successive *tuhars* namely, three period of purity. When the last formula is pronounced the *talaq* or divorce becomes irrevocable.

Table: 3.6 - Do you think triple divorce in one sitting should be banned?

Response	*Ulama*	*Social Activists*	*Lawyers*
Yes	99%	100%	100%
No	1%	-	-
Uncertain/Banned			

Table 3.6: When asked whether *Talaq-e-Bid'at* or the Oral triple divorce should be banned surprisingly 99 per cent Ulama supports ban and views that law proposing ban would bring relief to many women and there would be less cases of desertion through such divorce. Both Activists and Lawyers unanimously voiced ban on such practice. 100 per cent of the responses supports ban. As mentioned in Table 3, informs that all the Muslim countries imposed ban and any violation of the law by the husband is punishable by state. Many countries codified their Shariah law and stated a specific procedure to be followed to seek divorce, in the absence or violation of such procedure would lead to punishment.

Table 3.7: Do you think a woman is entitled to *Khula* without her husbands consent? If not how do you explain Prophet (PBUH) hadith (Bukhari) about Jamila? If husband's consent is necessary then what is the difference between *Khula* and *Mubaraat?*

Response	*Ulama*	*Social Activists*	*Lawyers*
Yes	29%	100%	58%
No	71%		16%
Uncertain/Banned			36%

Table 3.7: deals with one of the form of Divorce namely. *Khula*, which is absolute right of Wife to initiate divorce. Quran confers power on her to claim separation by Khula. Only 29 per cent of the Ulama say yes to accept that this is wife's whole and soul decision and husband's consent is not require where as 71 per cent of Ulama asserts that women is not given complete right and she needs husbands consent. 100 per cent Activist again responded that *Khula* should be practiced the way it is been mention in Hadiths concerning Jamila's case. Among the Lawyers 58 per cent says yes and 16 per cent says is negative. Ulama some directly denies existence of any such Hadiths and though they know the clear difference between the *Khula* and *Talaq-e-Mubaraat* but ironically insist on husbands consent for Khula expressing their fear that women are usually more emotional then men and their emotion would drive them to take such irrational step of *Khula* and this would lead to breaking up of family and children too will be affected. The so called fear which resides in the minds of Ulama is illogical and they could not counter the legality of rights given even in traditional Shariah. The legal science adopted while framing the laws measures all the pros and cons before codifying it into law, let me emphasise that Shariah is a legal science and science need to have empirical background and such arguments that women are emotional doesn't buy any legal sanctity. There can be many other circumstances which lead to women seeking divorce. Today women are educated and career oriented and equally aspires for professional and personal life. Awareness

and education can be one of the reasons but not because they are emotional entity.

Dr. Asgahr Ali Engineer in his book 'The Rights of Women in Islam' elaborately explains the right of *Khula*, Islam gives to the women. The word *Khula* literally means to disown or to repudiate, for a woman can repudiate her marriage. It has been referred to in the Quran in the following verses - Chapter 2, verse 229 of the Quran is cited as the basis for a woman's right to divorce in Islam - *khul*'.

> "Divorce may be (pronounced) twice, then keep (them) in good fellowship or let (them) go with kindness; and it is not lawful for you to take any part of what you have given them, unless both fear that they cannot keep within the limits of Allah; then if you fear that they cannot keep within the limits of Allah, there is no blame on them for what she gives up to become free thereby. These are the limits of Allah, so do not exceed them and whoever exceeds the limits of Allah these it is that are the unjust."

Chapter 4, verse 128 of the Quran also addresses this question

> "And if a woman fears ill usage or desertion on the part of her husband, there is no blame on them, if they effect a settlement between them, and reconciliation is better, and avarice has been made to be present in the (people's) minds; and if you do good (to others) and guard (against evil), then surely Allah is aware of what you do."

The case of Jamila, the wife of Thabit Bin Qais, reported by numerous authorities explains the *Khula* form of Divorce. Jamila was quite dissatisfied with her marriage though there was no quarrel between husband and wife. She stated to the Prophet PBUH that she did not find any fault with her husband on account of his moral or religion; it was just that she hated him. The Prophet allowed divorce provided she returned to her husband the orchard which he made over to her as her *mehr*. We also learn of repudiation of marriage by a woman called Burairah who had married Mugith. When she decided to obtain *Khula*, Mugith wept bitterly, tears rolling down his cheeks into his beard. The Prophet PBUH addressing ibn 'Abbas, his companion, said, "Don't you wonder about Mugith's passionate love for Buriarah and her equally passionate hatred for him?" The Prophet asked Burairah whether she could take him back. Burairah there upon asked the Prophet "Are you ordering me?" He said, "No, I am only recommending Mugith's case to you." Burairah thereupon said, "I do not need him." She persisted in asking for *Khula*. Thus, it was that Burairah turned down even the Prophet's recommendation and insisted on her right to repudiate her marriage.

After sighting the above incident during Prophet's lifetime it is clear that Khula does not require husbands consent and also woman needs no particular ground for divorce. In many countries Khula is allowed and woman only needs to apply in the court and she is not even require to produce any witnesses.

Table 4: Do you think father can give more than half of his inheritable property to his daughter or equal share in case- She is crippled and has no possibility of marrying or earning her livelihood?

Table 4: INHERITANCE

Response	*Ulama*	*Social Activists*	*Lawyers*
Yes	56%	97%	68%
No	44%	1%	22%
Uncertain/Banned		2%	10%

Table 4 on inheritance issue when asked to Ulama whether father can give more than half of inheritable property to his daughters or equal share in case she is physically handicapped and hence could not get marry or earn livelihood, 56 per cent supported such law to be there and 44 per cent though not completely denies but opines that father can gift to her daughter more than the share and also many Ulama emphasized that all children has rights and should take into account the consensus of other children before making such decision. Other children should not be deprived of their inheritance right. 97 per cent Activists overwhelmingly approves that father can more than half to his disable daughter. 68 per cent Lawyers too agrees in this case and 22 per cent percent still believe that it should not exceed the share described in Quran. 10 per cent are not certain about Shariah stand on this issue.

Table 4.1: Do you think the Quranic word *Ba'ada Wasiyatin....* (Sure: 4, Verse: 11) after making Will gives option to father to give more than half to his daughter specially if she is handicapped or does not get married?

Response	*Ulama*	*Social Activists*	*Lawyers*
Yes	16%	100%	10%
No	19%	-	33%
1/3rd of share / written proof	65%		67%

Table 4.2 asks whether wife and daughter will be entitled to equal share after the death of her husband in case they have contributed to family wealth. This is very crucial point to be brought about while framing a Muslim Law. There is need to acknowledge the economic contribution of the Muslim women in their family wealth. Today women are educated and earning and are contributing their skills in various fields. In return they are adding to the family income whether being daughter or wife.

Let us see what our respondent think about this important question. 65 per cent of Ulama says either women in the family be given some extra from the one-third or there need to be a written proofs of the income spend on family welfare which will make things undisputable. When asked to Ulama that mother, wife or daughter usually feels happy to make contribution and morally they would not like to write down and make a record of what they spend. Ulama did agree to this but still insist on written proof. Only 16 per cent Ulama agrees that wife or daughters are entitled for equal share.

19 per cent says they can not ask for more share than mentioned in the Quran. 100 per cent Activists unanimously calls for equal share while only 10 per cent of Lawyers affirms for equal share and 67 per cent opines the same as the Ulama. Shockingly 33 per cent says no to extra share and stick to the injunction of the Quran and does not analyse the changing circumstances of the modern period. Justice is done only when these women are given equal rights for contributing both financially and as a caretaker of the entire family. Right to equal share should be given in all properties by way of inheritance, movable and immovable.

Table 4.3: Do you think even a wife or daughter though not earning still contribute to family wealth by looking after and maintaining house or property? Should it not be counted as her contribution to family income as otherwise husband will have to employ servants to do the same?

Response	*Ulama*	*Social Activists*	*Lawyers*
Yes	8%	100%	79%
No	3%		
1/3rd of share / Moral duty of Husband	89%		21%

Table 4.3 the question raised in Table 4.3 sounds strange to the Ulama though but they did give an encouraging reply. When asked a wife or daughter though not earning still contribute to family wealth by looking after and maintaining house or property, Should it not be counted as her contribution to family income as otherwise husband will have to employ servants to do the same? 89 per cent of the Ulama responded, surprisingly, that her contribution should be acknowledge and husband either from the one-third of the share or being the moral duty of the husband should give his wife more than her share. Only 3 per cent says no and believes that it's the duty of the female member to look after the house. 100 per cent Activists and 79 per cent Lawyers agrees that their household work should be counted as economic contribution to the family. In 1994, the Iranian parliament enacted a law giving a divorced woman the right to monetary

compensation for the years she worked in her husband's home as a mother and housewife. This means in Islamic law a woman household work is not her moral obligation but if she does then one has to value her contribution by providing her financial compensation.

Table 4.4: Can an earning wife who contributes to family wealth be entitled to equal share in a property which husband has bought with his own and wife's income?

Response	*Ulama*	*Social Activists*	*Lawyers*
Yes	100%	100%	100%
No	-	-	-
Uncertain/ Banned	-	-	-

In response to Table 4.4 surprisingly we got a unanimous response from Ulama, Activists and Lawyers. If the husband buys a property having investment made by both the husband and wife then wife does has that much of right in the property additional to her share as a wife. 100% Ulama, Social Activists and Lawyers completely agrees and has consensus on this. This also proves that even in traditional Shariah law woman enjoy her complete right on her earnings and she should be given her due share as well as what ever she spends from her earning at her husband's place.

Table 5: MAHR

Table 5: Do you think – *Mahr* amount should be substantial enough to provide security to wife?

Response	*Ulama*	*Social Activists*	*Lawyers*
Yes	57%	100%	81%
No	43%		19%
Uncertain/ Banned			

Mehr which is the most important right of the Muslim woman at the time of marriage has been an issue of debate and discussion among the scholars and the activists. Table 5 deals with this important issue. The question asked is should Mehr amount be substantial enough to provide security to wife? 81 per cent of lawyers strongly supports such provision and express their concern on the rate of divorce. Lawyers believed that a good Mehr will provide security to woman and also to the marital life. Activists without any apprehension 100 per cent of them urge authority to implement the practice as soon as possible. Ulama too majority of them agrees that a woman can demand a substantial Mehr and 57 per cent agrees, while 43 per cent still believe and promote practice of *Fatimi Mehr* or *Sunnah Mehr* which is just a meager amount or just a formal requirement of marriage. They also believe substantial demand of *Mahr* will cause problems for girls and her family.

Among the Muslims it is the duty of the husbands to gift the marriage portion to the wife. As mentioned in the Quran "And give unto the women (whom ye marry) free gift of their marriage portions; but if they of their own accord remit unto you a part thereof, then you are welcome to absorb it (in your wealth). Another verse says "And those of ye seek content (by marrying them) give unto them their portions as a duty". In the first verse the words *sadaqa* and *nehla* are used for marriage portion or nuptial gift and in the second verse the word *ujur* plural of *ajr* is used to connote the same thing. The root word of *saduqa, sudaq* and *sidaq* all conveying the sense of dower is *sadaqa* means friend. The word sadaqa carries the sense of sincerity, friendship and companionship. Another Quranic injunction is "Let him who has abundance spend (on his wife) out of his abundance, and let him whose means of subsistence are scanty spend in accordance with what God has given him." Thus, what ordained here is that a man must spend on his wife according to his own capacity.

Similarly the word *nehla* means according to Imam Raghib in his dictionary *Mufradatul Quran* wrote *nehla* originates from *nahl* meaning bee and signifies that as the bee makes a gift of such a useful thing as honey without any consideration, in the same way Nehla is that sweet gift which is given to the woman willingly without any idea of consideration by the husband. In Quran a woman is ensured her rights and she is allowed to hold her own property and the husband is made to pay for her sustenance. Quranic injunction also says that she should share fully her husband's standard of living. The verse says "And if you wish to have (one) wife in place of another and you have given one of them a heap of gold, take nothing from it. Would you take it by slandering (her) and (doing her) manifest wrong?" From the verse it can be argued that there is no limit to giving *Mahr* to a wife. The word 'heap of gold' indicates this. Ibn Kathir, referring to Musnad Ahmad, narrates the story of Umar, the second Caliph, who sought to put a ceiling of 400 dirham on Mahr. This was challenged by a woman belonging to the tribe of Quraysh. She referred to the above verse and said when Allah had permitted to payment of a heap of gold who was he to put ceiling of 400 dirham on it? Umar had to take back his ordinance and admit that even a woman knew more than him.

The *Mehr* amount paid to her is her own. Neither her father nor her husband can claim it. She alone owns it in her own rights. The Quran also encourages the man to give her dower liberally and with pleasure and not with sense of compulsion. Also, if the wife wishes, she may allow her husband to enjoy part or all of it. But it will depend wholly on her discretion. Her husband cannot compel her to do so. The husband also cannot claim back the *Mehr* amount, even if he has given a heap if gold to the wife except in the case of the *Khula*.

Table 5.1: Do you think in view of inflationary economy 'Mahr" should be given in terms of gold, silver, real estate or in financial instruments like share, bonds, fix deposits etc?

Response	***Ulama***	***Social Activists***	***Lawyers***
Yes	100%	100%	100%
No	-	-	-
Uncertain/ Banned			

Table 5.1 the question deals with the Mahr to be given in various forms. Due to inflation when asked Mahr be given in terms of Gold, Silver, real estate or in financial instruments like share, bonds. Fix deposits etc. Ulama, Activists and Lawyers surprisingly all agreed and had consensus that Mahr can be given in the form of any instruments which will give the exact value even after many years. They also advised especially Ulama that Mahr should be in accordance with the capacity of the Husband. It shouldn't be less and something substantial.

Table 5.2: Do you think there should be no permission for *Mehr-e-Muwajjal*?

Response	*Ulama*	*Social Activists*	*Lawyers*
Yes	95%	59%	91%
No	5	41%	3%
Uncertain/ Banned			6%

Table 5.2 deals with a practice of Mahr-e-Muwajjal which means differ payment. The mahr may be paid immediately to the bride at the time of marriage or deferred to a later date, or a combination of both. 95 per cent Ulama does agree that it is necessary to have this provision because if the Mahr amount is substantial and groom has agreed upon it then he should be allowed to make partial payment at a given period of time mention during the Nikah and with the consent of the bride. 59 per cent Activists too agrees for this practice of Mahr but they urge that the period should not exceed more than one year. 41 per cent Activists fears that this will lead to violation of woman's immediate Mahr right and also one is not assured if the payment will be made. Husband may pressurise wife and may ask to forgo the rest of the amount. 91 per cent Lawyers too think that provision of differ payment should be there and this way woman can ask for more Mahr according to groom's capacity. 6 per cent Lawyers are not certain about this practice whether it will help or would create more problems.

Table 6: Marriage Registration

Table 6: Do you think marriage registration should be compulsory with registrar of marriage?

Response	*Ulama*	*Social Activists*	*Lawyers*
Yes	95%	100%	100%
No	5%	-	-
Uncertain/ Banned			

Table 6 shows the response of the target group when asked whether marriage registration should be made compulsory with the registrar of the marriage. A very good proportion of Ulama around 95 per cent of them agrees that Muslims should register their Nikah and if made compulsory then many problems can be solved. However, they urge that there should be proper machinery so that Muslims living in villages should also be able to register their Nikah. Only 5 per cent Ulama fears that in case, Nikah is not register since the word compulsory is mentioned, and according to Shariat the Nikah is performed then it can be considered as invalid. So registration should be made compulsory. 100 per cent Activists supports registration and 100 per cent Lawyers too demands for registration whether at district level or also at Panchayat level. Some Ulama along with Activists and Lawyers expressed the need to have a uniform marriage certificate.

Table 6.1: Do you think codification of Muslim Personal Law in India will help Muslim women to realise their Islamic rights?

Response	*Ulama*	*Social Activists*	*Lawyers*
Yes	96%	100%	100%
No	2%	-	-
Uncertain/ Banned	2%		

In Table 6.1 the most important question was raised that whether Codification of Muslim Personal Law in India will help Muslim women to realise their Islamic rights. The most encouraging response we received was from Ulama who strongly feels that if legal experts sit together and draft and also if it is placed in Parliament to approve its codification then it is definitely going to benefit the community at large scale and for long term. They want the court and judges to study Muslim Personal Law in dealing with Muslim cases. 100 per cent Activists and 100 per cent Lawyers are unanimous in their opinion and feels codification will be a great relief and it will safeguard women's rights. All of them is of the opinion that codified law will assure all marital, inheritance and property rights and it will definitely lead to decrease in destitution of Muslim women due to arbitrary practices of divorce. Muslim law based on Quranic principle is the need of the hour and also some reforms will give greater relief to Muslim women.

Conclusion

In the above analysis we have found that there is a change in the attitude of the Ulama though not significant. Since Ulama too are confronted with these issues in the community for which they too feel the need for long term solution but does not want to initiate any efforts towards it. One need not ignore the fact that large majority of Ulama still vehemently support existing Anglo-Mohammadan law and use the weapon of Fatwa to further alter the law. Throughout the interviews of the Ulama in different seminaries of Uttar Pradesh and Maharashtra, we can't say that they are completely anti-reforms or anti-codification. Because many Muftis and Ulama are not exposed to or they simply ignore, the real problems of the Muslim community due to their own constraint. After we shared with them the cases and expressed the inability of the social organisations to deal with Shariah issues on one hand and the irresponsible attitude of the Ulama on the other, they accepted that there has been not much efforts made to bring codified law for the community.

They shared during the interviews that how Imarat-e-Shariah and several Darul-Qada are researching and trying to explore the *fiqh* (Islamic Jurisprudence) and producing 'uncodified law' to solve the issues related to marriage and divorce. However, their claim does not reflect the ground reality. We have seen in the above Tables on Divorce and Polygamy that they knowingly promote un-Islamic and unjust practice over Quranic injunction. They do abrogation of the Quran by Ahadiths or by their *urf* (customary practices) to justify their rulings. In case of Oral triple divorce which they all accept is a sin but still insist on it to be valid if someone practices. Though they accept the element of flexibility in Shariah which they conform of having *ijma* and *Ijtihad* as one of the major factor while framing Islamic law but there is also sheer reluctance on part of Ulama to introduce any reform in Marriage and Divorce law. Also there are considerable differences of opinion among the Ulama belonging to old generation and the newly graduated Mufti or Alim. In spite of pressure from the Ulama circle there are few we found that they want to participate in framing law. They understand the dynamics of modern society and the need to have codified law so to guide the community to make progress at all level. Here I would like to quote Philosopher Allam Iqbal who urged "Ulama should form a vital part of a Muslim legislative assembly helping and guiding free discussion on question relating to law." As mentioned earlier the trend of Ulama has slightly undergone change due to the inevitable change occurring in the age of rationality. The educated Muslims now have an enquiring mind and sometimes freely questioning the existing authorities.

3

Islamic Family Laws in Other Countries

This chapter mainly deals with the whole legal mechanism introduced whether codification, implementation and reforms introduced in the Shariah law. It highlights the existing laws in other countries whether Islamic or those countries having Muslim Personal laws, and how it is in conformity or in non-conformity with the international conventions. The idea is to emphasise on the various Shariah law practiced and their implementation and amendments has resulted in great deal of re-emergence of Legal science since Nineteenth Century. The extent of diversity of the Islamic world, with current developments in the constitutional and international laws has tried to define justice more minutely because to maintain one's position and acceptability in the global fraternity, no country can implement law which negates International Convention of Human Rights. No doubt there is an intense struggle by the activists to uphold human rights especially woman's right through out the Muslim world due to its conditional support to CEDAW or other international Charters. This has led to gross violation of woman's right and the demand for secular or common law.

Since the emergence of secular ideology and the demand for secularisation of law need to be scrutinised whenever it is applied to modern Islamic law. After all, secularisation is not all that much concerned with emancipation from religious premises, or indeed with the alleged or suspected loss of importance suffered by religion in the modern age rather, the question is how, given the constant demands for democracy and the rule of law, political and legal institutions and processes can be reconciled with religious institutions which governs the Muslim masses.

Legal Profiles: Organisation

The legal profiles are organised in more detailed narratives. Although the aim is to cover all those aspects of (the application of) Muslim personal law that diverge from the classical application, the information in the legal profiles is limited to the extent that wherever such information is available, it has been included.

The categories included in the table and narrative versions of the legal profiles are as follows:

Legal System/History

Schools of *Fiqh*

Constitutional Status of Islam(ic) Law

Court System

Relevant Legislation

Notable Features

Notable Cases

Law/Case Reporting System

International Conventions (with Relevant Reservations)

Background and Sources

In the **Legal System/History** category, those aspects of the country's history that directly or indirectly impact upon the current application of Islamic family law are included. The colonial history, the period in which independence was gained, the influential factors in the framing of post-independence legislation, and the circumstances relating to inter-communal relations are all examples of the kind of material that is included in that section.

The **Schools of *Fiqh*** category refers to the predominant school(s) (sg. *maddhab*, pl. *madhahib*) of Islamic law within each country. As not all of the countries where Islamic law is applied to personal status have homogenous populations, this section could be referring to a Muslim minority (as in India or Israel) or a Muslim majority (as in Pakistan or Indonesia) state. Thus, the **Schools of *Fiqh*** category also includes a note of the other religious denominations represented in each country, whether they are in the majority or are a minority.

The **Constitutional Status of Islam(ic) Law** category refers to the place that religion or canonical law is given in each state's constitution. Thus, where there is a state religion that will be noted. Aside from Islam as the state religion (or possibly another religion in the case of Muslim-minority jurisdictions), there is also reference to whether or not the *shariah*, or a particular *maddhab*, or the principles of Islamic law/jurisprudence are explicitly named a/the main source of substantive law.

The **Court System** category covers the judicial establishment, noting whether or not there are separate *shariah* courts and/or separate courts for different sects, and whether ultimate appeal lies with the regular courts.

The **Relevant Legislation** category covers substantive personal status legislation based on Islamic law or applying to Muslims, whether there are comprehensive codes of personal status, as in many Arab states, or particular enactments for certain areas of law, as in South Asia. Some of the legislation applies to all citizens of a state regardless of religions, while other legislation applies only to Muslims. There is also note of the legislation covering the courts applying Islamic family law, whether this refers to family courts serving all communities, or *shariah* courts specifically constituted for matters concerning the application of Muslim personal status law. There may be some enactments not directly relating to Muslim personal law that still affects the rights of women.

The **Notable Features** category is based on the substantive legislation relating to Muslim personal status and succession. The features of the law covered in this category are not comprehensive; rather, the focus is on those aspects of the law that differ from classical interpretations of Islamic family law. Modern aspects of the law that are based on the views of other schools of law from that which predominates in a particular state are also noted wherever this constitutes a significant deviation in the contemporary application of the law. The ordering and content (where the information is available) of the **Notable Features** of modern Islamic family law are as follows:

Marriage Age: covers minimum marriage age or age of capacity, the calendar (lunar or solar) according to which the minimum marriage age is calculated, scope for judicial discretion, and penal sanctions, and any requirement of judicial permission or the bride's express consent in the circumstance of a significant age gap between the prospective spouses.

Marriage Guardianship: covers whether or not the *wali's* approval is an essential requisite for the ward (particularly the female ward) to marry, what powers the *wali* has, and what limitations there are to the powers of the wali or what recourse the ward may have in the face of the guardian's unreasonable objection.

Marriage Registration: covers the obligatory or voluntary registration requirements, liability and penal sanctions for non-compliance with obligatory registration, and other consequences of failure to register marriage, as well as procedures for validating unregistered marriages.

Polygamy: covers the modern restrictions on the husband's right to marry polygamously (such as requiring notification of existing and/or prospective wives or obtaining judicial permission and the basis for obtaining such permission), as well as whether or not a subsequent marriage by the husband creates a presumption of injury on grounds of which the wife may petition for a divorce.

Obedience/Maintenance: covers the modern legal conception (if any) of the wife's duty to obey her husband, the definition of *nushuz* (disobedience), how the husband's duty of maintenance is linked to the wife's obedience, and whether or not the wife may sue for arrears of maintenance and what limitations there are to her right to do so.

Talaq: covers modern limitations on the husband's right to unilateral repudiation, such as, invalidation of triple *talaq*, *talaq* on condition or by oath, the requirement of a particular formulation, the requirement that the wife be notified, the invalidation of extra-judicial *talaq* or the requirement of registration.

Judicial Divorce: covers the grounds on which a Muslim wife, and also a Muslim husband where applicable, may apply for judicial dissolution.

Post-Divorce Maintenance/Financial Arrangements: covers the financial consequences of divorce with particular attention to any additional financial rights for the wife legislated by states beyond the classical requirements of deferred dower and maintenance during the *'idda* period. Though the classical law generally only obliges the Muslim husband to support his wife during the waiting period after divorce, many states have attempted to legislate additional judicial rights for divorced women.

Child Custody and Guardianship: covers the regulation of post-divorce childcare. This includes the ages to which the divorced mother may retain custody over male and female children, any scope for judicial discretion relating to age of custody, and the limitations to her right to custody.

Succession: covers amendments to classical rules on inheritance, for example, obligatory bequest (*wasiyya wajiba*) in favour of orphaned grandchildren, or reforms allowing the spouse relict to share in the remainder (*radd*) of an estate.

The **Notable Cases** category includes summaries of rulings in some leading cases or cases of particular relevance to the application of Islamic family law and women's rights. Also included are cases that generated a great deal of publicity that may have had only a partial relation to Islamic family law but relate more specifically to gender roles or modern formulations of apostasy.

The **Law/Case Reporting System** category contains reference to the system of law reporting or case reporting where such information is available. While there is a long-standing and well developed system of case reporting in certain jurisdictions (for example, much of South Asia), there are other states where the legal system is not based on case law and where there is no official system of case reporting or there is an emerging system. In such states, there may be only practitioners' collections of notable cases and principles in *shariah* court decisions or judgements relating to Islamic family law, in which case that has been noted where such information was available.

The **International Conventions (with Relevant Reservations)** category covers four international Conventions and Covenants that directly relate to women's and children's rights. These are the International Covenant on Civil and Political Rights (ICCPR), the International Covenant on Economic, Social and Cultural Rights (ICESCR), the Convention on the Elimination of All Forms of Discrimination against Women (CEDAW), and the Convention on the Rights of the Child (CRC). The Covenants and Conventions to which each state is a signatory are listed, as are the accession dates and any relevant reservations. These may be directly relevant to the application of Islamic family law in that certain states adopting the CEDAW submitted reservations to certain provisions of the Convention on *shariah*-based grounds. They may also be indirectly related, such as reservations relating to unequal naturalisation regulations for men and women married to foreign nationals that have no basis in Islamic law.

Democratic and Popular Republic of Algeria

Legal History

The Algerian legal system is based on French and Islamic law. Algeria remained under French rule for 132 years, constituting the longest direct European colonisation of any region in North Africa. After a brutal eight-year struggle for independence, Algeria became a sovereign state in July 1962.

Under French rule, courts applied Maliki principles in matters relating to personal status and succession (unless the parties were Ibadi). Commentators note that the process of adjudication and interpretation in the Franco-Algerian courts led to distinctive developments in the area of family law. In 1916, a commission headed by the French jurist Marcel Morand was appointed to formulate a draft code of Muslim law. The draft code, *Avan-project de code du droit Musulman Algerien*, based mainly on Maliki principles but incorporating some non-Maliki (mainly Hanafi) provisions, was never formally passed into law although it did influence the application and administration of family law in Algeria. The government eventually issued a Marriage Ordinance in 1959, enacting some Maliki principles relating to family matters; the Ibadi minority was initially exempted from the Ordinance. The legislation may have been inspired by the codification of family law in Tunisia and Morocco in 1956 and 1958 under newly-independent national governments. Though the Marriage Ordinance did not introduce substantial changes to family law, there were some provisions based on Hanafi principles. The Ordinance established rules for solemnisation and registration of marriage, raised the minimum marriage ages for both parties, and established certain regulations relating to judicial dissolution and court orders for post-divorce reliefs; its application was specific to those who registered their option for state legislation.

The first Constitution promulgated in 1964 declared Islam the state religion. The new regime also amended the Marriage Ordinance of 1959, repealing or amending certain provisions such as the exemption of Ibadi marital relations from the terms of the Ordinance and the minimum marriage-age. The second Constitution adopted in 1976 reaffirmed Islam as the state religion. Periodic demands for comprehensive codification of personal status and inheritance laws eventually led to a draft code being presented to the National Assembly in 1980. After several years of debate, discussion and protest, the Family Code was enacted in 1984.

Schools of *Fiqh*: The Maliki school is the predominant *madhhab* in Algeria. There is an Ibadi minority. There are also small Christian and Jewish minorities.

Constitutional Status of Islam(ic) Law: The current Constitution was adopted on 19th November 1976 and has been amended several times, with the last revisions approved by referendum in November and signed into law in December 1996. Article 2 of the Constitution provides that Islam is the religion of the State.

Court System: The judiciary in Algeria is organised into three levels. *Daira* tribunals (numbering 183 in the late 1980s) are the courts of first instance for civil and certain criminal matters. The 48 *Wilaya* Courts in each province are organised into four chambers (civil, criminal, administrative and accusation) and are constituted by three-judge panels that must hear all cases. In civil suits, these courts have appellate jurisdiction over the decisions of lower courts. The highest level of the judiciary is the Supreme Court (with a Private Law chamber for civil and commercial cases, Social Division for social security and labour cases, a Criminal Court, and an Administrative Division).

Notable Features: The provisions of the Family Code 1984 are drawn from various schools of law, the Algerian draft code of Muslim law formulated by a commission headed by Marcel Morand in 1916, and parallel legislation from neighbouring countries (particularly Moroccan enactments). Article 222 of the Code specifies the *shariah* as the residuary source of law, thus allowing for selection of appropriate interpretations from any school of law or directly from the original sources of law (Quran and *sunnah*) or from secondary sources.

The minimum marriage age is 21 years for men and 18 for women, with scope for judicial discretion if necessity or benefit is established. Compulsion by the marriage guardian, whether the *wali* is the father or anyone else, is expressly forbidden, as is giving a woman into marriage without her consent. Nevertheless, the law does state that the contracting of a woman's marriage is the guardian's duty, whether he is the father or another close male relation (or the judge if there is no *wali*). The marriage guardian may not prevent his ward from contracting a marriage that is in her benefit, but a father may oppose the marriage of his virgin daughter if it is considered to be in her best interests. If the guardian opposes the marriage without valid cause, the judge may authorise it.

The Code of Civil Status governs procedural matters related to obligatory marriage registration. The Family Code does state that, if there is no register entry, a marriage may be validated by judgement of the court "if the elements which constitute the marriage are fulfilled in accordance with the provisions of the law." Following such judgement, the marriage shall be entered into the Register of Civil Status. A valid marriage is constituted by consent of the spouses before the *wali* and two witnesses, and the establishment of *mahr*.

Spouse's rights and obligations generally follow classical law. The husband is required to provide maintenance from the time the marriage is consummated so long as the wife remains in the matrimonial home, and is required to treat co-wives equitably. Maintenance is payable from the date that a claim is filed, though a judge may direct the payment of arrears of maintenance (on the production of valid evidence) for a period of not more than one year preceding the filing of the claim. The wife is required to obey and respect her husband and his family and suckle her offspring if she is able to do so.

On polygamy, classical injunctions regarding the equal treatment of co-wives are reiterated, with the additional proviso that the reason for contracting a polygamous marriage must be justified. It is not stated exactly how a just reason is defined. Prior notification of existing and future wives is required by the law. Any wife in a polygamous union may initiate legal action against her husband in case of harm (*darar*) or petition for divorce if her consent was not obtained.

Divorce is only established by a judgment of the court, and must be preceded by reconciliation efforts by the judge. Efforts at reconciliation are not to exceed three months. The wife may petition for divorce on the following grounds: non-payment of maintenance (requiring a court judgment ordering maintenance and upon condition that the wife didn't know of the husbands financial incapacity at the time of marriage); infirmity preventing conjugal relations; the husbands refusal to share his wife's bed for over four months; the husbands imprisonment for more than a year for a crime that brings disgrace to the family; the husbands absence without valid reason or provision of maintenance for over a year; any legally recognised harm (relating to the provision of maintenance or the contracting of a polygamous marriage, for instance); and any grave moral impropriety that is proved. The wife may also obtain a *khul* with her husbands consent in return for some compensation. In case there is any disagreement over the terms of the *khul*, the judge may order the wife to pay a particular sum that must not exceed the value of her proper dower. If the husband initiates divorce and the judge concludes the husband has abused his right of *talaq*, the wife is to be awarded damages; the law does not specify the upper limit for compensation to the arbitrarily divorced wife.

If the wife is granted custody of the children, the husband must provide for their accommodation in keeping with his means. A divorce is entitled to maintenance during her waiting period, a provision adapted from the Hanafi School. The divorces custody of her children ceases at 16 years for boys (or 10 if she remarries) and until the legal age of marriage (18 years) for girls (so long as the mother does not remarry or marries someone within the prohibited degrees to her daughter), with the proviso that the decision to terminate custody is in the wards best interests. Full guardianship reverts to the mother upon the father's death unless his will provides otherwise.

On succession, the Family Code introduced the obligatory bequest in favour of orphaned grandchildren by predeceased sons, as well as the Hanafi doctrine of *radd* (return), extended from its classical formulation to allow the spouse relict to share in the residue of the deceased's estate.

In the CEDAW Committees concluding comments to Algeria's initial report to the 20th CEDAW session in 1999, it is noted that, partly due to Algerias accession to the Convention in 1993, the Family Code 1984 is being revised. Some of the suggested changes may lead to the withdrawal of certain reservations submitted by Algeria upon accession to the CEDAW.

Law/Case Reporting System: Laws are published in the *Journal Officiel*.

International Conventions (with Relevant Reservations): Algeria signed the ICCPR and the ICESCR in 1968 and ratified them in 1989 with several interpretative declarations. The final declaration relates to Article 23(4) of the ICCPR on rights and responsibilities of spouses in marriage and divorce being interpreted in such a way that it does not impair "the essential foundations of the Algerian legal system".

Algeria signed the CRC in 1990 and ratified it in 1993 with the following interpretative declarations: to Article 14(1) and (2) on children's freedom of conscience and religion, as Algerian law stipulates that a child's education is determined by the religion of the father; and to Articles 13, 16 and 17 of the Convention on children's freedom of expression, right to privacy, and access to information, relating to particular provisions of the Algerian Penal and Information Codes and the interpretation of the provisions of the CRC in light of possible breaches of public order and decency and incitement of minors. The latter declaration also cites Article 26 of the Information Code which states that "national and foreign periodicals and specialised publications must not contain any illustration, narrative, information or insertion contrary to Islamic morality, national values or human rights or advocate racism, fanaticism and treason."

Algeria acceded to the CEDAW in 1996 with the following reservations: to Article 2, as Algeria reiterated its willingness to apply the provisions relating to the elimination of all discrimination by legislation and other appropriate means on condition that "they do not conflict with the provisions of the Algerian Family Code"; to Article 9(2) on equal nationality rights on the basis that the provision is inconsistent with the Algerian Nationality and Family Codes; to Article 15(4) relating to freedom of movement and freedom in choice of residence and domicile, stating that the provision "should not be interpreted in such a manner as to contradict the provisions of Article 37 of Chapter 4 of the Algerian Family Code"; and to Article 16 on equality of rights in personal status and family law, asserting that the provisions of that Article should not be taken to contradict the Algerian Family Code.

Background and Sources: Algeria, Initial Report to the Committee on the Elimination of Discrimination against Women, 1 Sept. 1998; CEDAW 20th Session, 19/01 to 05/02 1999, El Alami and Hinchcliffe, Islamic Marriage and Divorce Laws of the Arab World, London 1996; Christelow, Muslim

Law Courts and the French Colonial State in Algeria, Princeton, 1985; Knauss, The Persistence of Patriarchy: Class, Gender, and Ideology in Twentieth Century Algeria, New York, 1987; Lazreg, The Eloquence of Silence: Algerian Women in Question, New York, 1994; Mahmood, "Algeria" in Statutes of Personal Law in Islamic Countries, 2nd ed., New Delhi, 1995; Metz, ed., Algeria: A Country Study, 5th ed., Washington, D.C., 1994; Mitchell, "Family Law in Algeria before and after the 1404/1984 Family Code," in Islamic Law: Theory and Practice, ed. Gleave, London, 1997; Nasir, The Islamic Law of Personal Status, 2nd ed., London, 1990; Redden, "Algeria" in Modern Legal Systems Cyclopedia, Vol. 6, Buffalo, NY, 1990.

State of Bahrain

Legal History

Bahrain has had a long exposure to the British legal system and has a mixed legal system drawing from both English common law and codified systems and from Islamic law. The Ottoman Empire lost control over Bahrain in 1861; the territory became a British protectorate in 1880. Bahrain gained full independence from its protectorate status in August 1971. Upon independence, a Legislative Committee was appointed to establish an independent legal system. Since that time, Bahraini law has followed a similar pattern to other Arab states legislation, particularly Egyptian codes.

Personal law remains uncodified, and is administered by *shariah* courts regulated by the Bahrain Courts Law 1971. The Judicature Law also indicates the residuary sources of law in the absence of applicable provisions of law: judgments are to be derived from principals of the *shariah*; in the absence of applicable *shariah* provisions, on custom (with particular customs having precedence over general customs); and final resort is to natural law or the principles of equity and good conscience. The National Assembly was dissolved in 1975, and the Amir has ruled by decree since that time.

Schools of *Fiqh*: The Jafari School is the predominant *madhhab* in Bahrain, and there are significant Sunni minorities following either the Shafii or Maliki School.

Constitutional Status of Islamic Law: The Constitution of the State of Bahrain was adopted 26 May 1973. Article 1(a) affirms that "Bahrain is an Arab Islamic State". Article 2 affirms Islam as the religion of the State and identifies the *shariah* as a main source of legislation.

Court System: The judiciary is divided into regular and *shariah* courts. The *shariah* courts are divided into Shi'i and Sunni departments applying Jafari and Shafi'i or Maliki *fiqh*, respectively. These courts have jurisdiction over all disputes relating to Muslim personal status, except disputes over estates. Disputes over estates fall under the jurisdiction of the competent civil courts, though those courts are obliged to divide estates in accordance with Islamic law. The Junior *Shariah* Courts (Jafari and Sunni Departments) hear personal status cases in the first instance. The High *Shariah* Court of Appeal (Jafari and Sunni Courts) has appellate jurisdiction over Senior *Shariah* Court decisions. Each High *Shariah* Court consists of a president and a number of judges; sittings are validly held in the presence of two judges, one of whom must be the President of the Court or his deputy. A Decree Law (no. 8) 1989 establishing the Court of Cassation also directs that this Court has exclusive jurisdiction to decide cases filed simultaneously in the civil and *shariah* courts or before two *shariah* courts or to settle any dispute arising from conflicting judgments between such courts, as well as jurisdiction over civil and commercial matters and personal status suits involving non-Muslim non-Bahrainis.

Notable Features: Personal status law remains unlegislated. The *shariah* courts apply classical Islamic personal status law to Muslims without reference to state law.

Law/Case Reporting System: Laws are published in the *Official Gazette*. Case reporting is restricted to the judgments of the Court of Cassation, the highest court in Bahrain. There are no official publications of *Shariah* Court decisions.

International Conventions (with Relevant Reservations): Bahrain acceded to the CRC in 1992 without submitting any reservations.

Background and Sources: Amin, *Middle East Legal Systems*. Glasgow: Royston Ltd., 1985; El Alami and Hinchcliffe, Islamic Marriage and Divorce Laws of the Arab World, London, 1996; Ballantyne, Commercial Law in the Arab Middle East: The Gulf States, London, 1986; Mahmood, "Gulf" in Statutes of Personal Law in Islamic Countries, New Delhi, 1995; Redden, Bahrain in Modern Legal Systems Cyclopedia, Vol. 5, Buffalo, NY, 1990.

Peoples Republic of Bangladesh

Legal History

[see also: **Legal History, Republic of India** and **Legal History, Islamic Republic of Pakistan**] Bangladesh seceded from Pakistan in December of 1971. Following independence, the British-era legislation that had continued to be applied in Pakistan, as well as the post-1947 legislation enacted by Pakistan, remained the basis of Bangladeshi personal status laws. Pearl and Menski state that legal developments in Bangladesh and Pakistan since 1972 have been quite distinct. The prospect of a Uniform Family Code has been a subject attracting much lobbying by women's groups in Bangladesh, but there is no equivalent to India's constitutional directive regarding a Uniform Civil Code.

Schools of *Fiqh*: The Hanafi school is the predominant *madhhab* in Bangladesh. There are also Hindu and Christian minorities.

Constitutional Status of Islam(ic) Law: The Constitution was adopted on 4 November 1972. An amendment to the Constitution under President Ziaur Rahman in 1977 removed the principle of secularism that had been enshrined in Part II: Fundamental State Policy, replacing it with "absolute trust and faith in Almighty Allah." The Eighth Amendment of 1988 inserted Article 2A, affirming that "[t]he state religion of the Republic is Islam, but other religions may be practised in peace and harmony in the republic." Some women's groups challenged this move on the grounds that it risked exposing women to discriminatory laws.

At the same time, state law in South Asia has always afforded recognition to and left a sphere for the application of the family laws of different religious communities. Constitutional protection of women's rights and the assertion of gender equality comes under the Fundamental Principles of State Policy and is enshrined in Article 10 on the participation of women in national life as well as in Articles 26 to 29 of the section on Fundamental Rights affirming equality of all citizens before the law. This is balanced against the Constitutional protection of minority rights provided for in Article 41 on freedom of religion and the freedom of every religious community or denomination to establish, manage and maintain its religious institutions (subject to law, public order and morality). This affects the significant Hindu minority in Bangladesh (roughly equivalent in proportion to India's Muslim minority) in addition to Christian and Buddhist minorities.

Court System: The judiciary is organised at two levels, with subordinate courts and a Supreme Court with Appellate and High Court Divisions. The Family Courts Ordinance 1985 governs the application of the personal laws of all Bangladeshis through the state judiciary by the creation of Family Courts. The Family Courts have jurisdiction over personal status cases of all communities, though religious minorities are governed by their own personal laws. The Family Courts are convened in Assistant Judges Courts and have special procedures and reduced formalities. The Family Courts may hear suits *in camera* at the request of both parties, and the court fees are nominal, but lawyers and notaries fees considerably increase the costs associated with going to court. Under the terms of the Ordinance, Family Courts have exclusive jurisdiction to try and dispose of suits relating to the dissolution of marriage, the restitution of conjugal rights, dower, maintenance, and guardianship and custody.

The jurisdiction of the Family Courts is restricted so that if any criminal offence arises in the context of a civil case, it comes under the jurisdiction of Criminal or Magistrates Courts. This has created some inconsistencies within the legal system with Magistrates still hearing maintenance claims under Section 488 of the Criminal Procedure Code while Family Courts are supposed to retain exclusive jurisdiction to try and determine maintenance cases. The Bangladeshi legislation relating to family courts is quite similar to the legislation applicable in Pakistan, however, the Pakistani Family Courts have broader jurisdiction extending beyond civil suits.

Notable Features: [see also: **Notable Features, Republic of India** and **Notable Features, Islamic Republic of Pakistan**]

As elsewhere in South Asia, much of the Muslim personal law is unlegislated, the basis for the law being classical Hanafi *fiqh* except where this has been amended by legislation.

The Muslim Personal Law (*Shariaht*) Application Act 1937 continues to govern the application of Muslim family law in Bangladesh. (The pre-independence legislation that replaced this Act in 1962 only applied to West Pakistan.) According to the Act, Bangladeshis are subject to local custom and usage in matters relating to wills, legacies or adoption, unless a person declares his or her express preference for being governed by Islamic law. Thus, estates may validly devolve in proportions favouring women under customary law.

The Child Marriage Restraint Act 1929 has been amended by Ordinance in 1984 so that the minimum ages of marriage are 21 for men and 18 for women. The legislation provides penal sanctions for those who knowingly participate in the contracting of an under-age marriage, but does not invalidate such marriages.

The Muslim Marriages and Divorces (Registration) Act 1974 enacted to strengthen the inducements for civil registration states that "every marriage solemnised under Muslim law shall be registered in accordance with the provisions of this Act" and establishes the licensing of *Nikah* Registrars. The punishment for not registering a marriage is a prison sentence and/or a fine. Failure to register does not invalidate the marriage. It should also be noted that, although there is no legislation to this effect, there is a customary trend in Bangladesh towards encouraging the insertion of stipulations relating to delegated divorce in the marriage contract.

The issues of maintenance and obedience within marriage continue to be governed by classical law for the most part. Much legal development has occurred through case law. In *Nelly Zaman v. Giasuddin Khan* (34 DLR (1982) 221), the Court ruled that, with the passage of time, the husband's suing for forcible restitution of conjugal rights against an unwilling wife is both outmoded and untenable if considered with relation to the principle of equality of men and women enshrined in Articles 27 and 31 of the Constitution. "In the husband's unilateral plea for forcible restitution of conjugal rights as against a wife unwilling to live with her husband, there is no mutuality and reciprocity between the respective rights of the husband and the wife, since such plea for restitution of conjugal rights is not available to a wife as against her husband apart from claiming maintenance and alimony. A reference to Article 28(2) of the Constitution of Bangladesh guaranteeing equal rights of women and men in all spheres of the state and public life would clearly indicate that any unilateral plea of a husband for forcible restitution of conjugal rights as against a wife unwilling to live with her husband is violative of the accepted State and Public Principle and Policy" (34 DLR (1982) 221, at p. 222). With respect to arrears of maintenance, in *Rustom Ali v. Jamila Khatun* (43 DLR (1991) 301), the Court ruled (in accordance with classical Hanafi law) that a wife is not entitled to arrears of maintenance. Maintenance will only be allowed her from the date the suit is brought before the Family Court until three months from the decree of dissolution of marriage. The former wife or the child may not claim past maintenance unless the parties have a previously established agreement. In *Muhammad Hefzur Rahman v. Shamsun Nahar Begum* (15 BLD (1995) 34) relating to the maintenance of divorces, the Court ruled that a Muslim husband's responsibility to maintain his divorced wife does not cease with the expiry of the *idda*. The Court stated that the former husband is bound to provide his divorced wife with maintenance on a reasonable scale for an indefinite period, until her status as a divorce changes, that is, if she remarries. The ruling was based on an interpretation of a Quranic verse relating to provisions for divorced wives (2:241). The Supreme Court overturned the High Court's judgment on 3 December 1998, leaving the classical Hanafi interpretation intact for the moment.

The Bangladeshi Muslim Family Laws Ordinance, based on the Pakistani MFLO of 1961, has incorporated some amendments to the original legislation. There are administrative differences in terms of the governmental bodies that apply the provisions of the MFLO at the local level. Applications, appeals and conciliation procedures go to the Union Parishad, Pourashava or Municipal Corporation. This includes the application process for contracting polygamous marriages, the application process itself remaining the same (i.e., requiring the reasons for wanting to contract a polygamous marriage and certification attesting to the existing wife's or wives consent). Legislation introduced in 1974 to encourage and facilitate the registration of marriages has also been used to amend the MFLO and use registration as a method of controlling polygamy. The MFLO also establishes penalties for contracting polygamous marriages in contravention of the law. Polygamous marriages contracted without the permission of the relevant authorities are not rendered invalid, nor is there a penalty for failing to obtain the existing wife's consent (as long as the Council has permitted the polygamous marriage). In *Jesmin Sultana v. Mohammad Elias* (1997 (17) BLD 4), the Court ruled that Section 6 of the MFLO prohibiting the contracting of a polygamous marriage without the prior permission of the Arbitration Council is against the principles of Islamic law. The Court stated that Muslim jurists and scholars are nearly unanimous in the view that it is practically impossible to deal with co-wives justly, and so the Quranic injunction that a second wife may be taken under specific conditions is virtually a prohibition. The Court also noted that Tunisia has given legislative effect to this interpretation. Thus, the Court recommended that Section 6 of the MFLO should be repealed and replaced by a section prohibiting polygamy altogether. The Court also directed that a copy of the judgement be sent to the Ministry of Law for consideration. No action is known to have been taken on it.

The Dissolution of Muslim Marriages Act 1939 also remains in force in Bangladesh, with the amendments initiated in Pakistan by the Muslim Family Laws Ordinance 1961; that is, a polygamous marriage by the husband in contravention of the provisions of the MFLO is included as sufficient grounds for the first wife to obtain a decree of dissolution. A post-independence amendment to the provision relates to the exercise of the option of puberty, entitling a girl contracted into marriage by her father or other guardian before the age of 18 to repudiate the marriage (provided it has not been consummated) before attaining the age of 19. In addition, judicial *khul* granted by the courts without the husband's consent allows for women to obtain divorce by waiving their financial rights. In *Hasina Ahmed v. Syed Abul Fazal* (32 DLR (1980) 294), the Court ruled that a woman may be granted a *khul* by a judicial decision without the husband's consent.

Custody continues to be governed by the Guardians and Wards Act 1890 in Bangladesh. The Act stipulates that the courts are to be guided by the personal law to which the minor is subject. The courts are also directed to consider the age, gender and religion of the minor and the character and capacity of the proposed guardian, as well as considering the minor's own opinion if s/he is old enough to form an intelligent preference. For Muslims, the general rule is that the divorced mother is entitled to custody over male children until the age of 7 (classical Hanafi position) and over female children until puberty. Under the legislation, if the minor is very young or is a female, the courts are directed to give preference to the mother. In all cases, the interests of the ward are paramount. This has been confirmed by a number of judgements, such as *Muhammad Abu Baker Siddique v. S.M.A. Bakar & others* (38 DLR (AD) 1986). The Court's ruling contradicted the classical dictates of Hanafi law according to which the mother's custody over a boy ends at 7. The Court stated that "indeed, the principle of Islamic Law (in the instant case, the rule of *hizanat* or guardianship of a minor child as stated in the Hanafi school) has to be regarded, but deviation therefrom would seem permissible as the paramount consideration should be the child's welfare." The Court also pointed out that the rationale for the departure from classical positions is justified as there is no clear and distinct statement of the Quran or *sunnah* to rely upon, and also because the jurists themselves never reached any consensus. The *Zohra Begum v. Latif Ahmed Munawar* (1965 (17) DLR (WP) and PLD 1965 (Lah) 695) case, and other rulings deviating from classical law are also cited.

As there are detailed rules for the division of estates according to classical law, there is little legislation in this area. In general, property devolves upon the heirs according to Hanafi or Jafari rules of succession. The Muslim Family Laws Ordinance 1961 also introduced obligatory bequests in favour of orphaned grandchildren, allowing them to inherit from their maternal or paternal grandparents in place of their deceased mothers or fathers.

The Repression against Women and Children Act of January 2000 recognises offenses of sexual assault and sexual harassment. It also authorises a tribunal to decide to keep a woman in protective custody against her will for her safety.

Law/Case Reporting System: *Bangladesh Legal Decisions, Dhaka Law Cases, Dhaka Law Reports.*

International Conventions and Reports to Treaty Governing Bodies: Bangladesh acceded to the CEDAW in 1984 with a reservation relating to Article 2 regarding the elimination of discrimination against women and the Article 16(1) (c) regarding equality of rights in marriage and upon its dissolution; Bangladesh does not consider these provisions binding as they "conflict with the *shariah* law based on (the) Holy Quran and *Sunnah*."

Bangladesh signed the CRC in 1990 and ratified the same year, with reservations to Articles 14(1) on children's freedom of religion and 21 relating to adoption. The reservation to the latter states that the provision will apply subject to the existing laws and practices in Bangladesh.

Bangladesh acceded to the ICESCR in 1998 with a number of declarations. The interpretative declaration relating to Articles 2 and 3 of the Covenant states that equality of rights between men and women is to be implemented in so far as they agree with the Constitution of Bangladesh and, more specifically, subject to Bangladeshi state inheritance law.

Bangladesh acceded to the Convention on Consent to Marriage, Minimum Age for Marriage and Registration of Marriages in 1998 with reservations to Articles 1 and 2, stating that the treaty would be applied in accordance with the Personal Laws of different religious communities of the country, and allowing for a dispensation as to age, for serious reasons, in the interest of the intending spouses.

Background and Sources: Hossain, "Equality in the Home: Women's Rights and Personal Laws in South Asia," Human Rights of Women: National and International

Perspectives, ed. Cook, Philadelphia, 1994; Mahmood, Bangladesh in Statutes of Personal Law in Islamic Countries, 2nd ed., New Delhi, 1995; Monsoor, From Patriarchy to Gender Equity: Family Law and Its Impact on Women in Bangladesh, Unpublished PhD dissertation, SOAS, University of London; Pearl and Menski, Muslim Family Law, 3rd ed., London, 1998; Redden, Bangladesh in Modern Legal Systems Cyclopedia, Vol. 9, Buffalo, NY, 1990; Robinson, ed. The Cambridge Encyclopaedia of India, Pakistan, Bangladesh, Sri Lanka, Nepal, Bhutan and the Maldives, Cambridge, 1989.

Brunei (Negara Brunei Darussalam)

Legal History

For Muslim Bruneians, Islamic law is particularly influential in the area of family law. Sources of law are legislation (imperial statutes, common law, equity, etc.), Islamic law (Shafi'i views, or opinions of other three Sunni schools with the Sultan's approval), ancient custom and Malay custom.

During the fifteenth and sixteenth centuries, the Brunei Sultanate controlled the north-western coast of Borneo and parts of Kalimantan and the Philippines. European expansion from the sixteenth century led to the loss of Brunei's possessions to the Spanish and Dutch. In the nineteenth century, the Sultan of Brunei sought British aid in defending his coasts from piracy. The British explorer James Brooke was made Rajah of Sarawak in 1839 and the British annexed the island of Labuan in 1846. The Sultan accepted protectorate status under Britain by the late nineteenth century, formalised in 1906 by a treaty providing that the Sultan would seek the advice of the British Resident on all matters outside of local custom and religion. The Constitution was adopted in 1959 allowing for internal self-rule and establishing a Legislative Council, with the powers of the British Resident transferred to the Sultan and his appointed officials. A 1971 agreement ended Brunei's protectorate status, with Britain retaining control over defence and foreign relations. Brunei gained full independence in 1984.

The Mohammedan Laws Enactment 1912 promulgated under British rule was based on both custom and Islamic law. The Enactment covered limited aspects of family and criminal law and delineated the jurisdiction of *Kathis* Courts. It was followed by the Mohammedan Marriage and Divorce Enactment 1913 providing for registration through *kathis*. Both Acts were repealed by the 1955 Religious Councils, *Kathis* Courts and State Customs Act. Section VI of Act contains provisions on marriage and divorce applicable to marriages where both parties are Muslim and which were solemnised according to Muslim law. The Act also regulates the judicial application of Islamic family law, provides penalties for breach of its terms, etc.

Schools of *Fiqh*: The majority of the population is Shafi'i Muslims. There are also Buddhist and Christian minorities, as well as segments of the population adhering to indigenous religions.

Constitutional Status of Islam(ic) Law: The Constitution was promulgated 29th September 1959 (with some provisions suspended under the State of Emergency since December 1962 and others since independence on 1st January 1984). Article 3 declares Islam the state religion, "according to the Shafi'i sect". Article 3 also provides that "the Head of the religion of Brunei Darussalam shall be His Majesty the Sultan and *Yang Di-Pertuan* (Head of State)."

Court System: Brunei maintains separate *shariah* and regular court systems, with the former having jurisdiction over Muslim personal status. *Shariah* courts decide personal status cases or cases relating to religious offences following Shafi'i opinion, then legislation by the Religious Council (*Majlis*) under the terms of the 1955 Religious Council, State Customs and *Kathis* Courts Enactment. The Council may have recourse to non-*rajih* Shafi'i interpretations or positions from other schools of *fiqh* if required by *maslaha* and approved by the Sultan.

Notable Features: The minimum marriage age is not specified, but the legislation does provide that validity of marriage requires meeting all the conditions of validity according to the sect to which the parties belong. The *wali's* consent is also a requirement for validity of marriage. A marriage is void if both parties have not given consent. Marriage registration is obligatory, through *kathis* authorised as registrars, or solemnised by a *kathi* in the presence of a registrar. Polygamy is governed by classical law. Obedience and maintenance are governed by classical law, and a wife deemed to be *nashiza* is also liable to penal sanctions. In case of the husband's failure to maintain, the wife may apply to a *kathi* for a maintenance order, but sums and the time period for which the wife may claim arrears is not specified.

The legislation specifies that the husband may divorce his wife with one, two or three *talaqs* in accordance with Muslim law. The divorcing husband must report the divorce to the registrar within seven days. A woman may obtain a judicial dissolution according to Muslim law by applying to the *kathi* who will summon the husband. If the husband consents, the divorce is registered. If the husband refuses, the *kathi* may propose *cherai tebus talak* (*khul*), with the court assessing the sum payable by the wife to the husband according to the status and means of the parties. If the husband does not agree to granting a *khul* the *kathi* will appoint two arbitrators who may be given the authority to decree a divorce if parties agree to such a settlement. The wife may also be issued a certificate of presumption of death if husband is believed to have died or has not been heard from for an extended period of time. A woman divorced by her husband may apply to the *kathi* for *mattah* (*muta al-talaq*/consolatory gift) or maintenance (of a sum and for such period as the court sees fit). Child custody and guardianship is governed by classical law.

Succession is governed by classical law.

Notable Cases

Law/Case Reporting System: Case reporting is through the *Law Reports of Brunei*, continued in *Judgements of the Courts of Brunei Darussalam* from 1986.

International Conventions (with Relevant Reservations): Brunei acceded to the CRC in 1995, submitting that Brunei "expresses its reservations on the provisions which may be contrary to (Brunei's) Constitution and to the beliefs and principles of Islam, the State religion, and without prejudice to the generality of the said reservations, in particular expresses its reservations on articles 14, 20 and 21". (Article 14 relates to the child's freedom of religion and conscience and Articles 20 and 21 relate to adoption.)

Background and Sources: Hooker, Islamic Law in South-East Asia, Singapore, 1984; Ibrahim, The Status of Muslim Women in Family Law in Malaysia, Singapore and Brunei, Singapore, 1965; Mahmood, "Brunei" in Statutes of Personal Law in Islamic Countries, 2nd ed. New Delhi, 1995; Redden, "Brunei" inModern Legal Systems Cyclopedia, vol. 9, New York, 1990.

Arab Republic of Egypt

Legal History

The legal system is based on Islamic law and civil law (particularly French codes). Egypt attained independence from the Ottoman Empire in matters of administration of law and the judiciary in 1874. A reformist movement developed in the late nineteenth century, led by such prominent thinkers and commentators as the Grand *Mufti* Muhammad Abduh, Rashid Rida, and Qasim Amin. Changes in the interpretation and application of family law were an important part of the reformists' agenda.

The reform of the judicial administration began in 1875, leading to the establishment of *mukhtalatat* (mixed) and *ahli* (national) courts. As Egypt increasingly came under foreign influence, the legal system began resembling European systems to a greater extent. New legislation relating to penal, commercial and maritime law also reflected the growing influence of Europe, but personal law remained unreformed until 1920. (The renowned jurist Qudri Pasha prepared an unofficial code of personal status law based on the *rajih* (majority, dominant) views of the Hanafi school, a source still referred to in the *shariah* courts of some neighbouring states as a guide to Hanafi law.)

The *shariah* courts were integrated into the National Courts in 1956. There are judges trained in *shariah* presiding over family law cases within the National Courts. Appeals are heard by regular judges in the Court of Appeals and then the Court of Cassation.

From 1920 to the early 1950s, on the basis of recommendations made by several committees, the Egyptian legislature enacted a number of laws effecting important changes in legal principles relating to family law and succession. These included the Law of Maintenance and Personal Status (Law no. 25/1920), a law regulating minimum marriage age (Law no. 56/1923), a Law of Personal Status (Law no. 25/1929) on the dissolution of marriage and family disputes, the Civil Code of 1931, the Law of Inheritance (Law no. 77/1943), and the Law of Bequest (Law no. 71/1946). In 1976, a new law established rules for the enforcement of court-orders for payment of maintenance to wives, ex-wives, children and parents.

Through the 1960s and 1970s, despite various reports and proposals relating to legal reform, political events time and again pre-empted the enactment of new laws in this area. Finally, in 1979, after failing to achieve any consensus on matters of family law, Sadat unilaterally issued an emergency decree passing one of the proposals into law in 1979.

Law no. 44/1979 was popularly referred to as Jihan's Law or Jiji's Law. This controversial amendment introduced extensive changes to the two Egyptian Laws of Personal Status of 1920 and 1929, drawing from the interpretations of scholars of all four Sunni schools of law.

In May 1985, the 1979 law was struck down by the High Constitutional Court of Egypt on technical grounds and declared *ultra vires* the Egyptian Constitution; the initial emergency decree issued by Sadat had been issued in the absence of a true state of emergency and so was deemed invalid. A few months after the verdict, a Personal Status (Amendment) Law (Law no. 100/1985) was enacted to revise the 1920 and 1929 Laws on Personal Status. A number of the changes made by the 1979 law were reintroduced as well as some new provisions added. One element that was conspicuous by its absence in the 1985 legislation was the wife's automatic right to a divorce from her husband if he married polygamously. As a concession to religious conservatives, the presumption of injury occasioned by a polygamous marriage was removed, requiring the wife to establish that she has suffered harm from her husband's polygamous union if she wishes to divorce. Thus, the ground for divorce was no longer automatic but was left up to the discretion of the courts, as being the wife of a polygamous husband was no longer automatically equated with harm (constituting a return to the classical position).

The second compromise related to the requirement that the divorced wife in custody of minor children had exclusive rights to the rented marital home for as long as she retained custody (unless her former husband provided another dwelling). While the requirement to provide accommodation for the custodial mother was retained in the 1985 legislation, the former husband was given exclusive rights over his un-rented dwelling.

The Law of Personal Status was again amended in January 2000, giving women more options for divorce.

Schools of *Fiqh*: The Hanafi School is the predominant school of *fiqh*. Earlier on, Egypt was the home of the Shafi'i school and under the Fatimids, the ruling classes were Isma'ili. There is also a significant Coptic Christian minority in Egypt.

Constitutional Status of Islamic Law: The Constitution was adopted on 11 September 1971 and amended by referendum in May 1980. The amendment made Islamic law the principal source of legislation in Egypt. Article 2 of the Constitution reads in full: "Islam is the religion of the State and Arabic its official language. Islamic jurisprudence is the principal source of legislation."

Court System: *Shariah* courts were integrated into the national court system in 1956. Family law is administered within the National Courts by judges trained in *shariah* (with separate judges for and legislation applicable to cases involving Copts and Muslims). Appeals are heard by regular judges in the Courts of Appeal and, ultimately, the Court of Cassation.

Notable Features: There are a number of enactments relating to personal status, though the core of family law is formed by Laws no. 25/1920 and no. 25/1929 as amended by Law no. 100/1985. The Civil Code (no. 131/1948) drafted by Professor Abd al-Razzaq al-Sanhuri, the renowned Egyptian jurist who played a role in the drafting of legislation in a number of Arab states during the 1940s and 1950s, does not cover family law or succession, but does govern majority and civil status; Article 280 of the Civil Code directs that recourse should be had to the most appropriate opinion from the Hanafi school in the absence of any textual provision in the legislation.

The minimum marriage age is 18 for males and 16 for females (lunar calendar). Registration is compulsory but does not determine the validity of marriage. Courts may not hear cases where the parties have not attained the minimum marriage age, or where claim of marriage is disputed and there is no official documentation.

Guardianship is governed by the Civil Code but does not extend to the power of compulsion in marriage; a *wali* cannot prevent his ward from marrying for reasons relating to social status or the amount of dower, for example, as judges may authorise marriages if *walis* refuse.

Maintenance is due from the date of a valid marriage contract and valid retirement unless the wife apostasies, denies her husband conjugal rights without justification, or leaves the matrimonial home without his permission (except for circumstances permitted by rules of the *shariah*). However, leaving the home for lawful work does not constitute disobedience so long as the wife does not abuse this right, it is not contrary to the interests of her family, and her husband has not explicitly asked her to refrain from working. Maintenance is deemed to be a debt against the husband from the date that he fails to maintain until the debt is paid or excused, and claims for arrears of maintenance may not be heard for a period exceeding one year from the date of the claim.

Polygamy is permissible, with notification of the existing and intended wives. The existing wife may obtain a judicial dissolution on grounds of material or moral harm up to one year from the date of her knowledge of her husband's polygamous union if such harm makes cohabitation as husband and wife impossible.

Talaq expressed indirectly, while intoxicated or under coercion, or conditionally with the intent of forcing the taking of some action has no effect. A *talaq* to which a number is added verbally or by gesture is effective only as a single and revocable *talaq*, except for the third of three, *talaq* before consummation or in consideration of payment. A written and notarised certification of *talaq* must be produced within thirty days of repudiation and the notary must forward a copy of the certificate to the wife. Certain financial effects of *talaq* are suspended on the wife's knowledge of the repudiation if the husband is found to have concealed it.

The wife may obtain an irrevocable judicial divorce on the following grounds: serious or incurable defect of the husband (unless the woman married in full knowledge of the defect or it occurred after the contract and she implicitly or explicitly accepted it); harm making cohabitation as husband and wife impossible (if the harm is proved and reconciliation efforts fail); material or moral harm if the husband marries polygamously (subject to the aforementioned conditions); non-payment of maintenance; the husband's imprisonment for three years or more (after one year of the sentence has passed); and discord, if reconciliation efforts fail, with a financial settlement proportionate to the allocation of blame as determined by the arbitrators. A woman can also seek a divorce on the grounds of incompatibility, but in such case she forfeits all financial claims against her husband.

A divorce repudiated by her husband without cause or consent on her part is entitled to maintenance during her *idda* and compensation (*muta al-talaq*) of at least two years maintenance (with consideration for the husband's means, the circumstances of the divorce, and the length of the marriage); no upper limit for compensation is stipulated. Maintenance claims for the *idda* period can be heard up to one year from the date of the divorce. A divorcing husband must provide independent accommodation for his former wife who has custody of their minor children.

The divorced mother is entitled to custody of boys until the age of 10 and girls until the age of 12. Custody may be extended till the age of 15 for boys and till marriage for girls if the judge deems such an extension to be in the best interests of the ward.

On succession, notable reforms introduced by legislation in 1946 legalised bequests to heirs, and also established obligatory bequests to benefit descendants of predeceased sons (how low soever) and daughters. The doctrine of *radd* was also extended to allow the spouse relict to share in the residue of the deceased spouse's estate.

Notable Cases: Case no. 29 of 1980 in the Badari Court of Summary Justice for Guardianship of the Person (*Mahkama Juziyya lil-Wilaya alal-Nafs*) precipitated the 4th May 1985 judgement of the High Constitutional Court (*al-Mahkama al-Dusturiyya al-Ulya*) that the implementing resolution of Law no. 44/1979 (Jihan's Law) was unconstitutional on technical grounds as the initial emergency decree by which Sadat implemented the legislation was issued in the absence of a true state of emergency.

A 1993 *hisba* suit before the Giza Court of First Instance called for divorcing Professor Nasr Abu Zayd from his wife on grounds of his alleged apostasy. The Giza Court dismissed the suit and the petitioners appealed to the Cairo Court of Appeal (Department of Personal Status). The Appeals Court ruled in favour of the petitioners, and the case was brought before the Supreme Court in 1995. The Supreme Court ruled for divorcing Professor Abu Zayd from his wife. The case led to the passage of Law no. 3/1996 preventing claims by private individuals on the basis of *hisba*.

Law/Case Reporting System: Laws are published in *al-Jarida al-Rasmiyya*. Case reports of civil and criminal judgments of the Court of Cassation are published six times annually. Judges and practitioners indexes and summaries of the same are compiled less frequently. Parishioner's collections of principles in court rulings on *shariah* and personal status matters are also compiled.

International Conventions (with Relevant Reservations): Egypt signed the ICCPR and ICESCR in 1967 and ratified them in 1982. Egypt submitted a general declaration relating to the provisions of the *shariah* not conflicting with the text annexed to the instrument(s).

Egypt signed the CEDAW in 1980 and ratified it in 1981. One of the reservations submitted by Egypt relates to Article 9(2) on gender equality in nationality rights. "It is clear that the child's acquisition of his father's nationality is the procedure most suitable for the child and that this does not infringe upon the principle of equality between men and women, since it is customary for a woman to agree, upon marrying an alien, that her children shall be of the father's nationality." The next reservation is to Article 16 'relating to gender equality in family relations. The reservation relates to the status of the *shariah*; Article 16 is accepted insofar as it does not prejudice *shariah* provisions whereby women are granted rights "equivalent" to men's rights in order to "ensure a just balance between them." The reservation is made "out of respect for the sacrosanct nature of the firm religious beliefs which govern marital relations in Egypt and which may not be called in question and in view of the fact that one of the most important bases of these relations is an equivalency of rights and duties so as to ensure complementarity's which guarantees true equality between the spouses." The reservation to Article 2 states that, although "Egypt is willing to comply with the content of this article," it is with the proviso that "such compliance does not run counter to the Islamic *shariah*".

Egypt signed and ratified the CRC in 1990. Egypt submitted a general reservation concerning areas of conflict between the *shariah* (as one of the fundamental sources of Egyptian positive legislation) and the CRC, particularly in relation to provisions on adoption in Articles 20 and 21.

Background and Sources: Brown, The Rule of Law in the Arab World: Courts in Egypt and the Gulf, Cambridge, 1997; El Alami, "Law no. 100 of 1985 Amending Certain Provisions of Egypt's Personal Status Laws," Islamic Law and Society. Vol. 1(1), 1994: 116-136; El Alami, The Marriage Contract and Islamic Law in the *Shariah* and Personal Status Laws of Egypt and Morocco, London, 1992; El Alami and Hinchcliffe, Islamic Marriage and Divorce Laws of the Arab World, London 1996; Hill, *Mahkama*! Studies in the Egyptian Legal System: Courts and Crimes, Law and Society, London, 1979; Mahmood, Egypt in Statutes of Personal Law in Islamic Countries, 2nd ed., New Delhi, 1995; Najjar, "Egypts Laws of

Personal Status," Arab Studies Quarterly, Vol. 10, No. 3 (1988): 319-345; Nasir, The Islamic Law of Personal Status, 2nd ed., London, 1990; Pearl.

Federal Democratic Republic of Ethiopia

Legal History

Ethiopia was occupied by Italy from 1936 to 1941, although Eritrea came under Italian rule from 1886 to 1941. During WWII, the British defeated the Italians and established a protectorate over Eritrea. The 1950 UN Resolution to unify Eritrea and Ethiopia was implemented in 1952. The movement for Eritrean independence developed into an armed struggle in 1961. A Civil Code passed in 1960 governs civil, religious and customary law of marriages. Emperor Haile Selassie I (r. 1930, 1974) attempted to modernise the state, but the nation was struck by famine and a long-standing conflict with Eritrea; both factors are considered to have contributed to the 1974 military coup ending Selassie's rule.

Lieutenant Col. Mengistu Haile Mariam became the head of state and the government was oriented towards Marxism. All religions, including Ethiopian Orthodox Christianity, were officially placed on equal footing under new regime. The Eritrean People's Liberation Front won several strategic successes against Ethiopian in late the late 1980s and early 1990s, declaring the Provisional Government of Eritrea in May 1991. At the same time, 17 years of military rule under a junta (Derg) ended in 1991 amidst growing pressure from democratic opposition forces. From 1991 to 1995 a Transitional Government, a coalition of 27 political parties, ruled Ethiopia. A 1993 referendum in Eritrea resulted in a massive vote for independence.

A new Ethiopian Constitution was adopted in 1994 and elections were held in 1995 leading to election of Meles Zenawi as Prime Minister and Negasso Gidada as President. Federal Democratic Republic of Ethiopia established in August 1995.

Schools of *Fiqh*: The majority of Muslims are Shafi'i. The other major religion is Ethiopian Orthodox (or Monophysite) Christianity. There are also small Jewish and Animist minority communities.

Constitutional Status of Islamic Law: The current Constitution was adopted in 1995. Article 34 (on Marital, Personal and Family Rights), Section 5 states: "This Constitution shall not preclude the adjudication of disputes relating to personal and family laws in accordance with religious or customary laws, with the consent of the parties to the dispute." Article 78(5) also provides for the establishment or recognition of religious or customary courts, pursuant to Article 34(5).

Court System: Regular courts are organised at four levels. The Supreme Court has appellate jurisdiction and sits in Addis Ababa. The High Courts sits in the 14 provincial capitals have original and appellate jurisdiction. The awraja courts are convened in each of the 102 administrative subdivisions. Woreda courts are established in each of the 556 districts.

Under the 1944 legislation, *shariah* courts are organised into three levels: *Naiba* Councils serve as courts of first instance, *Kadis*. Councils as intermediate courts and the Court of *Shariah* as highest court.

Shariah courts have jurisdiction in two kinds of cases. The first are: marriage, divorce, maintenance, guardianship of minors, and family relationships; provided that the marriage to which the case pertains was concluded under Islamic law or the parties are all Muslims. The second are: cases concerning *awqaf*, gifts, succession, or wills, provided that donor is a Muslim or deceased was a Muslim at the time of his/her death.

Shariah courts have unclear legal status as the Mohammedan Courts Act 1944 establishing them was never actually repealed and yet the 1960 Civil Code makes no exceptions for Muslims or Muslim personal law. The Court of *Shariah* continues to sit as a division of the Supreme Court.

Notable Features: The Civil Code sets the minimum marriage age at 18 years for males and 15 for females, regardless of whether the marriage is contracted under civil, religious or customary law, though the new Family Law may have changed the minimum age to 18 for both males and females. Both the Constitution and the Civil Code state that consent to marriage obtained by violence renders marriage invalid, but the Civil Code provides that consent granted due to "reverential fear" of an ascendant or other person is not equivalent to consent obtained by violence.

Polygamy is abolished, backed by sanctions provided in the Penal Code. The Civil Code states that spouses owe each other "respect, support and assistance" and provides that the husband is the head of the family and determines the place of the marital home, the wife must obey him in all lawful things that he orders and he owes his wife protection. A marriage contract may be written settling the financial effects of marriage, as well as other reciprocal rights and duties, but cannot change any mandatory legal provisions and has no effect unless approved by family arbitrators or by courts.

Talaq is abolished. Under the Civil Code, all divorce law is uniform regardless of whether the marriage was contracted under civil, religious or customary law. Judicial divorce may be sought by either spouse for "serious causes" or "other causes". Serious causes are: adultery; desertion of the marital home without knowledge of that party's whereabouts for two years; a spouse's confinement to a lunatic asylum for minimum of two years; and judicial declaration of absence of a spouse. Couples seeking divorce for either serious or other cause must first appoint family arbitrators who will attempt to effect reconciliation and if efforts fail, arbitrators can grant a divorce, preferably on mutually agreed terms. If serious cause for divorce can be established for which one spouse bears the burden of fault, family arbitrators may divide common property unevenly. If no serious cause is established, property is divided unevenly to the disadvantage of the spouse who petitioned for divorce. Arbitrators decisions can be appealed to the court.

The Civil Code does not refer to support payments to former spouses. The Penal Code does make it an offence to refuse maintenance for either an existing or former spouse. Support payments are often granted to the wife during the course of divorce litigation and deducted from her share of communal property once it is divided.

The Civil Code provides that child custody and maintenance arrangements are to be made only with consideration for the interests of the ward. In the absence of any "serious reason", wards are to remain with the mother until the age of five.

Notable Cases

Law/Case Reporting System: Law reporting is through the *Federal Negarit Gazeta*.

International Conventions (with Relevant Reservations): Ethiopia acceded to the ICCPR and ICESCR in 1993, without reservations.

Ethiopia signed the CEDAW in 1980 and ratified it in 1981, with a reservation to Article 29(1).

Ethiopia acceded to the CRC in 1991, without reservations.

Background and Sources: CEDAW, Concluding Observations on Ethiopia's Combined Initial, Second and Third Periodic Report, January 1996; Redden, Ethiopia in Modern Legal Systems Cyclopedia, Vol. 6, Buffalo, NY, 1990; Ethiopia in Women of the World: Laws and Policies Affecting Their Reproductive Lives Anglophone Africa. Center for Reproductive Law and Policy and International Federation of Women Lawyers (Kenya Chapter), New York, 1997; Ethiopia, Combined Initial, Second and Third Periodic Report to CEDAW, 21 May 1993.

Republic of the Gambia

Legal History

The legal system is based on an amalgam of English common law, Islamic law, and customary law.

The Portuguese sent expeditions to Gambia in the mid-fifteenth century, and British trade in the region and exploration of the Gambia River began in the late sixteenth century. Gambia was incorporated into the British colony of Senegambia in 1765, but in response to growing French influence in Senegal, the British seized the Gambia River in 1888. In 1892, Banjul (then Bathurst) was established as the capital. Gambia gained independence in 1965. A republican constitution was adopted in 1970.

Marriage is governed by several regimes: customary, Islamic, Christian under the Christian Marriage Act 1862, and statutory under the Civil Marriage Act 1938. Colonial era legislation relating to Muslim personal law, the Mohammedan Marriage and Divorce Ordinance 1941, was retained after independence. The legislation is mainly of a regulatory nature.

The Law Reform Commission and the Women's Bureau of Gambia made proposals for the codification of Muslim personal status laws in the mid to late-1980s, but the suggestions were not adopted into law. Some of the provisions put forward in a proposed draft published in 1987 relate to establishing a minimum marriage age of 18 for males and 15 for females, broader grounds for divorce available to both parties (including irreparable breakdown) and limiting extra-judicial repudiation.

Schools of *Fiqh*: The majority of Gambians are Maliki Muslim. There are significant Christian minority communities, as well as followers of indigenous beliefs.

Constitutional Status of Islamic Law: The current Constitution was adopted in 1970, suspended in July 1994, revised and adopted by national referendum in August 1996 and reinstated January 1997.

The Constitution adopts no official religion. Article 7 identifies the following sources of law in addition to the Constitution: legislation; common law and principles of equity; customary law so far as it concerns members of the communities to which it applies; and *shariah* as regards matters of personal status and inheritance among members of communities to which it applies. Article 33(1) proclaims the equality of all persons before the law; Article 33(5c) exempts from the rest of Article 33 those laws relating to adoption, marriage, divorce, and burial, devolution of property on death or other matters of personal law.

Court System: The regular court system consists of the Supreme Court, High Court, Court of Appeal, and subordinate courts. Part 3 of the Constitution establishes *Cadi* Courts in such places as the Chief Justice determines. *Cadi* Courts are to be composed of a panel of one *Cadi* and two other scholars of *shariah* for hearings at first instance. For hearings on review, the panel is to consist of the *Cadi* and four *ulama*. The decision is made by the majority view of the panel. The jurisdiction of *Cadi* Courts applies to matters of marriage, divorce and inheritance where the parties or other persons interested are Muslims. Appeals of *Cadi* Courts decisions at first instance may be made within three months of the decision by applying to same court. There are two *Cadi* Courts (in Banjul and Kanifing).

Notable Features: The *Cadi* Courts apply classical Maliki *fiqh* to matters of personal status. The Mohammedan Marriage and Divorce Ordinance 1941 makes registration of both obligatory within one month, but registration does not determine validity.

Notable Cases

Law/Case Reporting System: Law reporting is through the *Official Gazette*. A loose-leaf collection of the Laws of Gambia was issued in 1990.

International Conventions (with Relevant Reservations): Gambia signed the ICCPR in 1979, with a reservation to Article 14(3)(d). Gambia signed the ICESCR in 1978 without reservations.

Gambia signed the CEDAW in 1980 and ratified it in 1993 without reservations.

Gambia signed and ratified the CRC in 1990, without reservations.

Background and Sources: Gambia Law Reform Commission and Gambia Women's Bureau, Law Reform Project No. 7: Muslim Marriages: Formation and Dissolution 1987; Gambia Women's Bureau, First and Second Workshops on the Legal Status of Women, October and November 1987; Redden, "Gambia," Modern Legal Systems Cyclopedia. Vol. 6, Buffalo, N.Y., 1990; Rubin and Cotran, "Gambia," Annual Survey of African Law, Vols. I and IV, 1967 and 1970.

Republic of Ghana

Legal History

The legal system is based on English common law and customary law. Over 100 distinct ethnolinguistic groups are represented in Ghana. Gold and later the slave trade attracted European explorers to the region; first the Portuguese in the late fifteenth century followed by Dutch, Danish, English and Swedish explorers. By the early nineteenth century, the British came to dominate the Gold Coast, extending their control further inland. By 1902 most of modern-day Ghana was a British crown colony, with Volta joining Ghana in 1956. The British policy of indirect rule utilised local chiefs in government and administration, thus traditional authorities retained their jurisdiction over the internal affairs of their communities. Following WWII, pressure for self-rule increased, and independence was gained in 1957.

Ghana became a republic under the 1960 Constitution and the first Prime Minister, Kwame Nkrumah, was elected

President. By 1964, Nkrumah had centralised power and limited opposition, had himself declared president for life and established a single-party state. A military coup in 1966 brought an end to Nkrumahs rule. Military rule continued until 1993, with brief periods of democratic civilian rule (1969-1972, 1979-1981). The fourth republican constitution came into effect in 1993, and in 1996, the first elected government to complete its first term was elected to a second term, under the former military ruler Jerry Rawlings.

British-era legislation relating to family law provided for civil registration under a monogamous regime under the Marriage Ordinance 1951. Until now, no single body of law regulates personal status matters. The colonial legislation applicable to Muslims, the Marriage of Mohammedans Ordinance 1907, is limited to administrative or procedural matters such as providing for registration of marriage and divorce. Muslim marriages are also affected by some other laws of universal application. Although the Ordinance has been retained, few Muslim marriages are registered under it and more commonly come under customary legal regimes.

The Ghana Law Reform Commission established in 1968 was given the task of reviewing statutory and customary laws and suggesting reforms. Its first programme identified inheritance and marriage law as among the main areas requiring attention. Among the successes of the Commission are counted the Maintenance of Children Decree 1977 and Intestate Succession Law 1985. The Maintenance of Children Decree establishes Family Tribunals to hear complaints about maintenance of children during the subsistence of marriage and after divorce. The Intestate Succession Law provides protection for children in communities where they are not entitled to shares of their deceased parents estates. The unification of family laws was identified in its 1996 report as a goal of the Commission. To that end, the Commission outlined a plan to assess the application and efficacy of existing legislation through questionnaires to be drafted in co-ordination with women's groups and NGOs.

Schools of *Fiqh*: The majority of Muslims are Maliki. The other major religions represented are Christianity and indigenous religions.

Constitutional Status of Islam(ic) Law: The current Constitution was approved on 28th April 1992, and adopts no official religion. Article 11 identifies the sources of Ghanaian law as: the Constitution; legislation; existing law; and common law. Existing law is defined as the written and unwritten laws of Ghana predating the current Constitution, as adapted to conform to the Constitution. Article 270(1) provides for the recognition of the institution of chieftaincy, together with its traditional councils under customary law. Article 272 states that the National House of Chiefs shall undertake a progressive study and codification of customary law to establish unified rules and evaluate such laws with the aim of "eliminating those customs and usages that are outmoded and socially harmful".

Court System: The higher courts are the Supreme Court (the highest court of appeal in civil and criminal matters), the Court of Appeal, the High Court, and ten Regional Tribunals. The lower courts are circuit courts and tribunals, community tribunals, juvenile and family tribunals; and traditional courts. Traditional courts include the National House of Chiefs, the Regional House of Chiefs, and the Traditional Councils.

Islamic law is applied by customary or traditional courts under the broader category of customary law.

Notable Features: The minimum marriage age is governed by classical or customary law. The Marriage of Mohammedans Ordinance specifies that marriage is solemnised in the presence of the bridegroom, the bride's *wali*, and two witnesses. The Criminal Code identifies causing someone to marry under duress as a misdemeanour. The Marriage of Mohammedans Ordinance provides for the registration of marriage and divorce among Muslims. Marriage must be registered within one week of solemnisation.

Polygamy is governed by classical or customary law. All customary marriages are defined as potentially polygamous under Ghanaian law.

The Criminal Code imposes the duty of maintenance of the wife and children on the husband.

Talaq is governed by classical or customary law. It is possible to terminate a customary law marriage by application to the court under the Matrimonial Causes Act, in which case grounds for divorce include those recognised in the personal law of the parties in addition to those enumerated in the Act. Under the Act, divorce may only be granted if the court concludes irreparable breakdown. Courts hearing suits for divorce among Muslims are directed to apply the Matrimonial Causes Act directing guidance by justice, equity and good conscience in determination of post-divorce reliefs and custody. The Courts are empowered under the Matrimonial Causes Act to grant maintenance in addition to the reliefs recognised under the personal law of the parties. The Matrimonial Causes Act provides that courts may grant custody according to the ward's best interests, and order provision for his/her education and maintenance out of the assets or income of either or both parents. Courts adjudicating Muslim divorces are required to apply the terms of the Matrimonial Causes Act.

Upon the death of a Muslim whose marriage was registered under the Marriage of Mohammedans Ordinance, property devolves according to Islamic law. The Wills Act 1971 provides for complete freedom of testacy, subject, however, to the customary law applicable to testator. Although Article 22 of the Constitution provides that the government shall endeavour to regulate the property rights of spouses to ensure equal cess of jointly acquired property and equal division of such property on divorce, there has been no legislative implementation of the directive as of yet.

Notable Cases

Law/Case Reporting System: Law reporting is through the *Official Gazette*. Decisions of the Supreme Court, Court of Appeal and High Court are published in *The Ghana Law Reports Digest*.

International Conventions (with Relevant Reservations): Ghana signed the CEDAW in 1980 and ratified it in 1986, without reservations.

Ghana signed the CRC in 1990 and ratified it in 1990, without reservations.

Background and Sources: Berry, ed., Ghana: A Country Study, Washington D.C., 1995; Ghana, Initial, second and third periodic report to CEDAW, 5th July 1991; "Ghana" in Women of the World: Laws and Policies Affecting Their Reproductive Lives Anglophone Africa, Center for Reproductive Law and Policy and International Federation of Women Lawyers (Kenya Chapter), New York, 1997; Ghana Law Reform Commission, Annual Reports, Accra (1971, 1979-1982, 1996); Mensa-Bonsu, "Family Law Policy and Research Agenda," The Changing Family in Ghana, ed. Ardayfio-Schandorf, Accra, 1996; Redden, "Ghana" in Modern Legal Systems Cyclopedia, Vol. 6, Buffalo, NY, 1990; Rubin and Cotran, Annual Survey of African Law, Vol. V, 1971.

Republic of India

Legal History

The Indian legal system is based in part on the English common law system. With respect to Muslim personal law as applied in India, the sources of law are Hanafi *fiqh* along with some resort to other schools, legislation, precedent, certain juridical texts (both classical and modern) that are considered authoritative, and custom.

During the British Raj, the colonial courts were directed to apply "indigenous legal norms" in matters relating to family law and religion, with "native law officers" advising the courts on the determination of those norms. A number of Hanafi sources (notably *al-Hidaya* and the *Fatawa Alamgiri*) were translated into English. The advisory positions of legal experts on Hindu and Muslim law were abolished in 1864. Legal commentators on the development of the indigenous system of "Anglo-Muhammadan" law (now more commonly referred to as Indo-Muslim law) attach varying degrees of significance to the subsequently authoritative position of these works (and the quality of the translations), the absence of judicial expertise in Muslim law, the introduction of principles of English law and procedure through judges trained in the English legal tradition and through interpretation of the residual formula of justice and right or justice, equity and good conscience to imply mainly English law, and to the position taken on customary law.

The status of the personal laws of minority communities and the plurality of religious laws in general, is much debated in India. Article 44 of the Constitution legislates a commitment to the gradual establishment of legal uniformity in India, the aim being that the state "shall endeavour to secure for the citizens a uniform civil code throughout the territory of India." This directive is considered a threat by elements of religious minority communities, who continue to be governed by their own personal laws in family matters, as applied within the superstructure of the Indian legal system.

Schools of *Fiqh*: The predominant *madhhab* is the Hanafi, with sizeable Shafii, Jaýÿfari and Ismaili minorities. India's minority religious communities also include Sikhs, Jains, Buddhists, Christians and Jews.

Constitutional Status of Islam(ic) Law: The Indian Constitution was adopted on 26th November 1949 and has been amended many times. The preamble of the Constitution affirms that India is a "sovereign socialist secular democratic republic". India's secularity is framed in terms of neither favouring nor officially adopting any particular religion, and Article 26 guarantees the freedom to manage religious affairs (subject to constraints imposed by the requirements of public order, morality and health) for every recognised religious denomination or sect. The aforementioned Article 44 of the Constitution contains the Directive Provision stating that Indian legislators shall aim to establish a uniform civil code throughout India. For the time-being, religious communities continue to be governed by their own personal laws (apart from Muslims, this applies to Christians, Zoroastrians, Jews and Hindus, as well as Buddhists and Sikhs who, for legal purposes, are classified as Hindus). Although the option of civil marriage exists, it is not often the only regime under which Indians marry. The difficulty of reconciling the secularity of the Republic and the objective of establishing legal uniformity with the protection of minority rights (also enshrined in the Constitution) has meant that, almost fifty years since the adoption of the Constitution, the goal of the directive principle in Article 44 is still far from being realised.

Court System: Muslim personal law is applied by the regular court system. As the majority of Muslims are Hanafi, courts presume that litigants are Hanafi unless the contrary is established.

There are four levels of courts in the judiciary. The first are civil courts with jurisdiction over arbitration, marriage and divorce, guardianship, probate, etc. The next level of courts is established in the subdivisions of each state, at the district level. Each district comes under the jurisdiction of a principal district civil court presided over by a district judge. There are State High Courts in each of the 18 states of the federation. The Supreme Court is constituted by one Chief Justice and not more than 17 judges.

The courts of first instance for personal status are generally the Family Courts, organised under the Family Courts Act of 1984. The Family Courts are deemed to be the equivalent of any district or subordinate civil court. Their jurisdiction is enumerated in the Act and covers suits for decrees of nullity, restitution of conjugal rights, judicial separation or dissolution, validity of marriage, matrimonial property, orders or injunctions arising out of the circumstances of marriage, legitimacy, maintenance, guardianship, custody, and access to minors. These courts have some criminal jurisdiction in terms of maintenance orders. Suits in these courts may be held *in camera* if the Family Court so desires or at the request of the parties to the case.

Notable Features:* With the exception of some enactments, most of the personal law applicable to Indian Muslims is uncodified and administered by state courts on the basis of Indo-Muslim judicial precedents. With one exception, the legislation regulating Islamic family law dates from the period of British colonial rule.

The Muslim Personal Law (*Shariaht*) Application Act 1937 directs the application of Muslim Personal Law to Muslims in a number of different areas mainly related to family law. The Act also directs the application of Muslim personal law in matters relating to intestate succession among Muslims. On the matter of Islamic inheritance law, as the Quran provides a systematic scheme for intestate succession, there has been no particular legislation in that area. The courts generally apply the classical rules relating to intestate succession.

The Child Marriage Restraint Act 1929 introduced under the British provided penal sanctions for contracting marriages below the specified minimum age, originally established at 18 and 15 years. As the Act currently stands in India (amended by Act 2 of 1978), the minimum marriage age is 21 for men and 18 for women. However, as registration is not compulsory in India, and as the Act does not instruct the dissolution of under-age marriages, such unions are not rendered invalid.

The Registration of Muhammedan Marriages and Divorces Act 1876 is still in operation in Bihar and West Bengal. Other states of the federation also have similar Acts, and there are facilities for voluntary registration. However, registration is not a requirement in India. The option of registering a marriage under the Special Marriage Act 1954 (under which all inter-religious marriages must be registered) also exists, in which case a different set of secular marriage and divorce laws would apply; it does not, however, appear to be very common to do so in practice. Registration may prove useful if recourse is had to the courts, but because it is not compulsory, other evidence may be used to prove the existence of an unregistered marriage. Upon signature to the CEDAW, India submitted a declaration affirming the government's commitment to the principle of obligatory registration of marriage, but stating that, for the present, the diversity and size of India's population make strict adherence to this principle impractical.

With regard to polygamy, the Criminal Procedure Code establishes that a woman who refuses to live with her husband on just grounds will still be entitled to maintenance and those just grounds, as defined in the Code, include the contracting of a polygamous marriage by the husband, even if the personal law applicable to the parties permits polygamy. This proviso only actually applies to Muslims as polygamy has been abolished for all other communities. In *Itwari v. Asghari* (AIR 1960 All 684), a suit for the restitution of conjugal rights by a Muslim husband against his first wife, the Allahabad Court stated that the onus was on the husband to prove that his second marriage did not constitute any insult or cruelty to the first wife. Although the Muslim husband has the right to contract a polygamous marriage, the Court held that it does not necessarily follow that the first wife should be forced to live with him under threat of severe penalties after the husband has taken a second wife. Even in the absence of proof of cruelty, the Court would not pass a decree for restitution of conjugal rights if it appeared that it would be unjust and inequitable to compel her to return to her husband under the circumstances of the case.

The Dissolution of Muslim Marriages Act 1939 introduced changes to the extremely restricted Hanafi rules on judicial divorce at the petition of the wife by the adoption and adaptation of certain Maliki principles. The nine grounds upon which a woman is entitled to obtain a decree of dissolution of her marriage under the Act are as follows: if the husband's whereabouts have not been known for four years; if the husband neglects to maintain the wife for two years; if the husband has been sentenced to seven or more years imprisonment; if the husband has failed to perform his marital obligations for three years; if the husband was impotent at the time of marriage and continues to be so; if the husband has been insane for a period of two years or suffers from a serious illness harmful to the wife; if the wife was contracted into marriage by her father or other guardian before the age of 15 and repudiates the marriage before she becomes 18 (provided the marriage has not been consummated); if the husband treats her with cruelty (including physical or other ill-treatment or unequal treatment of co-wives); and any other ground which is recognised as valid for the dissolution of marriage under Muslim law. On the other hand, apostasy by the Muslim wife, including conversion to another religion, does not in and of itself dissolve her marriage. The Act expressly extends the option of puberty to women who were contracted into marriage as minors by their fathers or paternal grandfathers, broadening the classical Hanafi rules. There has, however, been no substantial reform of the classical law relating to *talaq*. The Muslim husband retains the right to repudiate his wife extra-judicially, and from the available sources it appears that the most common form of divorce is the triple *talaq*. The stance of the pre- and post-independence courts has generally been to accept extra-judicial repudiation as "good in law, bad in theology". A major issue of concern is the determination of the time from which maintenance becomes due in cases where the *talaq* has not been communicated to the wife, but the validity of such repudiations has not been called into serious question. Pearl and Menski also note that the scarcity of case law reflects the fact that, in actual practice, the exercise of *talaq* doesn't often involve the courts.

With regard to maintenance upon divorce, classical Hanafi law has been modified in India by the Muslim Women (Protection of Rights on Divorce) Act 1986, passed following fierce protest by sectors of the Muslim community that viewed the Supreme Courts ruling in the Shah Bano case as a gross interference in matters of Muslim personal status. In *Mohammad Ahmed Khan vs. Shah Bano Begum* (AIR 1985 SC 945), the Supreme Court ruled that there was no conflict between classical Hanafi law, which only specifies the obligation to maintain a wife during her *idda* period, and the requirement to support a former wife unable to maintain herself established by state legislation. During the aftermath of the controversial judgement, the Congress government passed the Muslim Women (Protection of Rights on Divorce) Act. The Act entitles the divorced Muslim woman to "a reasonable and fair provision and maintenance to be made and paid to her within the *idda* period by her former husband." Although the Act itself provoked differing reactions as to what its effect would be, court practice allows the Muslim divorce to appeal to the courts if her former husband has not provided her with a reasonable sum for maintenance during her *idda* period. As in classical law, the *idda* period is defined as three menstrual cycles after the divorce; three lunar months if the wife is not subject to menstruation; or until delivery of the child or termination of pregnancy if the woman is enceinte. The Act also stipulates that the divorced wife is entitled to any outstanding dower, any property given her before or during marriage, and maintenance for children in her custody born before or after the finalisation of the divorce. There appears to be some modification to classical Hanafi law in the definition of a divorce entitled to claim such support, as the Act specifies that its application pertains to marriages conducted according to Muslim law where a Muslim woman has obtained a divorce from or has been divorced by her husband in accordance with Muslim law. The Act directs that if neither the former wife nor husband has the means to provide for her support, the responsibility of maintenance of the divorce falls on her relations, that is, those relatives that would stand to inherit from her. If she has no close relations or they are unable to support her, liability falls to the State *Waqf* Board. Section 5 of the Act also allows for a divorced Muslim woman and her former husband to declare to the Court their willingness to be governed by the provisions of sections 125 to 128 of the Code of Criminal Procedure relating to the maintenance of dependants unable to support themselves. In the first reported case relating to the Act (*Ali vs. Sufaira* 1988 (2) KLT), the Kerala High Court rejected a narrow interpretation of the legislation as only requiring Muslim men to support their divorced wives during the *idda* period. Rather, the Court stated that the appropriate interpretation of section 3(1)(a), "a divorced women shall be entitled to a reasonable and fair provision and maintenance to be made and paid to her within the *idda* period by her former husband", was that maintenance during the waiting period and reasonable and fair provision were two separate issues. Thus, the Court ruled that the Muslim divorce is entitled not only to maintenance for her waiting period, but also to a reasonable and fair provision to provide "for her future livelihood, from her former husband." This has since been confirmed by a large number of judgments.

Custody is governed by the Guardians and Wards Act 1890 applicable to all religious communities in India. The Act stipulates that courts are to be guided by the personal law to which the minor is subject. The courts are also directed to consider the age, gender and religion of the minor and the character and capacity of the proposed guardian, and the minors own opinion if s/he is old enough to form an intelligent preference. If the minor is very young or is female, the courts are directed to give preference to the mother. In all cases, the interests of the ward are paramount. In custody cases involving Muslims, courts tend to follow the general rule that the divorced mother is entitled to custody till seven years for boys (classical Hanafi position) and puberty for girls.

Law/Case Reporting System: Law reports are published in *Supreme Court Reports* (SCR), *All India Reporter* (AIR), *Indian Law Reports* (ILR), and a large number of state law reports.

International Conventions and Reports to Treaty Governing Bodies: India acceded to the ICESCR and the ICCPR in 1979 with a number of declarations, including one to the effect that the right of self-determination mentioned in common Article 1 is interpreted by India as applying only to peoples under foreign domination and not to sovereign independent states or a section of a people or nation.

India became a signatory to the CEDAW in 1980 and ratified it in 1993. India submitted a declaration regarding Articles 5(a) and 16(1) that reiterates India's commitment to abiding by the provisions "in conformity with its policy of non-interference in the personal affairs of any Community without its initiative and consent." India also registered a declaration regarding Article 16(2) on minimum marriage ages and compulsory registration; although India fully supports the principle, "it is not practical in a vast country like India with its variety of customs, religions and level of literacy."

India acceded to the CRC in 1992, with a declaration regarding the progressive implementation of Article 32 thereof on child labour, particularly with reference to paragraph 2(a) on the provision of a minimum employment age.

Background and Sources: Baxi, "People's Law in India," in Asian Indigenous Law in Interaction with Received Law, Chiba, ed. London, 1986; Diwan and Diwan, Women and Legal Protection, New Delhi, 1995; Engineer, The Shah Bano Controversy, Hyderabad, 1987; Anderson, "Islamic Law and the Colonial Encounter in British India," and Menski "The Reform of Family Law and a Uniform Civil Code for India," in Islamic Family Law, Mallat and Connors, eds. London, 1990; Mahmood, "India" in Statutes of Personal Law in Islamic Countries, 2nd ed., New Delhi, 1995; Malik, "Once Again

Shah Bano: Maintenance and the Scope for Marriage Contracts," Dhaka Law Reports Journal Section, Vol. 42 (1990): 34-40; Pearl and Menski, Muslim Family Law, 3rd ed., London, 1998; Redden, "India" in Modern Legal Systems Cyclopedia, Vol. 9, Buffalo, NY, 1990; Robinson, ed. The Cambridge Encyclopaedia of India, Pakistan, Bangladesh, Sri Lanka, Nepal, Bhutan and the Maldives, Cambridge, 1989.

Republic of Indonesia

Legal History

The Indonesian legal system is based on Roman-Dutch law, modified by custom and Islamic law. Sources of law are Islamic law, statutory legislation, presidential instructions, and official compilations of Islamic law.

European explorers arrived in the region in the sixteenth century, and the Dutch East India Company was founded in 1602. The Dutch established a trading post on the north coast of Java, later named Jakarta. The Dutch gradually asserted political and military control beyond Java from the eighteenth century until most of archipelago was under Dutch rule by the start of the twentieth century.

Under Dutch rule, the Netherlands Indies population was divided into Europeans, Natives, and Foreign Orientals. The Dutch established separate tribunals for Europeans and Natives. Indonesians were subject to *adat* law, with the Netherlands East Indies divided into several jurisdictions based on cultural and linguistic criteria. Dutch scholars identified and classified 19 different systems of customary law in the region. In areas under direct rule, there were European courts, native courts, and general courts for all of the population. In areas under indirect rule, there were native courts applying *adat* with very limited criminal jurisdiction and no jurisdiction over Europeans or foreigners. The basic principle was dominance of the received civil law system, and application of *adat* for natives as far as it was not replaced by statute. The first legislation relating to the application of Islamic law was an 1882 Royal Decree establishing a Priest Court for Java and Madura, although the Decree acknowledged that most Indonesians were also subject to *adat* law administered by native courts. The Priest Court had jurisdiction over Muslim family and inheritance law where all parties were Muslim and *awqaf*, and had concurrent jurisdiction with the native courts of Java and Madura. The Priest Court was composed of a President selected from the native courts officers and three to eight *qadis*, all appointed by the Governor-General. Subsequent legislation by Dutch authorities was also of a largely of regulatory and administrative nature. Independence was declared two days after Japanese occupying forces withdrew in 1945. Calls for the reform of marriage laws led to various proposals from members of government, women's groups and the National Institute for Law Reform from 1945 to 1973, but conflicting interests prevented any consensus being reached. The only statutory reform of Muslim personal status in that period was the enactment of the Muslim Marriage and Divorce Registration Law 1946 requiring registration. A new Marriage Law, the first that was applicable to all Indonesians, was eventually passed in 1974 amidst much controversy, particularly with regard to such issues as permission for divorce and polygamy. Some compromises made by the government included increasing the jurisdiction of *shariah* courts and eliminating registration as a requirement for validity of marriage. The Marriage Law is applied by the regular court system for religious minorities and by *shariah* courts for Muslim Indonesians.

Following the controversy over the Marriage Law, since the mid-1980s Compilations of Islamic Law in Indonesia (*Kompilasi Hukum Islam di Indonesia*) authored by officials from the Ministry of Religion and Supreme Court judges have been used to clarify points on personal law and inheritance for application by *shariah* courts. They are based on arguments from various schools, comparisons of application of Islamic law in different countries, decisions from religious courts, etc. The Compilations are presented as Presidential Instructions (Inpres) which have lower status that statute in the Indonesian legal system. A 1991 Compilation of Islamic Law directed the restriction of *hiba* (gifts) to a maximum of one-third of the donor's estate. While this represents a reassertion of classical interpretations, the Compilations also draw from eclectic sources, and Supreme Court judgements on appeal from the religious appellate courts diverge from classical law in many matters.

Schools of *Fiqh*: The majority of the population is Shafi'i Muslim. There are also Ahmadi minorities. The other recognised religious minorities are Roman Catholic, Protestant, Hindu and Buddhist. There are also significant minorities following tribal religions; they are not afforded any official recognition.

Constitutional Status of Islamic Law: The Constitution was promulgated in August 1945. It does not adopt any official religion, but Article 29(1) provides that "the State is based upon the belief in the One, Supreme God", also embodied in the Pancasila. Article 29(2) guarantees freedom of religion.

Court System: There are four judicial branches outlined in the Basic Law on Judicial Power 1970: general, religious, military and administrative courts. General courts include District Courts of First Instance, High Courts of Appeal, and the Supreme Court (*Mahkamah Agung*). Religious courts (*Pengadilan Agama*) are established side by side with District Courts. Religious courts are organised at two levels: courts of first instance in each district and appellate courts in all provinces (approximately 300 and 25, respectively; figures as of mid-1990s) and have jurisdiction over civil cases between Muslim spouses on matters concerning marriage, divorce, reconciliation, and alimony. Appeals from the religious appeals court (*Mahkamah Islam Tinggi*) go to Supreme Court, although the supervisory jurisdiction of regular courts over religious courts ended with the passing of the Law on Religious

Courts 1989. Religious courts have limited or special jurisdiction and secular courts have general jurisdiction. The competence of religious courts is not exclusive, and parties can apply to District Courts for adjudication on the basis of Dutch-derived civil law or local *adat*.

Notable Features: The minimum marriage age is 19 for males and 16 for females, with provision for marriage below the minimum age, subject to judicial discretion and parental consent. The free consent of marrying parties is a requirement for validity of marriage, unless the religious law governing the parties directs otherwise. The Marriage Law 1974 defines as legal a marriage "solemnised according to the laws of the respective religions and beliefs of each of the parties". Parties under 21 years require parental permission to marry; this refers to the consent of both parents, the surviving parent, or the guardian. Marriage registration is obligatory; the Marriage Registrar Office of the Department of Religious Affairs is responsible for the registration of Muslim marriages and the Civil Marriage Registrar Office of the Department of Internal Affairs for all other marriages. The basis of marriage is considered monogamy, but the Marriage Law does not prohibit polygamy for those religions that allow it (Islam, Hinduism, Buddhism). Polygamy is permissible with the consent of the existing wife or wives and with judicial permission, by fulfilling conditions specified by law, i.e., proof of financial capacity, safeguards that husband will treat wives and children equally; and a court inquiry into the validity of the reasons for wishing to contract a polygamous marriage (e.g., the existing wife's physical disfigurement, infertility, incurable disease). The law specifies that both spouses are equal and both are responsible for maintaining the home and caring for children. The permanent resident and domicile is to be decided by both parties. The husband as the head of the family is required to protect the wife and provide for her according to his means and the wife's duty is to manage the household.

The Marriage Law provides that divorce shall be carried out only before a Court of Law, after the Court has endeavoured to reconcile the parties. A husband married under Islamic law may submit a letter notifying the religious court of his intention to divorce and giving his reasons. If the husband's reasons accord with any of the six grounds for judicial divorce outlined in the Marriage Law and the court determines that reconciliation is not possible, the court will grant a session in order to witness the divorce. Either spouse may seek a judicial divorce (preceded by reconciliation efforts by the judge) on the following grounds: the other spouse's adultery; alcoholism, addiction to narcotics, gambling or "any other vice that is difficult to cure"; abandonment for two years without valid reason; cruelty or mistreatment endangering life; physical disfigurement or malady preventing performance of marital duties; constant disputes without hope of resolution; and sentencing to a prison term of five years or more. Property acquired during marriage is considered joint property, although the Marriage Law only directs that division is according to the law applicable to the parties. The court may order alimony for children or maintenance for the former wife. In terms of custody, the Marriage Law simply provides that in case of dispute over custody, the Court shall render its judgment; the father shall have responsibility for maintenance expenses, unless he is unable to bear such responsibility in which case the Court may order the mother to share such expenses.

Succession is governed by classical law. Some commentators have also noted that the Indonesian Supreme Court has often sought to equalise the rights of male and female inheritors.

Notable Cases

Law/Case Reporting System: There is no regular system of case reporting in Indonesia.

International Conventions (with Relevant Reservations): Indonesia signed the CEDAW in 1980 and ratified it in 1984 with a declaration regarding Article 29(1).

Indonesia signed and ratified the CRC in 1990, submitting a general reservation to the effect that Articles 1, 14, 16, 17, 21, 22 and 29 are to be applied in conformity with the Constitution of Indonesia. (The articles indicated relate to majority, children's freedom of religion and conscience, right to privacy, and right to access to information, adoption, and the direction of children's education.)

Background and Sources: Bowen, "You May Not Give It Away: How Social Norms Shape Islamic Law in Contemporary Indonesian Jurisprudence, "Islamic Law and Society, Vol. 5, No. 3 (Oct. 1998): 382-408; Hooker, A Concise Legal History of South-East Asia, Oxford, 1978; Hooker, Islamic Law in South-East Asia, Singapore, 1984; Indonesia, 2nd and 3rd Period Report to CEDAW, 12 February 1997; Katz and Katz, "The New Indonesian Marriage Law: A Mirror of Indonesia's Political, Cultural and Legal Systems," American Journal of Comparative Law, Vol. 23 (1975): 653-681; Katz and Katz, "Legislating Social Change in a Developing Country: The New Indonesian Marriage Law Revisited," American Journal of Comparative Law, Vol. 26 (1978): 309-320; Mahmood, Indonesia, in Statutes of Personal Law in Islamic Countries, 2nd ed., New Delhi, 1995; Pompe, "Islamic Law in Indonesia," Yearbook of Islamic and Middle Eastern Law, Vol. 4 (1998): 180-200; Redden, Indonesia in Modern Legal Systems Cyclopedia, Vol. 2, Buffalo, N.Y., 1990; Supriadi, "Indonesian Marriage Law," in The International Survey of Family Law, ed. Bainham, 1995: 279-285.

Islamic Republic of Iran

Legal History

Iran was ruled by a series of dynasties for 2,500 years. Shiism became the official religion under Safavid rule (1501-1722). The increasing influence of foreign powers in the region under the Qajars (1795-1925) began with a series of capitulations to Europeans, beginning with the Russians, in nineteenth century. In 1906 the first Constitution was promulgated. A series of laws were enacted thereafter, relating to criminal, civil, commercial, and family law. By 1936, legislation made secular education a requisite for serving judges. Major changes were introduced in the area of family law under Reza Shah with the passage of Family Protection Law 1967 (significantly amended in 1975) abolishing extra-judicial divorce, requiring judicial permission for polygamy and only for limited circumstances, and establishing special Family Courts for the application of the new personal status legislation. The 1979 Revolution brought end to Pahlavi dynasty (1925-1979). Supreme Judicial Council issued proclamation directing courts that all un-Islamic legislation was suspended. Council given remit to revise all existing laws to Islamise legal system, with Ayatollah Khomeinis *fatawa* serving as transitional laws.

Sources of law are Islamic law, constitutional law, legislation, informed sources such as custom, revolutionary principles, etc.

Schools of *Fiqh*: The Ja'fari school is the predominant *madhhab* in Iran. There are also Hanafi Muslim minorities, as well as Zoroastrian, Baha'i, Christian and Jewish minorities. The officially recognised religions are Sunni Islam, Zoroastrianism, Judaism, and various Christian denominations. Under a 1933 law relating to the rights of non-Shi'i Iranians, courts are to apply the personal status laws applicable to the litigants belonging to officially recognised religions.

Constitutional Status of Islam(ic) Law: The current Constitution was adopted on 2nd-3rd December 1979, with significant revisions expanding presidential powers and eliminating the prime ministership in 1989. Article 4 provides that all civil, penal, financial, economic, administrative, cultural, military, political, and any other laws must be based on Islamic criteria. Article 12 provides that the official state religion is Islam and the twelver Ja'fari school; other schools of law are to be accorded full respect and freedom of religious practice, including matters of personal status.

Court System: Special Courts established by the Family Protection Act 1967 were dissolved after the Revolution. The 1979 Constitution provides that the chief of the Supreme Court and the Prosecutor-General must be *mujtahids.* The Special Civil Courts were established in 1979 to adjudicate over matters relating to family law, succession and *awqaf.*

The court structure since the Revolution is as follows (numbers as of 1984):

Revolutionary Courts: (70 branches)

Public Courts: Civil Courts (205), Special Civil Courts (99), 1st Class Criminal Courts (86), 2nd Class Criminal Courts (156)

Courts of Peace: Ordinary Courts of Peace (124), Independent Courts of Peace (125), Supreme Court of Cassation (22)

Notable Features: The Civil Code provides that marriage before puberty is invalid unless authorised by the natural guardian.When authorised before puberty, minimum age is nine. The marriage of a virgin girl (even after puberty) requires permission of the father or paternal grandfather; a Special Civil Court may grant permission if the guardian refuses without valid reason. The Identity Office must be notified of all temporary or permanent marriages and their dissolution. Temporary marriage is permitted, and must be for fixed time period. Polygamy is permitted. Marital obedience and maintenance are governed subject to classical conditions.

A 12-article law on marriage and divorce passed in 1986 allows the wife the right to obtain a divorce if the husband marries without her permission or does not treat co-wives equitably in the court's assessment. A wife who is not *nashiza* may take the matter to court if her husband refuses to pay maintenance and the court will fix a sum and issue a maintenance order. Arrears of maintenance to the wife have precedence over all other liabilities against husband. (In temporary marriage, the wife is only entitled to maintenance if the contract stipulates such.) The husband may deny his wife the right to work in any profession "incompatible with the family interests or with the dignity of himself or of the wife". The wife's refusing conjugal relations where husband has contracted venereal disease not deemed disobedience.

Talaq is governed by classical Shi'i law, requiring a specific formula and two male witnesses. A conditional formula of divorce is invalid. 1992 amendments provide that registration of divorce without a court certificate is illegal. The wife may obtain a *khol* in return for consideration of more or less than nuptial gift (*mahr*). Judicial divorce is available on the following grounds: proven insanity of either spouse; husband's castration or inability to consummate marriage, (husband's lunacy or impotence are grounds whether they occurred before or after the contract); defect of the wife interfering with conjugal relations or her total blindness, contracting leprosy or becoming seriously crippled if they existed at time of contract; husband's non-maintenance, after failure to comply with maintenance order (whether he is unable or unwilling); and where continuation of marriage constitutes proven difficulty or hardship for the wife, if the husband refuses to divorce her. A 1992 amendment law extended the wife's access to divorce by the addition of the following grounds: husband's non-maintenance for up to six months for any reason; husband's bad behaviour, keeping bad company, etc. making the continuation of married life impossible for the wife; husband's incurable disease constituting a danger to the wife; husband's madness in cases where annulment of marriage would not be possible according to the *shariah*; husband's non-compliance with a court order to avoid demeaning or dishonourable employment; husband's conviction of five or more years; husband's addiction constituting a danger to his family and marriage; husband's desertion or leaving the marital home for six months without legitimate cause (legitimate cause being determined by the court); husband's conviction for a crime bringing dishonour to family (definition of a dishonourable crime to be determined by the court); husband's infertility for five years of marriage or his contracting a sexually transmitted disease; husband's disappearance for six months; and husband's polygamous marriage without his first wife's consent, if the court considers the co-wives are not being treated equally. To half of her husband's assets if the court finds the divorce was initiated by the husband and was not caused by any failure on the wife's part. A reform introduced in 1992 extended the divorced wife's financial rights from maintenance during *idda* and her deferred dower to the right to sue for payment for household services rendered to their husbands during marriage, although the measure is difficult to apply in practice partly because of the difficulty in assessing wages for housework.

The mother's custody ends at two years for boys and seven for girls; custody reverts to the father if the mother remarries. Mother may be granted custody in certain cases if the father is proven unfit to care for the child.

Succession is governed by classical law; descendants (how low so ever) of predeceased children of the propositus inherit in place of their parents. Children of Baha'i marriages are not recognised as legitimate and, therefore, are denied inheritance rights.

Law/Case Reporting System

International Conventions (with Relevant Reservations): Iran signed the ICCPR and ICESCR in 1968 and ratified both Covenants in 1975 without reservations.

Iran signed the CRC in 1991 and ratified it in 1994 with a general declaration and reservation to the effect that the Islamic Republic makes reservation to the articles and provisions which might be contradictory to the Islamic *shariah*, reserving the right not to apply any provisions incompatible with Islamic Laws and the international legislation in effect.

Background and Sources: Amin, Middle East Legal Systems, Glasgow, 1985; Haeri, "Divorce in Contemporary Iran: A Male Prerogative in Self-Will," in Islamic Family

Law, Mallat and Connors, eds., London 1990; Lawyers Committee for Human Rights, Report of, The Justice System of the Islamic Republic of Iran, Washington DC, May 1993; Mahmood, Iran in Statutes of Personal Law in Islamic Countries, 2nd ed., New Delhi, 1995; Mir-Hosseini, "Mariage et Divorce: Une Marge de Negociation pour les Femmes," Les femmes en Iran: Pressions Sociales et Stratgies Identitaires, Yavari-d'Hellencourt. Paris, 1998; Mir-Hosseini, Marriage on Trial: A Study of Islamic Family Law, Iran and Morocco Compared, London, 1993; Pakzad, "The Legal Status of Women in the Family in Iran," in In the Eye of the Storm: Women in Post-Revolutionary Iran, Afkhami and Friedl, eds., London, 1994; Ramaz, "Women in Iran: The Revolutionary Ebb and Flow," Middle East Journal, Vol. 47, No. 3 (1993): 409-428; Redden, Iran in Modern Legal Systems Cyclopedia, Vol. 5, Buffalo, NY, 1990; Taleghani, ed. and trans. Civil Code of Iran, Littleton, Colorado, 1995.

State of Iraq

Legal History

Iraq has a mixed legal system that draws on both Sunni and Shi'i *fiqh* for the law applied in *shariah* courts. The legal system as a whole also includes constitutional law, legislation and statutory provisions, usage and custom, judicial precedent, and authoritative juridical opinions. Iraq, the birthplace of the Hanafi school of *fiqh*, came under Ottoman rule in the seventeenth century. From 1850 a number of new civil, penal and commercial codes were adopted by the Ottomans, based on European (mainly French) models, but the OLFR 1917 was never implemented in Iraq as the Turks lost control over the region by the end of World War I when a British Mandate was established. The British administrators did not adopt the OLFR as it was not part of local law and because of the fact that Iraq had an almost equal proportion of Sunni and Shi'i inhabitants. A monarchy was established under King Faisal in 1921 following the Arab Revolt; Iraq gained full independence from its Mandate status in 1932. A military coup in 1958 brought an end to the monarchy and Iraq became a republic.

The Iraqi Law of Personal Status 1959 was based on the report of a commission appointed the previous year to draft a code of personal status and applies, according to Article 2, to all Iraqis except those specifically exempted by law, mainly relating to Christian and Jewish minorities. The ILPS provides that, in the absence of any textual provision, judgements should be passed on the basis of the principles of the Islamic *shariah* in closest keeping with the text of the ILPS. Article 1 of the Civil Code also identifies Islamic law as a formal source of law.

Schools of *Fiqh*: The Ja'fari and Hanafi are the predominant schools in Iraq. There are also Christian and small Jewish and Yezidi minorities.

Constitutional Status of Islam(ic) Law: The provisional constitution was adopted on 22nd September 1968 and came into effect from 16th July 1970. Article 4 of the current provisional constitution declares Islam the state religion. (A new constitution was drafted in 1990 but was not adopted.)

Court System: Courts of Personal Status hear all cases involving Muslims, whether Iraqi or not. These Courts have jurisdiction over marriage, divorce, legitimacy, succession, *awqaf*, etc. *Shariah* courts operate independently from the regular courts. The Code of Personal Status 1959 is a unified code applicable to Shi'a and Sunni Iraqis.

Notable Features: The minimum marriage age is 18 for men and women; judicial permission for under-age marriages may be granted at 15 years if fitness, physical capacity and guardian's consent (unless the guardian's objection is considered unreasonable) are established. No relative or third party has the power of compulsion; a marriage contract concluded by coercion is void if it has not been consummated. Likewise, no relative or third party may prevent a person having legal capacity from marrying. Court registration without charge is obligatory and requires documentation of age, identity, stipulation of the amount of dower, medical reports, etc.; unregistered marriages may be proven by the affirmation of both parties.

Polygamy is only permitted by judicial permission, obtainable on two conditions; the husband must show some lawful benefit and financial ability to support more than one wife. Permission is not to be granted if the judge fears unequal treatment of co-wives. The ILPS provides penalties of imprisonment and/or fines for non-compliance with its provisions relating to marriage guardianship, registration and polygamy.

Upon marriage, the husband is obliged to maintain his wife (in accordance with the circumstances of both spouses) subject to classical conditions. Maintenance for a wife who is not *nashiza* is deemed to be a debt from the time that the husband ceases to pay maintenance; the wife is not entitled to maintenance if she leaves the marital home without her husband's permission or lawful cause, or if she is imprisoned or refuses to travel with her husband without lawful cause. The wife's right to work is not expressly mentioned, although the implication is that she would require her husband's permission to do so.

Talaq must be confirmed by the *Shariah* Court's judgement or registered with the Court during the *'idda* period. *Talaq* by a man who is intoxicated, insane, feeble-minded, under coercion, enraged (*madhush*), or seriously ill or in death sickness is ineffective, as is*talaq* that is not immediate or is conditional or in the form of an oath. All *talaqs* are deemed single and revocable except the third of three.

The wife is entitled to request dissolution if the husband does not fulfil any lawful condition stipulated in the marriage contract. Either party may request dissolution upon the following grounds: such harm as makes continuation of marriage impossible; marital infidelity; if the marriage was contracted without judicial permission before either party attained 18 years; if the marriage was concluded outside of court by means of coercion and was not consummated; if the husband marries polygamously without judicial permission; and if any of the above grounds are not proven, then on grounds of discord (in which case the court must initiate reconciliation procedures; if reconciliation efforts fail and the husband refuses to pronounce *talaq*, courts may grant judicial divorce; if the wife is found to be at fault, her financial rights are then forfeit). The wife may request a judicial divorce upon following grounds: if the husband is imprisoned for three years; if her husband abandons her for two years without lawful reason; if her husband does not consummate the marriage within two years of the contract; husband's impotence or affliction (if this occurs after consummation, it must be confirmed by medical report); husband's infertility if the wife has no living son by him; husband's serious illness which would cause the wife harm; non-maintenance after a grace period of up to 60 days; husband's failure to maintain due to his absence, disappearance, concealing his whereabouts, or imprisonment for more than one year; and if the husband refuses to pay maintenance arrears after a 60-day grace period.

The wife may also request judicial separation before consummation in return for any dower and proven expenditure on the part of the husband for the purposes of the marriage. All judicial divorces are considered lesser irrevocable. The wife may also obtain a *khul* from her husband in return for consideration that may be more or less than her dower. The option of puberty is not specifically regulated, but is mentioned in the provision defining the waiting period. The former husband is obliged to maintain the divorced wife (even if she was deemed *nashiza*) during her *idda* period. According to legislation passed in 1983, the repudiated wife also has a right to live in the marital home without her former husband for three years provided that she was not disobedient, did not request or agree to the divorce, and does not own her own house or flat. The divorce is entitled to custody of boys or girls until the age of 10, extendible to 15 years if it appears to be in the minor's best interests. Upon attaining 15 years, the ward may choose which parent to live with, or choose any other relative if such choice appears reasonable to the court.

The original 1959 legislation on succession was based on Ottoman law regulating the inheritance to the right to *miri* (government) property. The Ottoman law, in turn based mainly on German law, equalised male and female inheritance rights. The 1959 legislation also introduced obligatory bequests to grandchildren by predeceased sons or daughters, as well as completes freedom of the testator to make a will within the limits of the bequeathable one-third of the estate. Amendments made in 1963 allowed female descendants of the deceased to completely exclude collateral male agnates. As well, the provisions relating to intestate succession were amended in 1963, repealing the Ottoman-inspired reforms and adopting the Shi'i system of classifying heirs; within the Shi'i system of classification, Sunni principles are applied to the division of estates amongst the heirs.

Law/Case Reporting System: Law reporting is through the Iraqi Official Journal, *al-Waqa'i al-Iraqiyya.*

International Conventions (with Relevant Reservations): Iraq signed the ICCPR and the ICESCR in 1969 and ratified both Conventions in 1971. The general declarations submitted by Iraq related to its entry not signifying recognition of the state of Israel, and to its entry not constituting entry to the Optional Protocol to the ICCPR.

Iraq acceded to the CEDAW in 1986, with a reservation relating to Iraq not considering itself bound by Article 2(f) and (g), Article 9(1) and (2), and Article 16. The reservation to Article 16 states concerns the provisions of the Islamic *shariah* according women rights equivalent to the rights of their husbands thereby ensuring a just balance between spouses.

Iraq acceded to the CRC in 1994 with a reservation to Article 14(1) relating to the child's freedom of religion, stating that "allowing a child to change his or her religion runs counter to the provisions of the Islamic *shariah*".

State of Israel

Legal History

Palestine remained under Ottoman rule from 1517 until 1917. The state of Israel was established in 1948 after the period of British Mandate rule from 1922 ended, followed by war with the Arab states. A majority of the Palestinian population became refugees in neighbouring Arab countries. Israel also has a significant Palestinian minority, a majority of who are Muslim.

The Israeli legal system is a mixture of English common law, British Mandate regulations, and, in personal status law, Jewish, Christian, and Muslim law. In matters of personal status, the system of shared jurisdiction in particular areas has allowed for legislation to intervene in the application of Muslim law (still based on the OLFR 1917 implemented by British Mandatory administration) by way of penal sanctions and procedural devices used to indirectly effect changes in the law. However, the core of personal status relating to marriage and divorce is still based on religious laws.

Schools of *Fiqh*: The Hanafi school is officially the main school of law, although this is a legacy of Palestine's Ottoman history. Much of the Muslim population, particularly in rural areas, is Shafi'i. Israel also has Christian and Druze minorities.

Constitutional Status of Islamic Law: The Basic Law on the Judicature regulates the creation of religious courts (*beit din*), which includes the Muslim Religious Courts. There is no formal constitution; some of the functions of a constitution are served by the Declaration of Establishment (1948), the basic laws of the parliament (Knesset), and the Israeli citizenship law, as well as other documents of constitutional significance.

Court System: Muslim, Druze, Christian and Rabbinical Religious Courts are separate. Muslim Religious Courts have exclusive jurisdiction over all matters concerning Muslim personal status. The Courts apply the Ottoman Law of Family Rights 1917 (as amended after being adopted in Palestine by ordinance in 1919) and have jurisdiction, with the consent of the parties involved, over adoption and inheritance.

Notable Features: The minimum marriage age is 17 for females under the Marriage Age Law 1950 and as determined by the personal status law applicable to the prospective grooms (18 years under the OLFR). There is scope for judicial discretion (granted to Civil Courts) if the wife in an underage marriage is pregnant or a child has been born (without a minimum age) or for special circumstances (specified by case law) from the age of 16 years for females. There are penal sanctions of imprisonment and/or fines for non-compliance for the husband, the person arranging the marriage, and the person officiating, though the law does not invalidate underage marriages. The *wali*'s permission is required for the marriage of a female below the minimum marriage age of 17 years.

Marriage registration is obligatory; non-registration does not invalidate the marriage according to religious law. The wife may insert a stipulation in the marriage contract that the husband may not take an additional wife and if he does so, she or the co-wife will be divorced. There is no forcible execution of an obedience judgement; maintenance claims between spouses or involving minor children are governed by the personal law applicable to the defendant, whether the case comes before the secular or religious courts. Claims for maintenance are not to be heard after the completion of the *idda* period after a divorce and arrears of maintenance cannot be claimed.

The OLFR invalidates *talaq* uttered under coercion or intoxication and also introduced the requirement of notification of divorce to the *shariah* court, but notification is procedural and does not affect the validity of a repudiation.

The Women's Equal Rights Law 1951 provides penal sanction of imprisonment for a husband's unilateral decision to divorce against his wife's will and in the absence of a court judgement permitting such repudiation, but the repudiation remains valid. Under the OLFR, judicial dissolution is available to the wife on the following grounds: defect or illness of the husband (failure to consummate marriage, impotence, infectious disease, and mental illness); non-payment of maintenance by an absent husband; discord and strife (after the appointment of arbitrators to form a family council, with such council empowered to determine fault should reconciliation efforts fail); and irregular/void marriage. The Age of Marriage Law also provides contracting of marriage of girl under 17 years as grounds for requesting a dissolution before the wife attains 19 years (or at the request of the wife's guardian or a welfare officer before she attains 18 years). A divorce who is not disobedient (*nashiza*) is entitled to deferred dower and maintenance during her *idda* unless she renounced such rights.

Compensation paid to the wife became a regular feature in divorce after the passage of the Women's Equal Rights Law establishing penal sanctions for the unilateral repudiation of wife against her will and without a court judgement. The Women's Equal Rights Law extended adjudication of the division of property to the regular civil courts. The Spouses (Property Relations) Law 1973 directs the application of the community property rule with the presumption that parties have an equal share in marital property if the parties opt for adjudication under state law. Under the Capacity and Guardianship Law 1962, in the absence of a specific agreement between spouses, the wife has preference in matters of custody over minor children until six years. Courts are to base judgements according to the wards best interests. Upon the death of one party, guardianship is to revert to the surviving parent. Courts are empowered to appoint guardians for minors, with the wards interests being the sole criteria for exercise of judicial discretion.

The Succession Law 1965 permits co-wives to share in the estate of the deceased husband. Muslims over 18 may opt for the application of *shari* inheritance law, otherwise, the Ottoman Law of Succession 1913 (initially equalising rights of male and female heirs to *miri* property, i.e., state-owned property granted to individuals) as amended by the Women Equal Rights Law (extending Ottoman legislation to *mulk* and movable property).

Notable Cases

Law/Case Reporting System: Law reporting is through the *Israeli Official Gazette*. Case reports of *shariah* court decisions are published in bulletins of the Muslim and Druze Divisions of the Ministry of Religious Affairs (*Majallat al-Akhbar al-Darziyya* and *Majallat al-Akhbar al-Islamiyya*).

International Conventions (with Relevant Reservations): Israel signed the ICCPR and ICESCR in 1966 and ratified them in 1991. Israel submitted a reservation to Article 23 of ICCPR relating to the establishment of gender equality in the area of family law. The declaration states that "matters of personal status are governed in Israel by the religious law of the parties concerned. To the extent that such law is inconsistent with its obligations under the Covenant, Israel reserves the right to apply that law".

Israel signed the CEDAW in 1980 and ratified it in 1991. Israel submitted a reservation to Article 7(b) relating to gender equality in the formulation and implementation of policy, including holding public office and performing public functions at all levels of government. The Israeli reservation states that, other than in the area of religious courts, the article has been fully implemented in Israel, and that the reservation concerns the inadmissibility of appointing women judges in religious courts where this is prohibited by the communal laws applicable to a particular community. Israel also expresses its reservation to Article 16 on gender equality in family law "to the extent that the laws on personal status which are binding on the various religious communities in Israel do not conform with the provisions of that article".

Israel signed the CRC in 1990 and ratified the Convention in 1991, without reservations.

Israel signed the Convention to Consent to Marriage, Minimum Age for Marriage and Registration of Marriages in 1962.

Background and Sources: Ibrahim, "The Status of Arab Women in Israel," Critique: Journal of Critical Studies of the Middle East, Vol. 12(1998): 107-120; Israel, Initial and Second Periodic Report to CEDAW, 8 Apr. 1997; Layish, "Reforms in the Law of Personal Status of the Muslims in Israel: Legislation and Application,"Recht van de Islam 12(1994), pp. 45-57; Layish, Women and Islamic Law in a Non-Muslim State: A Study Based on Decisions of the *Shariah* Courts in Israel, Jerusalem, 1975; Redden, Israel in Modern Legal Systems Cyclopedia, Vol. 5, Buffalo, NY, 1990; Reiter, "*Qadis* and the Implementation of Islamic Law in Present Day Israel," pp. 205-31 in Islamic Law: Theory and Practice, Gleave, ed., London, 1997; Welchman, "Family Law under Occupation: Islamic Law and the *Shariah* Courts of the West Bank," in Islamic Family Law, Mallat and Connors, eds., London, 1990.

Hashemite Kingdom of Jordan

Legal History

Jordan remained a part of the Ottoman Empire (see further: Turkey) until World War I and was then placed under an indirect form of British Mandate rule. The Ottoman legal system was retained; in 1927 many Ottoman laws (including the Ottoman Law of Family Rights 1917) were re-enacted with some alterations. The Hashemite Kingdom of Jordan was established as a fully independent state in 1947, with Islam as the state religion. The first Constitution was adopted the following year, and the state embarked on the process of developing a national legal system to replace the vestiges of Ottoman rule.

In 1947, a provisional Law of Family Rights was enacted and remained in force until it was replaced in 1951 by the new Law of Family Rights. Largely following the form of the OLFR, while some of the Egyptian reforms- notably regarding divorce- of the 1920s, the JLFR 1951 was the first in a series of codifications of Islamic family law issued in the 1950s by the national legislatures of newly independent Arab states. A new Constitution was adopted in 1952, retaining the religious and communal basis of jurisdiction in personal status matters. By this time, the Palestinian territory of the West Bank had come under Jordanian rule, including East Jerusalem, and until 1994, even during the Israeli occupation from 1967, the *shari'a* courts of the West Bank were under the authority of the Jordanian *Qadi al-Quda* and applied Jordanian law (see further: Palestinian territories).

A Civil Code and Civil Procedure Code were enacted in 1952 and 1953, the former replacing the Ottoman Majalla of 1876. The 1952 Civil Code was replaced in 1976, the new Code drawing from Syrian legislation (which in turn was modelled on the Egyptian Civil Code of 1948). The same year, the Jordanian Law of Personal Status replaced the 1951 JLFR. The JLPS revises the JLFR in a number of significant ways, providing for a more comprehensive code, while retaining reference to the classical Hanafi rules in the absence of a specific reference in the text. Discussions continue on the draft text of a new personal status law.

Court System: The Jordanian legal system draws from the Ottoman heritage in the communal jurisdiction of the religious courts of different communities over matters of personal status. In its civil court system it follows the French model. The *shari'a* courts are established in the Constitution along with the religious tribunals of other recognised communities and include first instance courts with a single *qadi* and the *Shari'a* Court of Appeal. The other two categories of courts established in the Constitution are the civil or regular courts (*nizamiyya*) and 'special tribunals'. The Constitution grants the *shari'a* courts exclusive jurisdiction in matters of Muslim personal status. Precise jurisdiction of and procedure in the *shari'a* courts is defined in the Law of *Shar'i* Procedure 1959; the rules governing qualification and functions of *shar'i qadis* and lawyers are to be found in the Law of Organisation of *Shari'a* Courts 1972 and the Law of *Shar'i* Advocates 1952 respectively, both of which have been amended a number of times.

Schools of Fiqh: The Hanafi *madhhab* is the dominant school in Jordanian law.

Constitutional Status of Islam(ic) law: The 1952 Constitution declares Islam to be the state religion. It does not specify the sources of legislation as a whole, although in regard to the *shari'a* courts it states that "the *shari'a* courts in the exercise of their jurisdiction shall apply the rulings of the *shari'a* law."

Notable Features: The minimum marriage age is 16 for men and 15 for women (all ages in the personal status law are calculated by the lunar calendar) and the Penal Code provides penalties for all those involved in carrying out underage marriages. An underage marriage can nevertheless be recognised as valid if the wife has fallen pregnant or given birth by the time of a suit to dissolve their marriage coming to court, or if both spouses have by that time reached the minimum age. In the event of a contract between a woman aged under 18 and a man 20 years or more her senior, the qadi is required to ascertain that the bride has freely given her consent to the marriage and that it is in her interest. The consent of the guardian is required for a female aged under 18 to marry, but not for a divorce or widow aged over 18; the law thus implicitly requires the consent of the guardian to the first marriage of a woman of any age, although the *qadi* can over-ride the *wali's* refusal if it has no justification in law. Criminal sanctions are provided for those violating the mandatory registration requirements for marriage and divorce.

There are no constraints on polygamy beyond the classical injunctions that a man must treat co-wives equitably and provide them with separate dwellings. The registration fee for a polygamous contract of marriage is higher than that for a monogamous union. The marriage contract requires a man to disclose his social status to the woman he is marrying, but there is no requirement that an existing wife be notified of a subsequent polygamous marriage by her husband.

The institution of the "house of obedience" is maintained but without forcible execution of an "obedience" ruling made against the wife beyond disqualifying her from maintenance rights against her husband.

As elsewhere in the region, *talaq* uttered by a man who is drunk, asleep, in a faint, coerced, or 'overwhelmed' (*madhush*) has no effect, while oaths on *talaq* and conditional *talaq* do not give rise to *talaq* if the intention was to get someone to do or not do something. A "triple *talaq*" as in *talaq* accompanied by a number in word or sign or- significantly- repeated in a single session has the effect of a single revocable *talaq* only. To give rise to the greater finality of irrevocable *talaq*, three *talaqs* must be pronounced not only separately but in three separate sessions.

Grounds for which the wife may petition for divorce are similar to those introduced elsewhere in the region from the time of the OLFR. They include failure to maintain, physical desertion or the absence of the husband for a year or more, a prison sentence of three years or more, "discord and strife", breach of a binding stipulation in the marriage contract, and various grounds associated with the mental and physical health of the husband (the latter also being entitled to petition for divorce on similar health grounds). The law allows either party to insert stipulations into the contract and to sue for dissolution if they are broken. Either spouse may also petition for divorce on the grounds of discord and strife.

The law provides for compensation for arbitrary *talaq* up to a maximum of the equivalent of a year's maintenance for the wife divorced 'without legitimate cause' and retains the classical rules requiring the ex-husband to pay for his divorced wife breastfeeding and undertaking custody of their children. A divorced mother is entitled to custody of her children until they reach puberty, subject to the classical conditions. During marriage, the wife has no financial obligations for her own upkeep and her medical expenses are included in the maintenance she is due from her husband. In the area of succession, changes to classical Hanafi law have been made in allowing the spouse relict to share in the *radd* or proportional return of the remainder of the estate to those holding fixed shares, should circumstances so permit; and in providing for the 'obligatory bequest' (*al-wasiya al-wajiba*) to orphaned grandchildren, although restricting this to the grandchildren through predeceased sons, not daughters.

Notable Cases: In 1989, an apostasy case against Toujan al-Faisal, journalist and parliamentary candidate, was heard in the first instance *shari'a* Court of south Amman. Jordan has no apostasy law but the petitioners sought that she should be declared an apostate, and divorced from her husband. Al-Faisal was standing in the elections at the time; the court eventually ruled no jurisdiction and on appeal in 1990 the *shari'a* court of appeal, which had agreed to hear the section of the petition relating to divorce on the grounds of alleged apostasy, found that there was no evidence of apostasy and dismissed the case.

Law Reporting: The Official Gazette. Practitioners' collections of principles of *shari'a* appeal court decisions.

International Conventions and Reports to Treaty Governing Bodies: Jordan is a party to both International Covenants. It signed the CEDAW in 1980 and ratified it in 1992 with the following reservations: Art. 9(2) regarding equal nationality rights for men and women, particularly in marriage; Art. 15(4) on equal rights regarding freedom of movement and choice of domicile (because "a wife's residence is with her husband"); and Art. 16(1) on equal rights in marriage and family relations. Jordan signed the CRC in 1990 and ratified it in 1991, with reservations to Articles 14, 20 and 22 concerning adoption and children's rights to freedom of choice of religion. Accession to Convention to Consent to Marriage, Minimum Age for Marriage and Registration of Marriage in July 1992.

Background and Sources: Redden, "Jordan" in The Modern Legal Systems Cyclopedia, volume 5, Buffalo NY 1990; Amin, "Jordan" in Middle East Legal Systems, Glasgow 1985; Mahmood, "Jordan" in Statutes of Personal Law in Islamic Countries, New Delhi 1995; Hinchcliffe and Alami, "Jordan" pages 79-114 in Islamic Marriage and Divorce Laws of the Arab World, London 1996; Welchman, "The Development of Islamic Family Law in the Legal System of Jordan," ICLQ 37 1988 868- 886; Gallagher, "Women's Human Rights on Trial in Jordan: The Triumph of Toujan al-Faisal," pages 209-231 and appended translation of article by Toujan al-Faisal, "They Insult Us... and We Elect Them!" pages 232-237, in Afkhami, Faith and Freedom, London 1995.

Republic of Kenya

Legal History

European colonial interest in Kenya began with Portuguese efforts to establish safe ports in the area of Mombassa from 1498. The Omanis captured Mombasa in 1696. British interests in the East African region in the mid to late nineteenth century led to the formation of the British East Africa Company. In 1895, within a decade of the founding of the East Africa Company, the area from the coast to the Rift Valley was declared the British East Africa Protectorate. Kenya gained independence in June 1963. Under the British protectorate, Kenya had parallel legal systems with African courts applying customary law, and appeals lying with the African Appeal Court, then with the District Officer and then a Court of Review. Muslim personal law was applied by Courts of *Liwalis*, *Mudirs* and *Kadhis*, with appeals lying with the Supreme Court (renamed the High Court after independence). The process of integrating the judicial system began in 1962 when powers of administrative officers to review African Courts' proceedings were transferred to magistrates. The process was completed by the passage of two acts in 1967. The Magistrates' Courts Act 1967 abolished African Courts and the Court of Review and established District and Resident Magistrate's Courts and a High Court. The *Kadhis'* Courts Act 1967 established six *Kadhis'* Courts for the application of Muslim personal status law.

In 1967, two Presidentially-appointed commissions began looking into marriage and divorce law and inheritance law. The commissions produced drafts of uniform family and inheritance codes to replace the existing customary, statutory, Islamic and Hindu laws then in force. The commission dealing with inheritance laws recommended a uniform code applicable with certain exceptions for customary laws. The bill based on its recommendations led to much heated debate. Criticisms included that the proposed law was too foreign, anti-Muslim, and afforded too many rights to women and illegitimate children. The bill was eventually passed in 1972. The marriage and divorce laws commission produced a draft code that was as uniform as the commission deemed feasible, but since the 1970s efforts to enact a uniform marriage law have been unsuccessful. Marriage law continues to be governed by several regimes: civil, Christian, Hindu and Muslim marriages are governed by separate legislation and communal laws and customary law marriages are also afforded official recognition.

The protectorate-era legislation relating to application of Muslim personal law has been retained. The Acts in force basically afford recognition to marriages solemnised under Islamic law, provide for the registration of Muslim marriages and divorces, delineate the jurisdiction and procedure of *Kadhis'* Courts and instruct the application of the principles of personal law applicable to the parties involved, without substantive codification of that law.

Schools of *Fiqh*: Kenya has a very diverse Muslim population due to Arab and South Asian settlement, local conversion and intermarriage, thus various schools represented. The majority are Shafi'i, and there are also sizeable Hanafi communities as well as Ja'fari, Isma'ili, Zaydi and Ahmadi minority communities.

Constitutional Status of Islam(ic) Law: The Constitution was adopted on 12th December 1963, and has been amended several times; most notably in 1964 when Kenya became a Republic and in 1991 when a multiparty system was restored. The Constitution does not provide for any official state religion. Article 66(1) to (5) provides for the establishment of *Kadhis'* Courts.

Court System: Local courts applying customary law were abolished in 1967 when reform and unification of the judiciary was completed. There are four levels of courts: Resident and District Magistrates' Courts (1st, 2nd and 3rd classes), Senior Resident and Chief Magistrates' Courts; a High Court and the Court of Appeal.

Islamic law is applied by *Kadhis'* Courts where "all the parties profess the Muslim religion" in suits relating to "questions of Muslim law relating to personal status, marriage, divorce or inheritance". There are eight *Kadhis'* Courts in Kenya, presided over by a Chief *Kadhi* or a *Kadhi* appointed by the Judicial Services Commission. Appeals lie to the High Court, sitting with the Chief *Kadhi* or two other *Kadhis* as assessor(s).

Notable Features: The minimum marriage age is governed by the Marriage Act for statutory marriages (requiring parties to be 16 years of age) and by the relevant personal laws applicable; for Muslims, neither the Mohammedan Marriage, Divorce and Succession Act nor the

Mohammedan Marriage Registration Act provide a specified minimum age. The applicable legislation refers only to Muslim law and does not specify any particular school. Although there are provisions for marriage registration, registration does not define validity and marriages conducted under statutory (includes the Marriage Act as well as the African Christian Marriage Act), customary, Muslim and Hindu law are all recognised. Polygamy is governed by classical law. Although it is a criminal offence to marry under statutory law and contract a subsequent marriage under Islamic or customary law, there are no legislative restrictions to polygamy outside of the statutory regime.

Talaq and judicial divorce are governed by classical law, as are post-divorce maintenance provisions. In matters of child custody and guardianship, *Kadhis'* Courts generally grant custody to the mother until 7 years for boys and 14 for girls at which point custody reverts to the father. The statutory legislation applicable (the Guardianship of Infants Act) directs that Courts must adjudicate with the interests of the ward as the primary consideration. And an increasing number of women are applying to the regular court system where custody over boys and girls under 16 is generally awarded to the mother.

Under the Law of Succession Act 1981, uniform legislation on intestate succession was made applicable to all Kenyans, with specific exemptions for the application of customary laws; a Muslim testator could provide in his/her will that the estate should devolve according to Islamic law. In 1990, an amendment was passed inserting an exemption for Muslims.

Notable Cases

Law/Case Reporting System: Case reporting is through the *Kenya Law Reports*, *Kenya Appeal Reports* and *Kenya Court of Appeal Decisions*.

International Conventions (with Relevant Reservations): Kenya acceded to the ICCPR and ICESCR in 1972, with a reservation to Article 10(2) of the ICESCR.

Kenya acceded to the CEDAW in 1984 without reservations.

Kenya signed and ratified the CRC in 1990 without reservations.

Background and Sources: Anderson, Islamic Law in Africa, London, 1954; Butegwa, "Kenyan Women's Awareness of their Rights: Report of a Field Study," in Women and Law in Kenya: Perspectives and Emerging Issues, Mbeo and Ooko-Ombaka, eds., Nairobi, 1989; Hirsch, Pronouncing and Persevering: Gender and the Discourses of Disputing in an African Islamic Court, Chicago, 1998; Kabeberi-Macharia and Nyamu, "Marriage by Affidavit: Developing Alternative Laws on Cohabitation in Kenya," in The Changing Family: Family Forms and Family Law, Eekelaar and Nhlapo, eds., Oxford, 1998; "Kenya" in Women of the World: Laws and Policies Affecting Their Reproductive Lives- Anglophone Africa, Center for Reproductive Law and Policy and International Federation of Women Lawyers (Kenya Chapter), New York, 1997; Mwangi, "The Application and Development of *Sharia* in Kenya: 1895-1990," in Islam in Kenya: Proceedings of the National Seminar on Contemporary Islam in Kenya, Bakari and Yahya, eds., Mombasa, 1995; Redden, "Kenya" in Modern Legal Systems Cyclopedia, vol. 6, Buffalo, NY, 1990; Rubin & Cotran, "Kenya" in Annual Survey of African Law, Vols. I-IV, 1967-1970.

State of Kuwait

Legal History

The Ottoman Empire ruled present-day Kuwait as part of Basra province from the late seventeenth century, and the Ottoman legal and judicial system functioning in Iraq was applied to Kuwaiti territory. However, the local rulers adhered to the Maliki School. In the late nineteenth century, a Treaty of Protection placed Kuwait under British extra-territorial control, and Kuwait became an administrative subdivision of British India. While the British did establish a western-style judicial administration, it only served the non-Arab inhabitants of Kuwait.

The British protectorate in of Kuwait ended in 1961, by which time Shaykh Abdullah al-Salim al-Sabah had begun the process of legal and judicial reform; the process of codification of was initiated by the country's leaders during the early 1960s. In 1959, Shaykh Abdullah enlisted the services of the renowned Arab jurist Abd al-Razzaq al-Sanhuri, leading to the enactment of a number of codes inspired by Egyptian and French models. While matters relating to civil and commercial law and procedure were codified in the 1960s, it was not until the 1980s that the Civil Code 1980 and the Kuwaiti Code of Personal Status 1984 were enacted.

Schools of *Fiqh*: The Maliki school is the official *madhhab* in Kuwait. There is also a significant Ja'fari Shi'a minority.

Constitutional Status of Islam(ic) Law: The Constitution was adopted on 11th November 1962. Article 2 states that "[t]he religion of the State is Islam, and the Islamic *Shariah* shall be a main source of legislation". Article 1(2) of the Civil Code also directs that, in the absence of a specific legislative provision, judges are to adjudicate according to custom (*urf*), and in the absence of an applicable principle of custom, be guided by the principles of Islamic jurisprudence (*fiqh*) most appropriate under the general and particular circumstances. Following the Iranian Revolution, Kuwait's rulers stated that they would begin Islamising the law and enacting laws which were fully in agreement with the *shariah*.

Court System: Under the 1959 Law Regulating the Judiciary, Kuwaiti courts are competent to hear all disputes concerning personal status, and civil, criminal and commercial matters. There are three levels of courts: courts of first instance (having several divisions, including personal status) in every judicial district; High Court (with five divisions, including personal status); and the Supreme Court (divided into the Division of High Appeal and the Cassation Division).

For the application of personal status laws, there are three separate sections: Sunni, Shi'i and non-Muslim (for the application of family laws of religious minorities). After judgements by the courts of first instance, appeals lie with the High Court, and then with the Cassation Division of the Supreme Court.

Notable Features: No substantive minimum marriage age is specified, rather, capacity to marry requires a party to have reached puberty and be of sound mind. The contract may not be registered where the female has not reached 15 years or the male 17 years. No claim arising from marriage shall be heard if either party is under-age at the time of the claim or if the claim is not established by official documentation of marriage. A woman who has been married previously or has attained 25 years has "freedom of choice" in marriage, however, she cannot conclude the contract herself and still requires her *wali* to do so, in accordance with classical Maliki rules. Polygamy is governed by classical law.

Maintenance is considered a debt against the husband from the date he fails to provide maintenance, up to a maximum period of two years arrears from the date of the claim. Judgements for obedience cannot be forcibly executed. A wife's going out to work is not deemed a violation of her marital obligations if her working is not contrary to her family's interests.

Talaq uttered by a man who is insane, feeble, under coercion, intoxicated, mistaken, disoriented, or enraged is not effective, nor are forms of *talaq* that are not immediate effective. *Talaq* to which a number is attached shall be effective as a single revocable *talaq*, except for the third of three. The wife may obtain a *khul* from her husband in return for appropriate recompense. The rules on *khul* include explicit prohibition of coercion in reaching a *khul* agreement and invalidate any condition of the settlement by the father stipulating his custody over children from the marriage.

The wife may seek a judicial divorce on the following grounds: the husband's non-maintenance; *ila*, should the wife request a divorce; the husband's absence of one year or more without proper justification (on the basis of *darar*/injury); and the husband's imprisonment for three years or more. Either spouse may apply for a judicial divorce on grounds of *darar*/injury caused by such word or action as makes continued matrimony impossible or for any breach of a valid stipulation recorded in the marriage contract; *darar* / injury is established by the testimony of two male or one male and two female witnesses and divorce on such grounds follows reconciliation efforts, with the possibility of an award being made as compensation for the aggrieved party. Annulment is available on following grounds: defect of either spouse such as makes cohabitation harmful or interferes with conjugal relations; and difference of religion arising from conversion or apostasy after marriage. The divorce is entitled to compensation equal to not more than one years maintenance in addition to maintenance during *idda*, except for cases of divorce for non-maintenance due to the husband's poverty, divorce for *darar*/injury caused by the, *khul*, or annulment at the wife's request. The divorced mother's right to custody ceases at puberty for boys and majority or age of marriage for daughters.

The 1971 Law on Obligatory Bequest introduced obligatory bequests to favour orphaned grandchildren; this applies to descendants through sons how low so ever and through daughters, the first generation only.

Notable Cases

Law/Case Reporting System: Laws and summaries of important Court of Cassation decisions are published in the Kuwaiti *Official Gazette*.

International Conventions (with Relevant Reservations): Kuwait signed the CRC in 1990 and ratified it in 1991 with a general reservation upon signature to all provisions of the Convention "incompatible with the laws of

Islamic *shariah* and the local statutes in effect"; and declarations upon ratification relating to Article 7 and its relation to Kuwaiti Nationality Law as applicable to orphans born in Kuwait and Article 21 on adoption as a system not recognised by the Islamic *shariah*, "the main source of legislation".

Kuwait acceded to the CEDAW in 1994 with reservations to Article 7(a) relating to gender equality in suffrage and eligibility for election ("inasmuch as the provision conflicts with the Kuwaiti Electoral Act under which the right to vote and run in elections is reserved for men") ; Article 9(2) on gender equality in nationality rights ("inasmuch as it runs counter to the Kuwaiti Nationality Act, which stipulates that a child's nationality shall be determined by that of his father"); and Article 16(f) on equal rights of guardianship, wardship, trusteeship and adoption ("inasmuch as it conflicts with the provisions of the Islamic *shariah*, Islam being the official religion of the state").

Kuwait acceded to the ICCPR and ICESCR in 1996. Kuwait submitted a number of interpretative declarations relating to the following Articles of the ICCPR: Articles 2(1) and 3, relating to the provisions of the Kuwaiti Constitution (especially Article 20 thereof), and the exercise of rights within the limits set by Kuwaiti law; and Article 23, relating to the supremacy of Kuwaiti national law ("which is based on Islamic law") in areas where there is conflict between national personal status laws and the provisions of the Convention. The reservation to Article 25(b) states that Kuwaiti electoral law restricts the right to stand and vote in elections to males. Kuwait also submitted two interpretative declarations and a reservation to the ICESCR. The interpretative declaration to Articles 2(2) and 3 is almost the same as Kuwait's first declaration to the ICCPR.

Background and Sources: Amin, Legal System of Kuwait, Glasgow, 1991; Amin, Middle East Legal Systems, Glasgow, 1985; Ballantyne, Commercial Law in the Arab

Middle East: The Gulf States, London, 1986; El Alami and Hinchcliffe, Islamic Marriage and Divorce Laws of the Arab World, London, 1996; "Kuwait,"Civil Society, Vol. 8, issue 90 (June 1999): 10-11; Mahmood, "Kuwait" in Statutes of Personal Law in Islamic Countries, 2nd ed., New Delhi, 1995; Nasir, The Islamic Law of Personal Status, 2nd ed., London, 1990; Pearl, A Textbook on Muslim Personal Law, 2nd ed., London, 1987; Redden, Kuwait in Modern Legal Systems Cyclopedia, Vol. 5, Buffalo, NY, 1990.

Lebanon (Lebanese Republic)

Legal History

The legal system draws *inter alia* on elements of Ottoman law, canon law, and codes based on French models. Lebanon became a part of the Ottoman Empire in 1516 and remained under Ottoman rule, with relative autonomy, for three centuries. It was under a French mandate from 1918 to 1943 and although French civil law had a great influence on the development of the Lebanese legal system and judiciary, the French authorities did not affect any substantive changes to the Ottoman Law of Family Rights 1917 or to uncodified aspects of personal law. During the 1920s, the borders of Lebanon were redefined and the Republic established. Lebanon has a very heterogeneous population, leading to the development of a highly complex system of power-sharing for the major religious communities. However, the proportion of Maronite Christians and Sunni and Shia Muslims in the population changed significantly over the span of half a century, and updating the census data providing the bases for the system of power-sharing is an issue that has proved difficult for the modern state of Lebanon to address.

The inequalities inherent in the power-sharing agreement which failed to adapt to changing circumstances, as well as the effects of the Palestinian struggle for self-determination, lead to a descent into civil war in 1975. Lebanon, which has a large Palestinian refugee population, accepted an

Arab-brokered peace accord in the early 1990s. During the late 1990s, there was considerable popular pressure for reform of laws regulation women's rights.

Schools of *Fiqh*: The Ja'fari and Hanafi schools are the predominant *madhahib* in Lebanon. There are also Druze, Ismai'li and Alawi/Nusayri minorities. Several Christian denominations are represented, including Orthodox and Catholic denominations and one Protestant church, and there is a small Jewish minority. There are over fifteen different officially recognised religious sects in Lebanon.

Constitutional Status of Islam(ic) Law: The Constitution was adopted on 23rd May 1926 and has been amended numerous times. The Constitution guarantees that the personal status and religious interests of the various recognised religious communities of Lebanon are to be respected.

Court System: Communal jurisdiction over personal status is recognised for Muslims, Druze, Christians and Jews. There are two levels of *Shariah* courts (with Sunni and Ja'fari Judges presiding over cases involving Sunni and Ja'fari litigants, respectively), *Shariah* Courts of First Instance and a Supreme *Shariah* Court in Beirut sitting with three *qadis* and a civil judge acting as Attorney-General. There are also two levels of Druze courts, the Courts of First Instance and a Supreme Court of Appeal.

Notable Features: The age of capacity is 18 years for males and 17 for females among Sunnis; scope for judicial discretion on the basis of physical maturity and the *wali's* permission is from 17 years for males and 9 for females. For Shia, the marriage age is real puberty for both, or 15 for males and 9 for females with judicial permission. For the Druze, the marriage age is 18 for males and 17 for females, or 16 and 15 with judicial permission. A mature female of 17 years may apply to the court to marry and the requirement of guardians permission may be waived if his objection appears unfounded. The *wali's* right of *ijbar* is retained for Lebanese Ja'faris.

Marriage registration is a requirement governed by the Family Rights Law and Sunni and Ja'fari *Shariah* Judiciary Act. The *Shariah* Court having jurisdiction over the domicile of either spouse has exclusive authority to solemnize marriage contracts and the personal status officer is only to record contracts solemnised according to the terms of legislation; a copy of the marriage contract must be sent to the Personal Status Administration for official registration. Failure to register does not invalidate Muslim marriages, but such marriages will not be recognised without a *Shariah* Court ruling.

Maintenance and disobedience are governed by classical law. There are no restrictions to polygamy other than classical injunctions to treat co-wives equally; there is express legal recognition of the validity of stipulations inserted into the marriage contract restricting the husband's right to marry polygamously (e.g. effecting the divorce of one or the other co-wife in case of breach of the stipulation).

Talaq uttered while intoxicated or under coercion is invalid while *talaq* upon condition (for Sunnis) or deferred until a future time are valid. A husband who repudiates his wife is obligated to inform the judge of his exercise of *talaq* within 15 days and then the Department of Personal Status. Failure to register with the Department of Personal Status does not invalidate the divorce, but the husband will be subject to criminal penalties. For the Shi'a, classical rules regarding a specific formula under particular conditions apply.

The wife may request a judicial divorce on following grounds: husband's failure to consummate the marriage; husband's affliction making cohabitation without harm impossible; husband's insanity; husband's failure to maintain and his concealment of his whereabouts, or his absence, disappearance or intermittent cohabitation with his wife; and either spouse may apply for divorce on grounds of marital discord (after reconciliation efforts) where a judicial decision determines fault and appropriate recompense for the aggrieved party. All judicial divorces for such grounds are irrevocable. For the Shia, judicial divorce is not recognised, though some Shii interpreters do accept judicial intervention. For the Druze, divorce is only possible by decision of a *Madhhab* judge. If the *Madhhab* judge finds no legal justification for the divorce, the husband will be obliged to pay damages to the wife. Druze may also annul marriage by mutual consent, before a judge and two witnesses, and this creates a permanent and indissoluble bar between the former spouses. Maintenance during the *idda* is obligatory except for the woman judged to be disobedient.

Among Sunnis, the divorced mother's right to custody ends at seven years for boys and nine for girls; at two years for boys and seven for girls for the Shia (unless the mother remarries) subject to the wards best interests; and at seven years for males and nine for females for the Druze.

Legislation relating to inheritance law directs the application of classical provisions relating to the division of *mulk* property for Sunni, Shi'i and Druze communities. Druze succession law is similar to the Sunni except that Druze does not exclude descendants of predeceased heirs. *Miri* property continues to be governed by the Ottoman Inheritance Law 1913, which gives equal portions to males and females.

Notable Cases

Law/Case Reporting System: Law reporting is through the *Journal Officiel*.

International Conventions (with Relevant Reservations): Lebanon acceded to the ICCPR and ICESCR in 1972 without reservations.

Lebanon signed the CRC in 1990 and ratified it in 1991 without reservations.

Lebanon acceded to the CEDAW in 1997 with a number of general reservations to Articles 9(2), 16(1)(c), (d), (f) and (g), and 29(1).

Background and Sources: Bilani, Najjar and El-Gemayel, Personal Status in The Lebanese Legal System, Vol. 1, ed. El-Gemayel, Washington D.C., 1985; El Alami and Hinchcliffe, Islamic Marriage and Divorce Laws of the Arab World, London, 1996; Mahmood, Lebanon in Statutes of Personal Law in Islamic Countries, 2nd ed., New Delhi, 1995; Nasir, The Islamic Law of Personal Status, 2nd ed., London, 1990; Nasir, The Islamic Law of Personal Status, 2nd ed., London, 1990; Redden, Lebanon in Modern Legal Systems Cyclopedia, Vol. 5, Buffalo, NY, 1990.

Libya (Socialist People's Libyan Arab Jamahiriya)

Legal History

The legal system includes elements of French, Islamic and Italian law. Libya became a part of the Ottoman Empire in 1551. Following the Italo-Turkish War (1911-1912), Italy annexed Libya in 1934 after exiling the most resistant elements of Libyan society, led by the Sanusiyya. Libya remained an Italian colony until World War II when the Allied forces and Libyan returnee fighters ousted German and Italian forces, following which the British and French shared control over the region. Libya gained independence in 1951, under its first king, Syed Idris al-Sanusi. A military coup in 1969 brought an end to the monarchy, and a republic was established under Colonel Muammar al-Qaddafi. The Revolutionary Command Council established a Committee for the Codification of Personal Law in the early years following the revolution.

While the Committee was still in deliberation, the RCC issued a decree identifying the *shariah* as the principal source of all legislation and establishing a High Commission to examine all existing legislation in order to make it consistent with *shari* principles. Legal provisions for the purpose of bringing legislation into accord with the *shariah* were to be based on *takhayyur*, *maslaha*, and custom and usage where the Maliki is the predominant school. Some of the recommendations of the Personal Law Codification Committee lead to the passage of the Law on Women's Rights in Marriage and Divorce in 1972, introducing innovative provisions on *khul*. The Penal Code 1953 was also amended by several laws passed in the early 1970s, making Libya the first country to introduce *hadd* punishments by state legislation. Penalties for various crimes such as theft, *zina*, *qadhf* and artificial insemination, were introduced by the amendments, although commentators note that the punishments have rarely been applied in practice.

A new Family Law was enacted in 1984 which raised the marriage age, restricted polygamy and divorce, and to a lesser extent evened the spouses mutual rights and obligations. Article 72 of the Family Law directs recourse to the sources of the *shariah* as a residual source of law in the absence of specific provisions in the legislation.

Schools of *Fiqh*: The Maliki School is the predominant *madhhab* in Libya. Libya also has a small Christian minority.

Constitutional Status of Islam(ic) Law: A Constitutional Proclamation was issued on 11th December 1969 and amended on 2nd March 1977. Article 2 declares Islam the official state religion. The state also protects religious freedoms "in accordance with established customs". Article 37 of the Proclamation stated that a permanent constitution is to be drafted, but it has yet to be produced. Article 2 of The Declaration on the Establishment of the Authority of the People issued in March 1977 provides that "[t]he Holy Quran is the Constitution of the Socialist People's Libyan Arab Jamahiriya". Colonel Qaddafi also elucidates his own political and social theories in the Green Book, based on a speech delivered in April 1975.

Court System: After the Revolution, Qaddafi abolished the dual system, and civil and *shariah* courts were merged in

1973. There are four levels of courts: summary courts, courts of first instance, appeal courts, and the Supreme Court. Courts of first instance have numerous divisions, including a personal status division. The courts of appeal (numbering three in 1987, at Tripoli, Benghazi and Sabha) and the courts of first instance are both constituted by three-judge panels with judgments confirmed by majority decisions. The *shariah* judges who once would have constituted the personnel of the *Shariah* Court of Appeals now sit in the regular courts of appeal, specialising in *shariah* appellate cases. The Supreme Court has five chambers: civil and commercial, criminal, administrative, constitutional, and *shariah*.

Notable Features: The minimum marriage age is 20 years for men and women. There is scope for judicial discretion on grounds of benefit or necessity and with the *wali's* consent, though no minimum age is specified. The marriage guardian may not force a ward of either sex into marriage or prevent his ward from marrying; if the guardian withholds consent, the ward may take the matter to court to obtain permission. Marriage registration is obligatory.

Polygamy is permitted with prior judicial permission, and on grounds of the husband's financial and physical ability. Amendments to the law on polygamy also permit the husband to marry polygamously with the written agreement of the first wife, or with judicial permission granted for serious reasons.

Maintenance is the husband's duty, within the limits of his ability, unless he is in hardship and his wife is wealthy. Either spouse may obtain a maintenance order, or be awarded interim maintenance during a suit if the plaintiff appears to be eligible according to a provision which clearly diverges from classical rules of Islamic law. No maximum time limit is specified for claiming arrears of maintenance.

With reference to divorce, Article 28 of the Code states that "[i]n all cases, divorce shall not be established except by a decree by the relevant court". *Talaq* uttered by a minor, insane, demented or coerced husband or without deliberate intent is invalid, as is *talaq* that is suspended or conditional. Any *talaq* to which a number is attached is considered single revocable (except the third of three). Judicial divorce is available on the following grounds: husband's failure to maintain without cause; husband's inability to maintain (of which the wife was ignorant at the time of the marriage, and after an appropriate grace period); husband's absence without justification; grounds of defect preventing fulfilment of the aims of marriage or other grave defect (whether such defect developed before or after the contract) and was not known to other party; and *hajr*, defined as the husband's sexual abstinence for four months or more without justification, after an appropriate grace period. Most of the above grounds for judicial divorce are available to men as well as women. Judicial divorce may be obtained if the parties do not agree to *talaq* by mutual consent and arbitration and reconciliation efforts fail and harm is established. If the harm is deemed to be the wife's fault, her deferred dower is forfeit, maintenance frozen and compensation is required; if it is deemed to be the husband's fault, he must pay the deferred dower and compensation. The wife may also obtain a *khul'* for appropriate compensation, which may include the forfeiture of maintenance rights, her deferred dower or custody over her children and courts are empowered to rule for *khul* if the husband retracts his offer of *khul* "due to obstinacy". Payment of compensation to the husband may be deferred if the wife establishes hardship. Annulment is effected due to difference of religion in cases of conversion where the wife becomes Muslim and the husband does not or if the husband becomes Muslim and his non-*kitabiyya* wife does not.

The divorcing husband must pay his wife maintenance for the *idda*, and for children in her custody. Compensation to the wife can be awarded by the court if the husband is considered to bear the responsibility for the causes of a *talaq*. The divorced mother's custody ends at the age of marriage for girls and puberty for boys.

The Law on Women's Right to Inheritance 1959 reiterates the application of classical law and introduces penal sanctions of imprisonment for anyone withholding from a woman her lawful share (until the payment of her share).

Notable Cases

Law/Case Reporting System: Law reports are published in the Official Journal, *al-Jarida al-Rasmiya*. Supreme Court decisions are published in *Majallat al-Mahkama al-Ulya*.

International Conventions (with Relevant Reservations): Libya acceded to the ICCPR and ICESCR in 1970 with a general declaration the effect that its accession shall in no way signify recognition of Israel or entry into dealings with Israel under the terms of the Covenants.

Libya acceded to the CEDAW in 1989 with reservations relating to the following: Article 2 being implemented "with due regard for the peremptory norms of the Islamic *shariah* relating to determination of the inheritance portions of the estate of a deceased person"; and to Articles 16(c) and (d) being implemented "without prejudice to any of the rights guaranteed to women by the Islamic *shariah*".

Libya acceded to the CRC in 1993 without reservations.

Background and Sources: El Alami and Hinchcliffe, Islamic Marriage and Divorce Laws of the Arab World, London, 1996; el-Alem, "Libya," Yearbook of Islamic and Middle Eastern Law, Vol. 1 (1994): 225-236; Layish, Divorce in the Libyan Family, Jerusalem, 1991; Mahmood, Libya in Statutes of Personal Law in Islamic Countries, 2nd ed., New Delhi, 1995; Mahmood, "Legal System of Modern Libya: Enforcement of Islamic Penal Laws," and Mayer, "Libyan Legislation in Defense of Arabo-Islamic Sexual Mores," in Criminal Law in Islam and the Muslim World: A Comparative Perspective," 1st ed., Mahmood, ed., New Delhi, 1996; Mayer, "Reinstating Islamic Criminal Law in Libya," in Law and Islam in the Middle East, Dwyer, ed., New York, 1990; Mayer, Islamic Law in Libya: Analyses of Selected

Laws Enacted since the 1969 Revolution, London, 1977; Metz, ed., Libya: A Country Study, Washington, D.C., 1989; Redden, Libya in Modern Legal Systems Cyclopedia, Vol. 5, Buffalo, NY, 1990.

Malaysia

Legal History

The legal system is based on English common law, with both Islamic law and *adat* constituting significant sources of law, particularly in matters of personal status.

Parts of present-day Malaysia were under Portuguese and Dutch control, and starting from Penang in the late eighteenth century, the region eventually came under British rule, formalised by the Anglo-Dutch Treaty 1824. Malaysia and Singapore were the eventual successor states to the Straits Settlements (Penang, Singapore, Malacca), Federated Malay States (Selangor, Perak, Pahang, Negri Sembilan) and Unfederated Malay States (Perlis, Kedah, Kelantan, Trengganu, and Johor). Sabah and Sarawak, formerly constituents of British Borneo, later joined Malaysia.

Under British rule, the first legislation regulating Islamic marriage in the Straits Settlements was the Mohammedan Marriage Ordinance 1880, mainly procedural in content. The Ordinance was amended in 1908 to make registration of marriage and divorce compulsory, non-compliance being punishable by fine or imprisonment. A 1923 amendment directed the application of Islamic law to intestate succession of Muslims insofar as local custom would permit, and without disinheriting non-Muslim kin. The Ordinance continued to be applied in Penang and Malacca until State Acts were passed in 1959. The first codification of Malay customary law (a mixture of *adat* and Islamic law) came in 1915 with enactment of Laws of the Malay Courts 1915 in Sarawak.

The region was occupied by Japanese forces from 1942 to 1945, with control reverting to the British after WWII. A legislative assembly was established in 1955 and independence achieved in 1957. From 1948, the States were granted jurisdiction over application and legislation of *shariahh* and from 1952 to 1978, new laws were promulgated in the eleven Muslim-majority States of Malaysia and Sabah, generally entitled Administration of Islamic/Muslim Law Enactments and covering the official determination of Islamic law, explanation of substantive law, and jurisdiction of *syariah* courts. New laws relating to personal law were enacted in most States between 1983 and 1987.

Efforts by Kelantan State to pass a *Syariah* Criminal Code Enactment 1993 relating to the application of *hadd* penalties resulted in a stand-off between the Federal and State governments. It was passed by the State legislature but never brought into force. It was a matter of much controversy as criminal matters are within Federal and not State legislatures jurisdiction.

Schools of *Fiqh*: The majority of Muslims are Shafii, with Hanafi minorities. There are also significant Buddhist, Hindu and Christian minorities and a high proportion of followers of indigenous religions, particularly in Sabah and Sarawak (both States are Muslim-minority).

Constitutional Status of Islam(ic) Law: The Constitution was adopted on 31st August 1957 and has been amended several times. Article 3(1) declares Islam the official state religion as well as guarantees religious freedom. Articles 3(3) and (5) provide that the Ruler of each State is the head of the religion of Islam by the Constitution of that State. In the absence of a Muslim ruler (in the States of Malacca, Penang, Sabah and Sarawak) or in the Federal Territories (Kuala Lumpur and Labuan) *Yang di-Pertuan Agong* (Head of State) is declared the head of the religion of Islam.

The Ninth Schedule of the Constitution outlines the legislative lists. Malaysia is a federation of 13 States with both State and Federal level executive and legislative powers; civil law (and family law as a subset of civil law) come under the federal legislature's jurisdiction, but persons of the Malay race are defined as Muslims under the Constitution and the States are empowered to make personal laws governing Muslims and laws relating to religious offences, and to establish and regulate *syariah* courts for the application of Islamic law. Personal status law relating to non-Muslims is within the Federal legislature's jurisdiction (governed by the Malaysian Law Reform (Marriage and Divorce) Act 1976 that repealed all previous statutes on marriage and divorce governing non-Muslims). Clarification of points of Islamic law comes under the jurisdiction of each State's *Majlis* (Council of Religion and Malay Custom). The *Majlis* generally issue *fatawa* that are in keeping with Shafi'i tenets except where such may conflict with public interest. In such instances, the Councils (with the approval of State authorities) may follow minority Shafi'i views or interpretations from other three major Sunni *madhahib*.

Court System: There are three levels of *syariah* courts in a system parallel to and independent of the civil courts: *Syariah* Subordinate Courts, *Syariah* High Court and *Syariah* Appeal Court.

Syariah Subordinate Courts have jurisdiction as indicated by state legislation over criminal suits liable to punishment up to 2,000 ringgit and/or imprisonment up to two years and civil suits in which the value of the subject in dispute is up to 100,000 ringgit or not estimable in cash.

The *Syariah* High Court has appellate jurisdiction over Subordinate Court decisions in civil suits of 500 ringgit or more and criminal suits. The *Syariah* High Court has original jurisdiction as indicated by state legislation in criminal suits and civil jurisdiction over betrothal and marriage, divorce, nullification or separation, marital property claims, maintenance of dependants, legitimacy, guardianship and custody, testate and intestate succession, gifts *inter vivos* and *awqaf*, in cases where all the parties are Muslims.

The *Syariah* Appeal Court has appellate jurisdiction over decisions arising out of the *Syariah* High Court's original jurisdiction; all appeals are heard by the Chief *Syarie* Judge and two other members and decisions are by majority opinion.

In September 2000, the government announced that it would establish a separate family court.

Notable Features: The minimum marriage age is 18 for males and 16 for females, with provision for judicial permission for underage marriages. A valid marriage requires both parties consent as well as the consent of the *wali* or *syariah* judge if no *wali* is available; compulsion of wards or unreasonable objection to their valid marriage is punishable by fine and/or imprisonment.

Marriage registration is obligatory; both parties must apply to the Registrar for permission to marry at least seven days before the wedding. Marriage is not to be solemnised except in the *kariah masjid* of the woman's normal residence or by special permission to marry elsewhere. The Registrar is required to record the value and contents of items of dower given and promised at the solemnisation of marriage. There is provision for the appointment of Registrars in public offices as well as in *kariah masjid*. Non-registration is punishable by fine and/or imprisonment although it does not determine the validity of marriage.

Polygamy is allowed with judicial permission, contingent upon application to the court and a hearing with existing wife or wives. The court requires proof of necessity (e.g., first wife's sterility, physical infirmity, wilful avoidance of restitution order, etc.); proof of financial capacity; guarantee of equitable treatment of co-wives; and proof that the proposed marriage will not lower the standard of life of the existing wife or wives and other dependants. Contravention of the application procedure and permission requirements is punishable by requiring immediate payment of any outstanding dower to the existing wife or wives and by fine and/or imprisonment.

The wife's right to maintenance is subject to classical definitions of obedience. The wife may obtain a maintenance order from the court in cases where her husband fails to provide maintenance; the levels and period for which the wife might sue for arrears are not specified. The wife's disobedience can result in restitution order or punishment of fine.

Extra-judicial repudiation is punishable by fine and/or imprisonment. A husband wishing to pronounce *talaq* is required to apply for judicial permission, outlining his reasons as well as the amounts of payments of *nafkah edah* (*idda* period maintenance), *mutaah* (consolatory gift) and *maskahwin* (dower) he intends to make and provisions for the division of *harta sepencarian* (matrimonial property). If a court hearing determines the consent of the other party and the irretrievability of the breakdown, the court advises the husband's pronouncement of a single *talaq* and registers the divorce. If the other party disagrees or the court is not convinced of irretrievable breakdown, the court begins conciliation efforts. The conciliation committee has up to six months to effect a conciliation; if the committee fails to do so, it issues a certificate of its failure, including any recommendations regarding custody, maintenance, division of property, etc. (The Act only provides penalties for extra-judicial repudiations and does not refer to their validity; courts tend to adjudicate on the validity of a *talaq* pronounced outside of court on the basis of classical law.)

The wife may apply for judicial dissolution on the following grounds: the husband's disappearance for over one year; failure to maintain for three months; sentencing to three years or more in prison; failure to perform marital obligations for one year; continued impotence, if the wife was unaware of it upon marriage; mental illness lasting two years or leprosy, vitalgo or communicable venereal disease; the wife's repudiation of a marriage concluded by her father or grandfather before she attained 16, if she is below 18 years and the marriage was not consummated; cruel treatment; husband's refusal to consummate for four months; invalidity of her consent (obtained under duress, mistaken, etc.); and any other grounds for dissolution or nullification recognised in *hukm shar*. A wife divorced without just cause may apply for maintenance during her *idda* and *muta*, levels of which are to be set by the court.

The court also divides assets acquired by joint effort during marriage, and may also order the division of assets acquired by sole efforts, with consideration of the contribution made by the other party in terms of housework and caring for the family, though the other party will in all cases receive the smaller portion. The divorced wife is also entitled to reside in the marital home during the *idda* or until the expiry of her custody or her remarriage, if the former husband cannot provide other suitable accommodation.

The divorced mother is entitled to custody over boys until seven years and girls until nine years, subject to classical conditions. The court may extend custody to nine and eleven years respectively upon the *hadina* application. After the expiry of the *hadinah*'s custody, the father becomes custodian, with the proviso that wards having reached the age of discernment may choose with which parent to live, unless the court directs otherwise.

Succession is governed by classical law as modified by Malay custom. This is particularly important in rural areas and with reference to the inheritance of land, as all Malay *adat* have specific rules on inheritance of land and such rules are often inconsistent with Islamic law. For example, inheritance in Malaccan *adat* is matrilineal.

Notable Cases

Law/Case Reporting System: Case reporting of Federal Court and High Court decisions is through the *Malayan Law Journal*. Law reporting is through the Federal and State *Official Gazettes*. Some *Syariah* Court judgements are included in some issues of the *Syariah Law Journal* of the International Islamic University of Malaysia.

International Conventions (with Relevant Reservations): Malaysia acceded to the CEDAW in 1995 with a number of reservations relating to discriminatory aspects of customary and personal status laws and discrimination to appointments in public office (particularly relating to the offices of *mufti* or *qadi*). These reservations were withdrawn in 1998. The reservation to Article 11 on elimination of discrimination against women in employment still stands, stating that "Malaysia interprets the provisions of this article as a reference to the prohibition of discrimination on the basis of equality between men and women only".

Malaysia acceded to the CRC in 1995 with a general reservation to Articles 1, 2, 7, 13, 14, 15, 22, 28, 37, 40(3) & (4), 44 and 45, declaring that "said provisions shall be applicable only if they are in conformity with the Constitution, national laws and national policies of the Government of Malaysia." (The articles mentioned relate to majority, measures to eliminate discrimination against children, birth registration and nationality rights, children's freedom of expression, religion, and association, adoption, right to education, children's rights and liberties in criminal law, the system of reporting to the CRC and co-operation with UNICEF.)

Background and Sources: Hooker, Islamic Law in South-East Asia, Singapore, 1984; Ibrahim, Family Law in Malaysia and Singapore, Singapore, 1984; Kamali, "Islamic Law in Malaysia: Issues and Developments," Yearbook of Islamic and Middle Eastern Law, Vol. 4 (1998): 158-179; Mahmood, Malaysia in Statutes of Personal Law in Islamic Countries, 2nd ed. New Delhi, 1995; Redden, Malaysia in Modern Legal Systems Cyclopedia, Vol. 9, New York, 1990; Selangor, Administration of Islamic Law Enactment 1989 and Islamic Family Law Enactment 1984 (as at 15th September 1991), comp. by Legal Research Board, Kuala Lumpur, 1992; Siraj, "Women and the Law: Significant Developments in Malaysia," Law and Society Review, Vol. 28, No. 3 (1994): 561-581.

Republic of Maldives

Legal History

The Republic of Maldives was never under direct British

rule. As the British came to control virtually all of the area of the Indian Ocean by the late nineteenth century, the Maldivian Sultan established an agreement with the Governor of Ceylon in 1887. This agreement allowed the Maldives to enjoy the status of a protected state without actually becoming a protectorate. Thus, the British only controlled external affairs and had no jurisdiction to involve themselves in the internal matters of the islands (although it is said that attempts at interference in internal affairs were made at times). The Maldives obtained full independence from their protected status under the United Kingdom in July 1965.

The legal system is based on an admixture of Islamic law and English common law, with the latter being more influential in some areas, such as commercial law. With relation to personal status, the basis for the law is the *shariah*, as adapted to the modern Maldivian judicial system. Much of what is known about the legal history of the Maldives is of an anecdotal nature and is drawn from the works of travellers who had visited the islands at different times. There are indications that Persians had visited the islands by the sixth century, and there are also numerous accounts of European travellers such as the Frenchman Franois Pyrard who was shipwrecked in the Maldives in 1602. One of the most well-known travelogues including the Maldives is that of ibn Battuta who served as the chief *Qadi* of the islands for over a year. From his own account, he attempted to enforce certain *hadd* penalties, e.g., for theft (though it is not clear whether he actually introduced or reinstated them); some of these punishments were unknown to the Maldivians and later fell into disuse. Article 7 of the Maldivian Constitution prohibits the infliction of physical injury.

Schools of *Fiqh*: Maldivians are mainly Shafi'i with a Ja'fari minority, though the Maliki school predominated until the sixteenth century. The only non-Muslim Maldivian residents are expatriates as Maldivian citizenship is only granted to Muslims.

Constitutional Status of Islam(ic) Law: Before conversion to Islam, Arabic and Persian sources indicate that women often served as rulers of the Maldives. Historical records indicate that there has long been some form of democracy in the Maldives, with the Sultans role being similar to that of a Constitutional monarch. The Sultan was aided by a number of councils, of which he (or she) was an equal member. There is evidence of Sultans being deposed for deviating from normal procedures and precedents against the advice of their counsellors. There have been at least three Sultanas in the Maldives. The accounts of women rulers date back to the fourteenth century. There have also been a number of cases where men have served in the office of Sultan in the name of the legitimate female successors. Ibn Battuta said of this that "[i]t is a strange thing about these islands that their ruler is a woman, Khadija Where (her father) was deposed, none of the royal house remained but Khadija and her two younger sisters, so they raised Khadija to the throne."

The first written constitution of the Maldives was adopted in 1932 and was based on customs and conventions and the traditional modes of administration. The Maldives were established as a republic in 1953 but the sultanate was restored the following year. After a referendum on the issue in April of 1968, the sultanate was abolished and the Maldives again established as a republic.

The current Constitution came into effect on 1st January 1998. Article 1 identifies was adopted identifies Maldives as a democratic republic based on the principles of Islam. Article 7 states that Islam is the state religion. Article 16 allows for criminal defense in accordance with *shariah*. Article 23 protects property rights, except as provided by law or *shariah*. Article 25 allows for limits on free expression for the purpose of protecting the basic tenets of Islam; Article 38 states that the President is the supreme authority to propagate the tenets of Islam; Article 156 states that law includes the norms and provisions of *shariah*.

Court System: The Republic of the Maldives has a highly decentralised system of administration; a result of geographic exigencies as the country is made up of approximately 200 inhabited and almost 1,000 uninhabited islands. The administrative units are organised into 19 atolls, with each atoll governed by an atoll chief (*atholhuvarin*) appointed by the President. There is also a magistrate or *ghazi* on each inhabited island who deals with legal and criminal matters. Serious cases are referred to the courts in Male, the capital and twentieth administrative unit. The High Court sits in Male and, in addition to being the ultimate court of appeal, also handles any politically sensitive cases; there are also eight lower courts in Male dealing with theft, debt or property cases. There are no jury trials. Judges are appointed by the President and removable by him, and they must be Muslims. *Shariah* is incorporated into legal system.

Notable Features: According to custom, the minimum age for marriage is 15; the Law on the Protection of the Rights of the Child discourages marriage before the age of 16.

In the case of divorce, children under seven years will, primarily, remain with their mother; if this is not deemed appropriate (if, for example, the mother is to remarry and have other children), custody will be offered to the maternal grandmother, the paternal grandmother or the father, in descending order of priority. Children over the age of seven years can choose in whose custody they wish to remain.

Law/Case Reporting System: Government Gazette

International Conventions and Reports to Treaty Governing Bodies: The Maldives signed the CRC in 1990 and ratified it in 1991. Reservations made upon signature relate to the Islamic *shariah* being one of the fundamental sources of Maldivian Law and not recognising the system of adoption, as well as to the provision relating to children's freedom of religion because "the Constitution and the Laws of the Republic of Maldives stipulate that all Maldivians should be Muslims". The reservations to Articles 14 and 21 were reiterated upon ratification.

The Maldives acceded to the CEDAW in 1993, with general reservations regarding any provisions contradictory to the *shariah* or Maldivian tradition and legal and constitutional autonomy.

Background and Sources: Initial reports of States parties due in 1993 : Maldives 05/08/96. CRC/C/8/Add.33; Bell, The Maldives Islands: Report on a Visit to Male, January 20 to February 21, 1920, Colombo, 1921; Ellis and Amarasinghe, Guide to Maldives, Buckinghamshire, England, 1995; Ibn Battuta, Travels in Asia and Africa 1325-1354, trans. Gibb, Exeter, 1983; Maloney, People of the Maldives Islands, New Delhi, 1980; Redden, Maldives in Modern Legal Systems Cyclopedia, Vol. 9 Buffalo, N.Y., 1990; Robinson, ed. The Cambridge Encyclopaedia of India, Pakistan, Bangladesh, Sri Lanka, Nepal, Bhutan and the Maldives, Cambridge, 1989.

Morocco, Kingdom of (and Western Sahara)

Legal History

Spanish and Portuguese power in Morocco and the Western Sahara was in its ascendancy in the fifteenth century, with several coastal areas being the subject of rival claims. By the early twentieth century, the British acknowledged Morocco as part of the French sphere of influence, with Morocco being divided between Spain and France in 1904. A French protectorate was established in 1912. Spanish Morocco faced fierce resistance and a revolt in 1920 nearly succeeded in driving the Spanish out, when a French and Spanish alliance re-established Spanish authority in 1926. Morocco gained independence from France in 1956 and Spain relinquished authority over most of its Moroccan holdings during the same period. The status of the Western Sahara remains unresolved, with contesting claims on the part of the Moroccan state and the Polisario Front (Popular Front for the

Liberation of the Saquia el-Hamra and Rio de Oro) which proclaimed a government in exile of the Sahrawi Arab Democratic Republic (SADR) in February 1976. The region was divided between Morocco and Mauritania in April of that year, with Morocco taking over the remaining one-third of the territory soon after Mauritania succumbed to pressure from Polisario in 1979 and abandoned its claims. Preparations for a long-delayed UN-sponsored referendum on the future of the territory continue.

Under French and Spanish rule, the colonial legal systems influenced local developments outside of the sphere of family law. *Shariah* courts continued to apply Maliki *fiqh* during the first half of the century (in addition to local tribunals applying customary law). Following independence in 1956, a Law Reform Commission was established in order to draft a code of personal status. A Code was passed into law within the next year, based on dominant Maliki doctrines as well as *takhayyur*, *maslaha*, and legislation from other Muslim countries (perhaps most importantly the Tunisian Code of Personal Status 1956). Article 82 of the Code directs that "[w]ith regard to anything not covered by this law, reference shall be made to the most appropriate or accepted opinion or prevailing practice of the school of Imam Malik". Major amendments to the Codes provisions relating to marriage guardianship, polygamy, *talaq* and *muta al-talaq* were made in 1993.

Schools of *Fiqh*: The Maliki school is the predominant *madhhab* in Morocco. There are also Jewish and Christian minorities.

Constitutional Status of Islam(ic) Law: The Constitution was adopted on 10th March 1972, and has undergone major revisions in 1992 and 1996. Article 6 declares Islam the official state religion and guarantees freedom of worship for all citizens.

Court System: There are four levels of courts; 27 *sadad* courts, 30 regional courts, 9 courts of appeal and the Supreme Court in Rabat [figures as of late 1980s]. The *sadad* and regional courts are divided into four sections: *shariah*; rabbinical; civil, commercial and administrative; and penal. *Sadad* courts are courts of first instance for Muslim and Jewish personal law. *Shariah* sections of regional courts also hear all matters of Islamic law affecting Moroccan Muslims.

Notable Features: The minimum marriage age is 18 years for males and 15 for females. There is scope for judicial discretion for males under 18 if there is fear of immorality. Marriage of a minor below the age of majority (*rushd*) requires the guardians consent, and if the guardian refuses, the parties may take matter to court.

Compatibility of age in marriage is the sole right of the wife. The marriage guardian is not to contract the marriage of his ward unless she authorises it. The *walis* right of coercion (*ijbar*) under certain circumstances was revoked under the 1993 amendments to the Code. The ward may take the matter to court if her guardian refuses consent for her marriage, and if a ward of the age of majority has no father, she may choose either to appoint a *wali* of her choice or contract her own marriage.

The provisions relating to registration include the requirement of a notarised contract before two witnesses. Preliminaries include the filing of documents attesting to the identity, age, domicile, guardians name, husband's personal status, and proof of dissolution for previously married women, as well as specification of the dower.

Polygamy is not permitted in case of fear of unequal treatment. There is a requirement of notification for the second wife, and the 1993 amendments to the Code also require notification of the existing wife. A woman who did not insert a stipulation restricting her husband's right to marry polygamously in the marriage contract and whose husband does so may request a judicial divorce on grounds of harm.

The Code specifies maintenance as one of the rights of the wife, and obedience as one of the rights of the husband.

Talaq must be registered in the presence of two male witnesses and, under the 1993 amendments, in the wife's presence (unless she fails to appear at the summons), within the jurisdiction of the marital residence. If *talaq* is found to have been exercised while the wife is menstruating, the judge shall oblige the husband to revoke it. *Talaq* uttered while intoxicated, under coercion, enraged, upon condition, by oath or with intention to coerce is ineffective. *Talaq* to which a number is attached is effective as a single revocable repudiation (except third of three). The wife may seek a judicial divorce on the following grounds: husband's non-maintenance; husband's grave and incurable or long-term defect though such right is forfeit if the wife married in full knowledge of the defect or if it occurred after the contract and she implicitly or explicitly accepted it; such harm caused by the husband as makes cohabitation impossible (after reconciliation efforts); husband's absence for over one year without valid reason; and husband's oath of abstinence if he does not comply with a judicial decision allowing four months grace period. All judicial divorces are irrevocable except divorce granted because of the husband's oath of abstinence or inability to maintain. Regulations relating to *khul* are based on classical law. The divorcing husband is obliged to pay compensation if the *talaq* was on his part. The 1993 amendments to the Code add to this that the *qadi* shall assess the injury sustained by the arbitrarily divorced wife in awarding compensation, with no upper or lower limits set to compensation awards. The divorced mother has right of custody until puberty for sons and until marriage for daughters.

Matters of testate and intestate succession are covered in Books V and VI of the Code of Personal Status, respectively. Obligatory bequests were introduced in favour of orphaned grandchildren by predeceased sons, how low so ever.

Notable Cases

Law/Case Reporting System: Law reports are published in the *Bulletin Officiel.*

International Conventions (with Relevant Reservations): Morocco signed the ICCPR and ICESCR in 1977 and ratified both in 1979 without submitting any reservations.

Morocco signed the CRC in 1990 and ratified it in 1993, with a reservation to Article 14 according children freedom of religion, "in view of the fact that Islam is the State religion".

Morocco acceded to the CEDAW in 1993. Morocco submitted the following declarations: Morocco confirmed its willingness to apply the provisions of Article 2 on the elimination of discrimination provided that they do not "prejudice the constitutional requirement that regulates the rules of succession to the throne(and) do not conflict with the provisions of the Islamic *shariah*"; Morocco also stated that, with respect to Article 15(4), "Morocco declares that it can only be bound by the provisions of this paragraph, in particular those relating to the right of women to choose their residence and domicile, to the extent that they are not incompatible with Articles 34 and 36 of the Moroccan Code of Personal Status". Morocco also submitted the following reservations: Morocco's reservation relating to Article 15(4) states that "the Law of Moroccan Nationality permits a child to bear the nationality of its mother only in the cases where it is born to an unknown or to a stateless father, when born in Morocco"; Morocco also expressed reservations regarding Article 16 stating that equality in family law "is considered incompatible with the Islamic *shariah*, which guarantees to each of the spouses rights and responsibilities within a framework of equilibrium and complementary in order to preserve the sacred bond of matrimony".

Background and Sources: El Alami and Hinchcliffe, Islamic Marriage and Divorce Laws of the Arab World, London, 1996; Blanc and Zeidguy, compiled by Moudawana:

Code de Statut Personnel et des Successions edition Synoptique Franco-Arabe), 1996; Mahmood, Morocco in Statutes of Personal Law in Islamic Countries, 2nd ed., New Delhi, 1995; Mir-Hosseini, Marriage on Trial: A Study of Islamic Family Law, Iran and Morocco Compared, London, 1993; Nasir, The Islamic Law of Personal Status, 2nd ed., London, 1990; Pearl, A Textbook on Muslim Personal Law, 2nd ed., London, 1987; Redden, Morocco inModern Legal Systems Cyclopedia, Vol. 6, Buffalo, NY, 1990; Welchman, "Islamic Marriage and Divorce Laws of the Arab World by El Alami and Hinchcliffe," (book review) Yearbook of Islamic and Middle Eastern Law, Vol. 3 (1996): 547-550.

Federal Republic of Nigeria

Legal History

The legal system is based on English common law, Islamic law, and customary law.

Lagos was annexed by Britain in 1861. The Oil Rivers Protectorate was established by treaties with Yoruba rulers. By 1900 the British controlled all of present-day Nigeria. Due to the system of indirect rule, traditional authorities retained powers over their communities. The British introduced a statutory monogamous marriage regime with 1914 Marriage Act.

Nigeria gained independence from Britain in 1960. A military coup in 1966 marked beginning of long period of military rule punctuated by brief periods of civilian rule (1979-1983, 1999).

The Muslim Fulani Usman dan Fodio led a *jihad* (Fulani *Jihad* or Sokoto *Jihad*) against the Hausa aristocracy in the Kingdom of Gobir in northern Nigeria in the early nineteenth century, establishing a new empire with its capital at Sokoto under which an elaborate *shariah* court structure developed. The British adapted Emirs Judicial Councils from the existing judicial structures in northern Nigeria; these continued to serve as appellate courts in the emirates until the establishment of the *Shariah* Court of Appeal in 1959. Judicial reforms initiated in the late 1960s created grades of *alkalis* (*qadis*) courts; initially there were four grades and as of reforms in the late 1970s, three grades. The first instance courts established were Area Courts Grades 2 and 1, then the Upper Area Court and the Upper Area Court of Appeal, with the highest state level appellate jurisdiction lying with the *Shariah* Court of Appeal in each state.

Schools of *Fiqh*: About half the population is Muslim, about 40 per cent Christian, and about 10 per cent practice traditional indigenous religions or no religion.

Constitutional Status of Islam(ic) Law: The current Constitution was adopted in 1999. Six new states were established in 1996, bringing the total number of states to 36, in addition to the Federal Territory of Abuja. Part 2.10 of the Constitution states that "The Government of the Federation or of a State shall not adopt any religion as State Religion".

Court System: The Supreme Court is the highest federal court, with appellate jurisdiction over the lower federal courts and the highest state courts. Each state has its own judicial system, including Magistrates or District Courts (first instance in civil and criminal matters) and a High Court (original and appellate jurisdiction). The Constitution also provides that states may establish lower and appellate customary courts having limited civil jurisdiction. The northern states have separate *shariah* courts to administer Islamic personal law.

The Constitution provides for establishment of higher *shariah* courts. Article 236(1) establishing Court of Appeal provides that of at least 15 judges, no less than three shall be well-versed in Islamic law and no less than three in customary law; Court of Appeal hears appeals from Federal High Court, State High Courts, *Shariah* Courts of Appeal, and Customary Courts of Appeal. Article 259(1) provides for *Shariah* Courts of Appeal for any States requiring them. *Shariah* Courts of Appeal consist of a Grand *Kadi* and as many *Kadis* as State Assembly prescribes, with at least two *Kadis* hearing appeals.

The 1999 Constitution also provides that the Federal Government is to establish a Federal Shariah Court of Appeal and Final Court of Appeal; however, the Government had not yet established such courts.

Notable Features: In terms of child custody, the Matrimonial Causes Act 1970 is applicable to custody suits arising out of the dissolution of civil, customary and Islamic marriages; in all custody matters, the Act directs that the interests of the child shall be paramount.

Shariah courts apply classical Maliki *fiqh* to matters of personal status and succession.

Notable Cases

Law/Case Reporting System: Decisions of higher *shariah* courts are published in *Shariah Law Reports* (Zaria, Nigeria) and *Islamic Law Reports* (Katsina, Katsina State); both are published irregularly. Case reporting of higher court decisions is published in *All Nigeria Law Reports* and *Supreme Court Digest*. Law reporting is through *Official Gazette of the Federal Republic of Nigeria*, and State *Official Gazettes.*

International Conventions (with Relevant Reservations): Nigeria acceded to the ICCPR and ICESCR in 1993, without reservations.

Nigeria signed the CEDAW in 1984 and ratified it in 1985, without reservations.

Nigeria signed the CRC in 1990 and ratified it in 1991, without reservations.

Sultanate of Oman

Legal History

Omani tribes adopted the tenets of Ibadi Islam in the seventh-eighth century, European incursions into the area of present-day Oman began with the Portuguese in the early sixteenth century. The expulsion of the Portuguese in 1650 was followed by a period of ascendancy of Omani power in

Gulf and Indian Ocean region; by the end of the 1600s, the Omani empire included Bahrain and Zanzibar. The decline of the empire began in the following century. Omani leaders signed treaties of protection with the British in 1798 and 1800 as French interest in Indian Ocean increased and a series of treaties and agreements concluded with the British in the nineteenth century brought Oman under increasing British influence, with an 1891 treaty bringing Oman under British protection. The sovereignty of the Sultanate of Oman and Muscat was formally recognised in 1951 under Sultan Said ibn Taimur.

Efforts at judicial reform began with the overthrow of the previous Sultan (Said bin Taimur, r. 1932-1970) by his son Qaboos in a bloodless coup supported by the British. Since that time, Oman has adopted a number of codes relating to commercial, criminal, labour, and tax laws, among other areas. Personal status remains unlegislated. Efforts at regulating the *shariah* courts were unsuccessful, leading to the establishment of separate courts and judicial tribunals to enforce state law beginning in the 1970s. There are both *shariah* and state courts now, with the former applying Ibadi law within an increasingly limited area of jurisdiction, and the latter applying those laws promulgated by royal decree. Ultimate appeal lies with the Sultan. There have been tentative efforts at establishing a more representative form of government. Sultan Qaboos introduced a *Majlis al-Istishari* (consultative council) in 1981, an informal advisory body comprised entirely of appointed members. This was replaced by a *Majlis al-Shura* in 1990 with members chosen by the Sultan from slates of three citizens put forward by notables of each district. The new *Majlis* is empowered to review legislation and state development plans and adopt and recommend amendments by a two-thirds majority.

Schools of *Fiqh*: Oman is the only state in which the Ibadi School is the predominant *madhhab*. There are also Sunni and Shi'i minorities, as well as Hindu and Christian (mainly expatriate) communities.

Constitutional Status of Islam(ic) Law. In November 1996 a Basic Law, in effect a constitution was decreed by Sultan Qaboos to regulate several important areas of governance. Chapter 1 of the Basic Law is entitled. The State and the System of Government. Article 2 declares Islam the official state religion, and provides that the *shariah* is "the basis for legislation".

Court System: The judiciary is comprised of *shariah* courts, magistrate courts, and several specialised courts and tribunals. *Shariah* courts hear civil and minor criminal cases, and judgments are made according to Ibadi doctrine. The Court of Appeal in Muscat staffed by three *qadis* hears appeals from the first instance *shariah* courts. The highest level of judiciary is Complaints Committee.

Since the 1970s, the jurisdiction of *shariah* courts has been reduced. Magistrates Courts hear misdemeanor cases. The Criminal Court in Muscat hears cases involving felonies and serves as appellate court. Other specialised courts and quasi-judicial tribunals in various areas of land, commercial, labour and tax law apply state-issued legislation.

The Sultan issued several royal decrees to establish a law on judicial authority and to affirm the independence of the judiciary as called for in the 1996 Basic Charter. The decrees formally establish the judiciary as an independent, hierarchical system composed of a Supreme Court, an appeals court, primary courts (one located in each region), and, within the primary courts, divisional courts. Within each of the courts there are to be divisions to handle commercial, civil, penal, labour, taxation, general, and personal cases (the latter under *Shariah*). The general prosecutor, which currently falls under the Royal Omani Police Chief Inspector, is to become an independent legal entity. Implementation of these decrees is expected to take place during 2000.

Notable Features: Classical Ibadi *fiqh* is applied to personal status matters.

Notable Cases

Law/Case Reporting System: Law reports of Royal Decrees and Ministerial Decisions are published in the *Official Gazette.*

International Conventions (with Relevant Reservations): Oman acceded to the CRC in 1996 with a number of reservations. The reservation to Article 21 states that a general reservation is submitted to provisions that do not accord with Islamic law or the Sultanates state legislation, particularly those provisions relating to adoption. The reservation to Articles 14 and 30 states that Oman does not consider itself bound by those provisions that grant children the freedom of religion or that "allow a child belonging to a religious minority to profess his or her own religion".

Background and Sources: Amin, Middle East Legal Systems, Glasgow, 1985; El Alami and Hinchcliffe, The Uncodified Law in Islamic Marriage and Divorce Laws of the Arab World, London, 1996; Ballantyne, Commercial Law in the Arab Middle East: The Gulf States, London, 1986; Mahmood, Gulf in Statutes of Personal Law in Islamic Countries, 2nd ed., New Delhi, 1995; Redden, Oman in Modern Legal Systems Cyclopedia, Vol. 5, Buffalo, NY, 1990; Riphenburg, Oman: Political Development in a Changing World, London, 1998.

Islamic Republic of Pakistan

Legal History

[see also: **Legal History, Republic of India**] The legal system is based on English common law with provisions to accommodate Pakistan's status as an Islamic state, most notably in the area of personal status, but also to some extent in the areas of criminal law and commercial law.

After the partition of India in 1947, the legislation relating to Muslim family law introduced in British India continued to govern personal status. A seven-member Commission on

Marriage and Family Laws was established in 1955 with a remit to consider the personal status laws applicable in the new state and determine the areas needing reform. The Commission submitted its report in 1956, suggesting a number of reforms, including, for example, the consideration of all triple *talaqs* (except for the third of three) as single, revocable repudiations. The report led to much debate, with many leading *ulama* (including Maulana Abul Ala Maududi, leader of the *Jamaat-i-Islami*) opposing its recommendations. The Muslim Family Laws Ordinance 1961 adopted some of the provisions of the Report of the Marriage and Family Laws Commission, aiming to reform divorce law and inheritance law relating to orphaned grandchildren, introduce compulsory marriage registration, place restrictions on the practice of polygamy, and reform the law relating to dower and maintenance in marriage and divorce, as well as to amend existing legislation with relation to marriage age. Again, various sectors of the *ulama* regarded this as unjustified interference or tampering with the classical law. When the first Constitution of Pakistan was finally promulgated in 1956, it included a provision that came to be referred to as the repugnancy clause. This clause stated that no law repugnant to Islamic injunctions would be enacted and that all existing laws would be considered in light of this provision, in order to institute appropriate amendments. This repugnancy provision has been retained and actually strengthened in the succeeding Constitutions.

After a military take-over in 1999, the Constitution was again suspended. During 2000, discussions continued about possible amendments to the Constitution.

Schools of *Fiqh*: The predominant *madhhab* is the Hanafi, and there are sizeable Ja'fari and Isma'ili minorities. The legal status of the Ahmadis is somewhat unclear. They self-identify as Sunni Muslims, but were declared non-Muslims by the state. In 1974, then-Prime Minister Zulfiqar Ali Bhutto finally conceded to a long-standing campaign waged by conservative religious elements agitating for the official designation of Ahmadis as non-Muslims. There have been Ahmadi initiatives to adopt a modified version of the Muslim Family Laws Ordinance 1961 to be applied to Ahmadi personal status cases. There are also Christian, Zoroastrian, Hindu, Sikh and Jewish minorities in Pakistan.

Constitutional Status of Islamic Law: The third Constitution was adopted on 10th April 1973, suspended in 1977, and re-instituted in 1985; it has undergone numerous amendments over time. It was suspended again in 1999 and remained suspended at the time of writing.

Article 1 of the Constitution declares that Pakistan shall be known as "the Islamic Republic of Pakistan" and Article 2 declares Islam the state religion. In 1985, the Objectives Resolution contained in the preamble of the Constitution was made a substantive provision by the insertion of Article 2A, thereby requiring all laws to be brought into consonance with the Quran and *sunnah*. Chapter 3A establishes the Federal *Shariaht* Court and stipulates that the Court shall take up the examination of any law or provision of law that may be repugnant to the "[i]njunctions of Islam, as laid down in the Holy Quran and the *Sunnah*". If a law or provision is determined to be repugnant, the Court is to provide notice to the federal or provincial government specifying the reasons for the decision. The Court may also examine any decisions relating to the application of the *hudud* penalties which have been decided by any criminal court, and may suspend the sentence if there is any question as to the correctness, legality or propriety of any finding, sentence or order or the regularity of the proceedings. The Supreme Court also has a *Shariaht* Appellate Bench empowered to review the decisions of the Federal *Shariaht* Court and consisting of three Muslim Supreme Court judges and up to two *ulama*. Part IX of the Constitution is entitled Islamic Provisions and provides for the Islamisation of all existing laws, reiterating that no laws shall be enacted which are repugnant to the injunctions of Islam. An explanation appended to Part IX clarifies that, with respect to personal law, the expression "Quran and *Sunnah*" means the laws of any sect as interpreted by that sect.

The Islamic provisions also provide for the creation of an Islamic Ideology Council of 8 to 20 members appointed by the President. They must have "knowledge of the principles and philosophy of Islam as enunciated in the Holy Quran and *Sunnah*, or understanding of the economic, political, legal or administrative problems of Pakistan." The Islamic Council is meant to represent various schools of thought as far as that may be practical, and at least one woman should be appointed. Its function is to make recommendations to the *Majlis-e-Shoora* (Parliament) and the Provincial Assemblies "as to the ways and means of enabling and encouraging the Muslims of Pakistan to order their lives individually and collectively in all respects in accordance with the principles and concepts of Islam as enunciated in the Holy Quran and *Sunnah*." The Council also determines for the federal and provincial governments whether or not proposed laws are repugnant, and compiles for them in suitable form "such Injunctions of Islam as can be given legislative effect."

Court System: The judiciary is composed of three levels of federal courts, three divisions of lower courts, and a Supreme Judicial Council. There are district courts in every district of each province, having both civil and criminal jurisdiction though they deal mainly with civil matters. The High Court of each province has jurisdiction over civil and criminal appeals from lower courts within the provinces. The Supreme Court sits in Islamabad and has exclusive jurisdiction over disputes between or among federal and provincial governments, and appellate jurisdiction over High Court decisions. There is also a Federal *Shariaht* Court established by Presidential Order on 26th May 1980. This Court has exclusive jurisdiction to determine, upon petition by any citizen or the federal or provincial governments or on its own motion, whether or not a law conforms to the injunctions of

Islam. An Islamic advisory council of *ulama* assists the Federal *Shariaht* Court in this capacity.

The West Pakistan Family Courts Act 1964 continues to govern the jurisdiction and functioning of the Pakistani Family Courts; the Act was never applied to East Pakistan before Bangladeshi independence. Appeals from the Family Courts lie with the High Court only. The Family Courts have exclusive jurisdiction over matters pertaining to the dissolution of marriage, dower, maintenance, the restitution of conjugal rights, the custody of children, and guardianship.

Notable Features: The West Pakistan Muslim Personal Law (*Shariaht*) Application Act 1962 repealed the 1937 Muslim Personal Law (*Shariaht*) Application Act as well as provincial legislation on the application of Muslim personal law. The new Act directs the application of Muslim personal law, notwithstanding any custom or usage, to all questions of personal status and succession where the parties are Muslims. One particular provision of the new legislation states that, "[t]he limited estates in respect of immovable property held by Muslim females under the customary law are hereby terminated"; this constitutes the opposite stance to customary land law to the 1937 enactment, and so the new Act provides that it will not apply retrospectively.

The Child Marriage Restraint Act 1929 introduced penal sanctions for contracting child marriages. The minimum marriage age as the Act currently stands is 18 for males and 16 for females. Despite the provision of penalties for contracting under-age marriages, such unions are not rendered invalid. The issue of marriage guardianship is governed by classical law; according to the Hanafi school, an adult woman may contract her marriage without a *wali*, but the influence of custom is strong, as shown by the events surrounding the Saima Waheed case. In *Abdul Waheed v. Asma Jehangir* (PLD 1997 Lah 331), the question put before the Court was whether or not an adult Hanafi Muslim woman may contract herself in marriage without the consent of her *wali*. In this particular case, the woman was an adult Hanafi Muslim of 22 years of age who contracted a marriage with a college lecturer without the knowledge of her parents. Her father disapproved of her choice and attempted to file a suit under the *Zina* Ordinance 1979. The majority judgement of the Lahore High Court held that the basic essential requirement for the validity of the contract was the woman's consent to the marriage, and not that of the *wali*. However, the tone of the discussion, including the recognition of the customary role of the *wali*, the endorsement of *purdah* (i.e., separation of men and women in public life), the focus on moral decline, the setting of the judgement (largely in terms of *shariah* law, with little reference to the Constitution) and the call for legislation on the matter, all indicate that the classical Hanafi position and customary dictates are not in full accordance. As well, the decisions of the Federal *Shariah* Court on matters relative to family law were held to be binding on the High Courts, while the Constitution had expressly barred the Federal *Shariah* Court from interfering with Muslim personal law. Some commentators predict this may lead to a "gradual erosion of the protective features of the MFLO 1961".

The Muslim Family Laws Ordinance 1961 introduced reforms to various aspects of the classical law. The reforms concern the registration of marriage and divorce, inheritance rights of orphaned grandchildren, restrictions on polygamy, consideration of every *talaq* (except the third of three) as single and revocable, formalisation of reconciliation procedures in disputes relating to maintenance or dissolution of marriage, and recovery of *mahr*, along with specified penalties for non-compliance.

The MFLO introduced marriage registration and provides for penalties of fines or imprisonment for failure to register. However, a Muslim marriage is still legal if it is contracted only according to the religious requisites. The MFLO also instituted some limited reforms in the law relating to polygamy, with the introduction of the requirement that the husband must submit an application and pay a fee to the local

Union Council in order to obtain prior written permission for contracting a polygamous marriage. The application must state the reasons for the proposed marriage and indicate whether the applicant has obtained the consent of the existing wife or wives. The chairman of the Union Council forms an Arbitration Council with representatives of the existing wife or wives and the applicant in order to determine the necessity of the proposed marriage. The penalty for contracting a polygamous marriage without prior permission is that the husband must immediately pay the entire dower to the existing wife or wives as well as being subject to a fine and/or imprisonment; any polygamous marriage contracted without the Union Council's approval cannot be registered under the MFLO. Nevertheless, if a man does not seek the permission of his existing wife or the Union Council, his subsequent marriage remains valid. Furthermore, the difficulty in enforcing resort to the application process to the Union Council, combined with the judiciary's reluctance to apply the penalties contained in the MFLO (as indicated by the case law), tend to restrict the efficacy of the reform provisions. This has led some observers to describe the provisions requiring the permission of the Arbitration Council as a mere formality.

Efforts were also made to reform the classical law as it relates to the exercise of *talaq*. The MFLO requires that the divorcing husband shall, as soon as possible after a *talaq* pronounced "in any form whatsoever", give the chairman of the Union Council notice in writing. The chairman is to supply a copy of the notice to the wife. Non-compliance is punishable by imprisonment and/or a fine. Within thirty days of receipt of the notice of repudiation, the chairman must constitute an Arbitration Council in order to take steps to bring about a reconciliation. Should that fail, a *talaq* that is not revoked, either expressly or implicitly, takes effect after the expiry of ninety days from the day on which the notice of repudiation was delivered to the chairman. If the wife is pregnant at the time of the pronouncement of *talaq*, the *talaq* does not take effect until ninety days have elapsed or the end of the pregnancy, whichever is later. The classical law regarding the requirement of an intervening marriage in order to remarry a former husband who has repudiated the same woman three times is retained. Failure to notify invalidated the *talaq* until the late 1970s and early 1980s, but the introduction of the *Zina* Ordinance allowed scope for abuse as repudiated wives were left open to charges of *zina* if their husbands had not followed the MFLOs notification procedure. Thus, judicial practice has, since the early 1980s, recognised as valid repudiations in contravention of the notification procedure. The rules regarding notification and arbitration apply, *mutatis mutandis* and so far as applicable, to delegated divorce (*talaq al-tafwid*), or to marriage dissolved other than by *talaq*. The chairman of the Union Council will also constitute an Arbitration Council to determine the matter in cases where a husband fails to maintain his wife or wives, or fails to maintain co-wives equitably (at the application of one or more wife or wives, and in addition to their seeking any other legal remedy). Any outstanding dower or maintenance not paid in due time is recoverable as arrears of land revenue. Also, where no details regarding the mode of payment of *mahr* are recorded in the marriage contract, the entire sum of the dower stipulated therein is presumed to be payable as prompt dower.

The MFLO also introduced a significant reform to the classical law of inheritance by allowing for orphaned grandchildren by predeceased sons or daughters to inherit from their maternal or paternal grandparents.

The Dissolution of Muslim Marriages Act 1939 continues to govern divorce in Pakistan. The Act has been amended by the Muslim Family Laws Ordinance 1961 to include the contracting of a polygamous marriage in contravention of the MFLO in the grounds entitling a woman to a decree for the dissolution of her marriage. Another amendment raises the age at which a woman has to have been married by her father or other guardian to exercise her option of puberty from 15 to 16; thus, the option of puberty may be exercised if the girl was married before the age of 16 if she repudiates the marriage before the age of 18 so long as the marriage was not consummated. The "judicial *khul*" is a significant feature of divorce law in Pakistan. It is welcomed by some as giving women the right to divorce regardless of grounds, provided that she is prepared to forgo her financial rights (i.e., repaying her dower). It is criticised by others who point out that judges may rule for a judicial *khul* in cases where women are clearly entitled to a judicial divorce under the terms of the DMMA without losing their financial rights. In *Khurshid Bibi vs. Mohd. Amin* (PLD 1967 SC 97), the question for the Supreme Court to determine was stated as follows: "(Is) a wife, under the Muslim law, entitled, as of right, to claim *khul*, despite the unwillingness of the husband to release her from the matrimonial tie, if she satisfies the Court that there is no possibility of their living together consistently with their conjugal duties and obligations." The Supreme Court stated that the Muslim wife is indeed entitled to *khul* as of right, if she satisfies the Court that she would be forced into a hateful union if the option of *khul* was denied her by her husband.

In terms of maintenance during and after marriage, the classical law is applied. The post-independence changes to the Indian Criminal Procedure Code that allow a divorced wife who is unable to support herself to claim maintenance from her former husband have not been reflected in the Criminal Procedure Code of Pakistan. While the Indian Criminal Procedure Code was extended so as to apply to divorces, no such reforms have been made to Section 488 of the Criminal Procedure Codes of either Pakistan or Bangladesh.

Child custody continues to be governed by the Guardians and Wards Act 1890. The Act stipulates that the courts are to be guided by the personal law to which the minor is subject. The general rule for Muslims is that the divorce is entitled to custody until seven years for males (classical Hanafi position) and puberty for females. The courts are also directed to consider the age, sex and religion of the minor and the character and capacity of the proposed guardian, as well as considering the minor's own opinion if s/he is old enough to form an intelligent preference. If the minor is very young or is a female, the courts are directed to give preference to the mother. In all cases, the interests of the ward are paramount.

The *Qanun-e-Shahadat* (law of evidence) Order 1984 replaced the Evidence Act 1872, though it essentially restates the original legislation, but as it was intended to bring the law of evidence closer to Islamic injunctions, there were changes which specifically impacted upon women. The Order introduced changes to the law as it relates to the presumption of legitimacy. The original Evidence Act did not provide for a minimum period of gestation, and the maximum was 280 days. Now, the minimum gestation period is set at six months and the maximum at two years, bringing the provision into accordance with the majority position in classical Hanafi *fiqh*. With regard to the changes introduced relating to women's testimony, practice since the Order's issuance has been for instruments pertaining to financial or future obligations to be attested by two men, or one man and two women while courts may accept or act on the testimony of one man or one woman in all other cases.

The Offence of *Zina* (Enforcement of *Hudood*) Ordinance 1979 introduced the concepts of fornication and adultery into criminal law. The Pakistani Penal Code had not afforded any recognition to fornication as a crime, and adultery was only defined as an offence under section 497 if a man had intercourse with the wife of another man without his permission; the woman involved bore no criminal liability. The *Zina* Ordinance provides for severe penalties for committing adultery or fornication, and reiterates the classical distinction between married and unmarried parties in determining punishments. Thus, the *hadd* punishment for a married person convicted of *zina* is *rajm*, stoning to death, a penalty that has not been carried out by the state, and the *hadd* for an unmarried person found guilty of *zina* is one hundred lashes in a public place. The Ordinance also makes a distinction between *ta'zir* and *hadd* punishments for *zina*, as *hadd* punishments are generally more severe and require a more rigorous standard of proof. If the accused confesses to the crime, or if there are four pious adult Muslim male eye-witnesses to the actual act of penetration, the *hadd* penalty may be applied. Often the higher standard of evidentiary requirements is not met, and if there are other complications as well (appeals, retractions of confessions, etc.), the usual course has been to apply *ta'zir* punishments, defined as imprisonment for up to ten years, thirty lashes, and a fine.

The Enforcement of *Shariah* Act 1991 affirms the supremacy of the *shariah*, (defined in the Act as the injunctions of Islam as laid down in the Holy Quran and *Sunnah*) as the supreme law of Pakistan. The Act states that all statute law is to be interpreted in light of the *shariah* and that all Muslim citizens of Pakistan shall observe the *shariah* and act accordingly. Section 20 of the Act states that "[n]otwithstanding anything contained in this Act, the rights of women as guaranteed by the Constitution shall not be affected."

Law/Case Reporting System: The decisions of Pakistani courts are published in *Pakistan Legal Decisions* (PLD), *Civil Law Cases* (CLC), *Monthly Legal Digest* (MLD) and a number of other law reports.

International Conventions and Reports to Treaty Governing Bodies: Pakistan signed the CRC in 1990, and ratified the Convention the same year. The reservation made upon signature regarding the CRC being interpreted in light of Islamic legal principles and values was withdrawn in 1997.

Pakistan acceded to the CEDAW in 1996, with a general declaration to the effect that Pakistan's accession to the Convention is subject to the provisions of the national Constitution.

Background and Sources: Ali, "Is an Adult Muslim Woman *Sui Juris*? Some Reflections on the Concept of

"Consent in Marriage" without a *Wali* (with Particular Reference to the Saima Waheed Case)," Yearbook of Islamic and Middle Eastern Law, 1996; Carroll, "Quran 2:229: A Charter Granted to the Wife Judicial *Khul* in Pakistan," Islamic Law and Society. Vol. 3: 1 (1996); Lau, Case Note on the Saima Waheed Case, Yearbook of Islamic and Middle Eastern Law, 1996; Mahmood, Pakistan in Statutes of Personal Law in Islamic Countries, 2nd ed., New Delhi, 1995; Pearl, "Three Decades of Executive, Legislative and Judicial Amendments to Islamic Family Law in Pakistan," in Islamic Family Law, Mallat and Connors, eds. London, 1990; Pearl and Menski, Muslim Family Law, 3rd ed., London, 1998; Mehdi, The Islamisation of the Law in Pakistan, Richmond, Surrey, 1994; Redden, Pakistan in Modern Legal Systems Cyclopedia, Vol. 9, Buffalo, NY, 1990; Robinson, ed. The Cambridge Encyclopaedia of India, Pakistan, Bangladesh, Sri Lanka, Nepal, Bhutan and the Maldives, Cambridge, 1989.

Palestine/Palestinian Territories of West Bank and Gaza Strip

Legal History

The Palestinian territories of the West Bank, including East Jerusalem, and the Gaza Strip are that part of Palestine not included in the territory on which the state of Israel was established in 1948. Legally the territories share a history of Ottoman law and custom, and British Mandate legislation along with *shari'a* and customary rules. From 1948-1967 the West Bank including East Jerusalem was ruled by Jordan while the Gaza Strip was administered by Egypt.

After 1967 Israeli military orders regulated large areas of life for Palestinians in both the West Bank and Gaza Strip while Israel purported to illegally annex the territory of East Jerusalem. Since the bilateral PLO-Israeli 'Oslo Accords' set the framework of the current peace process, the unification of laws in the two areas has been on the agenda of the Palestine national Authority, established under the terms of the agreements. Currently Jordanian law governs personal status for Muslims in the West Bank; East Jerusalem Muslims have recourse either to that law or to the law applied in the Israeli *shari`a* system, which comprises the Ottoman Law of Family Rights as amended by Israeli legislation since 1948; and Gazan Muslims are governed by personal status law issued during the Egyptian administration of the Strip.

Some regulations have been issued since the 1994 Oslo Accords by the Palestinian Qadi al-Quda, which are applied in both areas. The most appropriate opinion of the Hanafi school is the residual law in Muslim personal status matters in both areas. Recognised Christian communities apply their own personal status laws in their own tribunals. Work is reported to be proceeding on the text of a Palestinian personal status law, a matter of substantial interest in different sectors of Palestinian civil society.

Schools of *Fiqh*: The Hanafi School is the predominant *madhhab* in Palestine, as well as in Jordan and Egypt, the states whose legislation continues to govern personal status in the West Bank and Gaza, respectively.

Constitutional Status of Islam(ic) Law: The draft Basic Law for the transitional period (which has not yet been ratified by Yasser Arafat, the President of the PNA) provides that "the principles of the Islamic *shari`a* are a principal source of legislation" (Art.4/2) and that "matters of personal status are to be dealt with by *shari`a* and religious courts" (Art. 92/1).

Court System: Regular courts including magistrates' and first instance courts with High Courts with appellate jurisdiction for civil and criminal matters. Complexities in unifying courts and laws in the two areas of the West Bank and Gaza Strip are one of the challenges facing the Palestinian Authority. The *shari'a* courts in both areas apply personal status law, using the execution offices in the regular court system. A *shari'a* court of appeal for the West Bank has been established under the PA which sits for the moment in Nablus, with Jordan maintaining direction of the *shari'a* first instance and appeal courts in East Jerusalem. The *shari'a* court of appeal in the Gaza Strip is also now under PA jurisdiction.

Notable Features: For the rules of Muslim personal status currently applicable in the West Bank see under Jordan. For Muslim Palestinians marrying under Israeli law in East Jerusalem see under Israel. In the Gaza Strip, the Egyptian-issued Law of Family Rights sets puberty as the minimum age of marriage with no marriage allowed of a female aged under 9 or a male aged under 12. The Palestinian Qadi al-Quda issued an administrative decision in 1995 raising these ages to a minimum of 15 for the female and 16 for the male, as in the Jordanian law. All ages are calculated according to the lunar calendar.

The LFR assumes that there is a guardian and that where there is not, the *qadi* acts as guardian for the woman in marriage. Marriage registration is mandatory but failure to register does not invalidate the marriage.

Polygamy is governed by classical law, but the woman is allowed to stipulate in the contract that the husband shall not take another wife while married to her, and may seek divorce if he subsequently breaks the terms of that stipulation.

The rules of maintenance and obedience are maintained in their classical form.

On *talaq*, standard reforms to the classical Hanafi rules, as implemented in Egypt in the 1920s, have been included in the LFR; extra-judicial *talaq* is valid but registration is obligatory. The same rules on judicial divorce apply as in the West Bank, except that a wife is entitled to petition for divorce on the grounds of injury, and a husband is not entitled to apply on grounds of 'discord and strife'.

There has been no amendment in the LFR to the classical Hanafi rules on post-divorce maintenance, or on arrears pre-dating submission of the maintenance claim.

Law/Case Reporting System: Palestinian Official Gazette.

International Conventions (with Relevant Reservations): N/A (until statehood is formally recognised and implemented, Palestine cannot become a state party to international instruments).

Background and Sources: El Alami and Hinchcliffe, Islamic Marriage and Divorce Laws of the Arab World, London, 1996; Welchman, "Family Law under Occupation: Islamic Law and the Shariah Courts of the West Bank," in Islamic Family Law, Mallat and Connors, eds., London, 1990; Welchman, Islamic Family Law: Text and Practice in Palestine, Jerusalem (WCLAC) 1999.

Republic of the Philippines

Legal History

The term Moros (Filipilno Muslims) is a label given by the Spanish in the sixteenth century to thirteen ethno-linguistic groups, mainly concentrated in south-western Philippines. Under Spanish rule, colonial authority was not extended to the Moro areas due to considerable resistance on the part of the local population. Spain lost the Philippines to the United States who ruled the area from 1899 to 1946. The US military rulers initially obtained the acknowledgement of the Sultan of Sulu in the Bates Agreement, preserving the Sultan's jurisdiction over Moros.

The United States policy eventually changed, limiting the powers of traditional authorities and encouraging Christian Filipino settlement in Muslim areas. The 1914 Organic Act for the Department of Mindanao and Sulu extended state laws to the area, within certain limits, and redrew existing boundaries to establish provinces and municipalities. The Philippine Commission Act 1915 allowed for assessors such as *kalis*, *panditas*, or Muslims well-versed in local laws and customs, to sit with Moroland Courts, and permitted the modification of US law in cases where the parties were Muslims. The principle of exemption continued, but over time came to be limited to the area of family law.

After independence, a separatist movement emerged among students and intellectuals in the late 1960s, gaining popular support after the eruption of communal violence in Cotabato in 1970. The movement developed into an armed struggle for secession after President Ferdinand Marcos declared martial law in 1972. The conflict continued into the mid-1970s, with a cease-fire declared and Libyan-brokered peace talks held in 1976. The settlement offered to the separatists included a Muslim Autonomous Region in 13 provinces, but negotiations broke down. Marcos began implementing parts of the Tripoli Agreement unilaterally, including passing a Code of Muslim Personal Laws in 1977.

A new round of talks began under President Corazon Aquino in 1986. After much debate, an Organic Act was passed in 1989 allowing for the creation of an autonomous region in Muslim Mindanao, followed by a plebiscite in which four provinces (Lanao del Sur, Maguindanao, Sulu and Tawi-Tawi) opted for inclusion in the Autonomous Region for Muslim Mindanao (ARMM). A final Peace Accord was signed between the government and the Moro National Liberation Front in September 1996.

Schools of *Fiqh*: Muslims of the Philippines are almost all Shafi'i. The majority of the population is Roman Catholic, and there are Protestant and Buddhist minorities.

Constitutional Status of Islam(ic) Law: The current Constitution was adopted on October 15th 1986. Article II, Section 6 states that "the separation of Church and State shall be inviolable". Article III, sec. 5 guarantees the free exercise of religion and states that there shall be no religious test for exercising civil and political rights. Article X relates to local government and Section 1 thereof states that "there shall be autonomous regions in Muslim Mindanao and the Cordilleras as hereinafter provided", to which Sections 15 to 21 relate. Under Section 20, personal, family and property relations to be subject to the legislative power of each autonomous region.

Court System: *Shariah* courts are organised at two levels. The *Shariah* Circuit Courts in five *shariah* judicial districts have exclusive original jurisdiction over: cases relating to offences defined in the (Muslim) Family Code and civil actions between Muslims married under the terms of Family Code (relating to marriage, divorce, betrothal, dower, division of property upon divorce, maintenance and consolatory gifts, restitution of marital rights and disputes over communal property).

The five *Shariah* District Courts, each presided over by one judge, have exclusive original jurisdiction over: custody, guardianship, legitimacy, paternity and filiation cases arising under the Family Code; the disposition, distribution and settlement of estates or wills of Muslims and the appointment of executors; petitions for declaration of death or absence or correction of entries in Muslim civil status registers; and actions arising from customary contracts between Muslims. The District Courts also have appellate jurisdiction over *Shariah* Circuit Court decisions. Decisions of *Shariah* District Courts are final.

An Office of Jurisconsult in Islamic Law is constituted under the supervision of the Supreme Court. The Jurisconsults Office shall, upon the written request of any party on any question concerning Muslim Law, issue legal opinions based on recognised authorities, and shall compile and publish all legal opinions issued.

Notable Features: The minimum marriage age is 15 years for males and puberty for females (a female is presumed to have attained puberty at 15 years). The *Shariah* District Court may authorise the marriage of a female between 12 and 15 years if she has attained puberty, upon petition of her *wali*. The marriage of minors is defined as betrothal and may be annulled by either party within four years of attaining puberty if the marriage was not voluntarily consummated and neither the father nor paternal grandfather served as *wali*. There is a penalty of imprisonment or fines or both for illegal solemnisation of marriage. Validity of marriage requires the free consent of marrying parties and the presence and consent of the *wali*.

Marriage registration is obligatory, backed up by penal sanctions of fines for failure to register any change in civil status. The Family Code states that no Muslim man may take more than one wife "unless he can deal with them with equal companionship and just treatment as enjoined by Islamic law and only in exceptional cases". The grounds for determination of exceptional cases are not specified.

The husband's rights and obligations in marriage relate to fixing the residence of the family (subject to classical conditions) and providing maintenance. The wife may not work without her husband's consent, but may take the matter to an arbitration council in case her husband withholds his consent.

Divorce may be effected by *talaq*, *ila*, *zihar*, *li'an*, *khul*, *tafwid* or *faskh*, according to the Family Code. Divorce by *talaq* must be effected by the husband in a single repudiation during the wife's *tuhr*. Any *talaq* to which a number is attached counts only as a single revocable repudiation until the expiry of the *idda*. A woman may seek a judicial divorce on the following grounds: in cases of the husband's oath of abstinence (*ila*), *zihar* (likening of his wife to his relations within the prohibited degrees), *li'an* (imprecation of adultery); or a decree of *faskh* on the following grounds: husband's failure to maintain her for six months; husband's conviction to one years imprisonment; husband's impotence or abstention from conjugal relations for six months; husband's insanity or affliction with an incurable disease injurious to his family; husband's cruelty; and any other cause valid under Muslim law. Until the passage of the Family Code, Muslims were the only Filipinos with a possibility for legally ending a marriage.

The divorced wife is only entitled to maintenance during *idda*, in addition to maintenance for the duration of nursing if the divorced mother continues to nurse her child for two years. The divorced mother has the right to custody over sons and daughters until seven years after which age the ward may choose to reside with either parent. The custody of an unmarried female ward who has reached puberty reverts to father, and the son in the same circumstances resides with the mother.

Succession is governed by classical law, as defined in the Family Code.

Notable Cases

Law/Case Reporting System: Law reporting is through the *Official Gazette.*

International Conventions (with Relevant Reservations): Philippines signed the ICESCR and ICCPR in 1966, ratifying the former in 1974 and the latter in 1986 without reservations.

Philippines signed the CEDAW in 1980 and ratified it in 1981 without reservations.

Philippines signed and ratified the CRC in 1990 without reservations.

Philippines signed the Convention on Consent to Marriage, Minimum Age for Marriage and Registration of Marriages in 1963 and ratified it in 1965 without reservations.

Background and Sources: Hooker, Islamic Law in South-East Asia, Singapore, 1984; Mahmood, Philippines, in Statutes of Personal Law in Islamic Countries, 2nd ed., New Delhi, 1995.

State of Qatar

Legal History

From its early history, the region now known as Qatar has come under Persian, Portuguese, Ottoman and British influence. Qatar was considered a part of Bahrain by the British until the 1860s, although the ruling al-Khalifah family of Bahrain only exercised limited control over Qatar. In 1868, a treaty of co-operation was signed between Britain and the al-Thani tribe settled around Doha; the treaty outlawed warfare at sea and directed that any conflicts be referred to the British Resident in the Gulf. Wahhabism became influential in the region due to an alliance forged between the al-Thani tribe and Wahhabis and their allies in the late eighteenth century; the al-Thani tribe became the ruling family of the region by the 1893 after Shaykh Jasim al-Thani, appointed Governor by the Ottomans in 1879, asserted his own rule.

The Ottoman Turkish garrison was expelled from Doha and relations with Britain were further strengthened by the 1916 Treaty of Protection making Qatar a British protectorate. The Treaty of Protection continued in force until 1971 when Qatar declared its independence. Since that time, a Penal Code, Civil and Criminal Procedure Codes, and Laws on Judicial Organisation have been adopted. Personal law remains uncodified, administered by the *shariahh* courts.

Schools of *Fiqh*: The Hanbali School is the predominant *madhhab* in Qatar.

Constitutional Status of Islam(ic) Law: The Amended provisional basic regulation was passed on 19 April 1972, replacing the Provisional Constitution adopted in 1970. Article 1 declares Islam state religion and provides that "the Islamic *Shariah* Law shall be a fundamental source of its legislation". Article 9 guarantees equal public rights and requires equal public duties without distinction for race, sex or religion.

Court System: Qatar maintains a dual system of civil and *shariah* courts. The first civil courts were established in 1962. The *shariah* courts jurisdiction has increasingly been limited to family law matters (marriage, divorce, wills, succession), though they retain some criminal jurisdiction.

Shariah courts are staffed by *qadis* who administer uncodified (mainly Hanbali-Wahhabi) personal status law and are organised into two levels: *Shariah* Courts of First Instance and the *Shariah* Court of Appeal.

Notable Features: Classical Hanbali *fiqh* is applied to personal status matters.

Notable Cases

Law/Case Reporting System: Law reporting is through the *Official Gazette.*

International Conventions (with Relevant Reservations): Qatar signed the CRC in 1992 and ratified it in 1995, submitting a general reservation to any "provisions incompatible with Islamic Law" upon signature and confirming it upon ratification.

Background and Sources: El Alami and Hinchcliffe, The Uncodified Law in Islamic Marriage and Divorce Laws of the Arab World, London, Mahmood, Gulf in Statutes of Personal Law in Islamic Countries, 2nd ed., New Delhi, 1995.

Kingdom of Saudi Arabia

Legal History

Saudi Arabia was never directly colonised although parts of the present-day state had come under nominal or intermittent Ottoman control since the sixteenth century. Turkish garrisons were at times stationed in Mecca, Medina, Jeddah and other centres, but the Ottomans only exercised limited powers and local rulers had a high degree of autonomy in internal affairs. The Ottomans final efforts at occupying eastern Arabia in 1871 to forestall the growing British influence at their borders in the Arabian Gulf eventually failed. The basis of the Wahhabi state of Saudi Arabia was established in 1902 when Abd al-Aziz al-Saud and his followers gained control of Riyadh, signalling the beginning of the third period of Saudi-Wahhabi dominance in the region. Abd al-Aziz consolidated his territorial gains over the next decade, expanding out of the surroundings of Riyadh and the eastern part of the region into the areas where the Ottomans were expelled. The Kingdom of Saudi Arabia was declared on 22nd September 1933 over those lands that had come under Abd al-Aziz's control by conquest and by forging numerous alliances.

Following the 1979 seizure of the Grand Mosque in Mecca, the decline in oil prices in the 1980s, and the effects of the second Gulf War, tentative efforts have been made to establish a more representative form of governance. A *Majlis al-Shura* (Consultative Council) was introduced by King Fahd in 1993. The *Majlis* had 61 appointed members; in 1996 this was increased to 90 members. Although the *Majlis* has no legislative powers, it may examine government policies and propose laws or amendments to existing laws. Decisions or suggestions from the *Majlis* are first sent to the Council of Ministers for review, and then to the King for his approval.

The main sources of Saudi law are Hanbali *fiqh* as set out in a number of specified classical scholarly treatises by authoritative jurists, other Hanbali sources, other schools of law, state regulations and royal decrees (where these are relevant), and custom and practice. Royal decrees have been used to direct courts to base judgements on several authoritative classical treatises by Hanbali jurists (e.g., *al-Mughni* of ibn Qudamah). A resolution of the Supreme Judicial Council passed in 1928 also directed the courts to rely on particular Hanbali sources in civil matters, ranked as follows: *Sharh Mutaha al-Iradat* of al-Bahuti, *Kashshaf al-Kina an Matn al-Ikna*of al-Bahuti, commentaries of al-Zad, commentaries of al-Dalil, and if no suitable provision is found, then secondary sources in Hanbali legal manuals, and lastly, reference to authorities of other *madhahib*. If no answer is found in officially sanctioned sources, resort may be had to *ijtihad*. Traditional areas of law continue to be governed by *shariah* law while certain spheres of law relating to corporate, tax, oil and gas, immigration law, etc. have been regulated by royal decrees and codes.

Schools of *Fiqh*: The Hanbali school is the official *madhhab* in Saudi Arabia. There is also a Shi'i minority adhering to the Ja'fari school.

Constitutional Status of Islam(ic) Law: Saudi Arabia has no formal constitution. The functions of a constitution are served by the Basic Law articulating the government's rights and responsibilities issued by King Fahd in March 1992. Article 1 of the Basic Law declares Islam the official state religion and the Quran and *sunnah* the Constitution. The Basic Law also provides that "[t]he state protects the rights of the people in line with the Islamic *shariah*," affirms the independence of the judiciary and states that administration of justice is based on "*shariah* rules according to the teachings of the holy Quran, the *sunnah*, and the regulations set by the ruler provided that they do not contradict the holy Quran and *sunnah*". Article 9 of the Basic Law states that "the family is the kernel of Saudi society, and its members shall be brought up on the basis of the Islamic faith". Article 26 provides that the state protects human rights "in accordance with the Islamic *Shariah*".

Court System: *Shariah* Courts have general and residual jurisdiction, i.e., jurisdiction over any case or matter the jurisdiction over which has not been expressly assigned to another tribunal. There are four levels of *shariah* courts: Minor Courts, General Courts, Cassation Court, and the Supreme Judicial Council. Civil claims may also go to the *Amarah* in which case the Amir attempts to guide the parties in a dispute to a compromise; the matter is ultimately referred to the courts if a settlement is not reached. There are also a number of specialised tribunals for settling disputes in specific areas, such as commercial or labour law; these specialised tribunals are formed under various ministries outside of the Ministry of Justice. The highest appellate tribunal in all matters, the Board of Grievances, is also independent of the Ministry of Justice, and since its re-organisation in 1982 has been made directly responsible to the King.

Notable Features: Standard Hanbali *fiqh* is applied to personal status cases.

Notable Cases

Law/Case Reporting System: Law reporting is through the *Official Gazette.*

International Conventions (with Relevant Reservations): Saudi Arabia acceded to the CRC in 1996 with a general reservation to "all such articles as are in conflict with the provisions of Islamic law."

Background and Sources: El Alami and Hinchcliffe, "The Uncodified Law" in Islamic Marriage and Divorce Laws of the Arab World, London, 1996; Mahmood, "Gulf" in Statutes of Personal Law in Islamic Countries, 2nd ed., New Delhi, 1995; Redden, "Saudi Arabia" in Modern Legal Systems Cyclopedia, Vol. 5, Buffalo, NY, 1990; Vassiliev.

Republic of Senegal

Legal History

The legal system is based on the French civil law system. Senegal gained independence from France in 1960. Prior to the enactment of the Family Code in 1972, family relations were governed by Christian, Islamic and customary laws, or under the civil code. Work on codification of a uniform personal status law began in 1961 with a comprehensive listing of customary laws applied in Senegal, and the publication of 68 officially recognised customary regimes. A commission for codification was established in 1961 and began by issuing a questionnaire investigating customary practices. A 27-member committee was given the task of drafting a single code for all Senegalese that would minimise any aspects not uniformly applicable, would be appropriate to modern social conditions, would compromise on matters likely to cause conflict between traditional laws and modern statutes, and observe proscriptions related to family law in the Quran.

The Family Code that was drafted passed into law and came into force on January 1st 1973. The Code regulates marriage, divorce, succession and custody, with separate section for Muslim succession law. As of 1993, the government established a working group to adapt national legislation to conform with the international instruments ratified by Senegal.

Schools of *Fiqh*: The majority of the population is Maliki Muslim. A minority of the population follows indigenous religions or is Christian (mainly Roman Catholic).

Constitutional Status of Islamic Law: The Constitution was adopted on 3rd March 1963 and has been revised numerous times. Article 1 declares that Senegal is a secular state.

Court System: Senegal took steps to abolish separate customary courts and establish a unified judicial system after independence in 1960. Tribunals of first instance and assize courts decisions are appealable to courts of appeal. The Supreme Court or Court of Cassation is the highest appellate court.

Notable Features: The minimum marriage age is 20 years for males and 16 for females, with provision for judicial discretion for permitting underage marriages for serious reasons. Each party must give free consent, even minors, and parties under 21 years require parental consent. Lack of free consent or parental consent is grounds for nullification of marriage.

Marriage registration is obligatory. If a marriage is to be contracted under one of the customary regimes recognised in Senegalese law, the parties must inform the officer of civil status one month prior to the marriage. Non-registration is punishable by a fine but does not determine the validity of a marriage.

Polygamy is permitted, but the groom must register his option for a monogamous, limited polygamous or polygamous (up to four wives) regime upon the registration of his first marriage, and the option is for life. It may only be altered to lower the number of wives further. Wives are entitled to equal treatment in polygamous unions.

The husband is identified as the head of the family. The choice of residence lies with the husband, and the wife is required to live with him, unless she is authorised by a judge to reside elsewhere. Although maintenance is defined as an obligation of both spouses during the subsistence of marriage, the obligation is principally that of the husband and his failure to maintain is provided as a ground for the wife to seek dissolution. Since the 1989 reforms of the Family Code, the husband has not been permitted to forbid his wife from working.

Extra-judicial divorce is not permitted. Either party may seek a judicial dissolution on the following grounds (preceded by reconciliation efforts by the judge): the other party's declared absence; adultery; sentencing for a crime bringing dishonour to the family; failure to fulfill a legal condition stipulated upon marriage; abandonment of the family or conjugal home; maltreatment rendering continuation of marital life impossible; medically established sterility; grave and incurable illness discovered since marriage; incompatibility making continuation of conjugal life intolerable; and for the wife, the husband's failure to maintain her. In case the husband sought the divorce on grounds of incompatibility or incurable illness of the wife, the obligation to maintain is transformed to obligation to pay alimony. In case the divorce is judged to be the exclusive fault of one party, the judge may grant the other party appropriate compensation.

Custody is determined by judgment of the court and may be granted to either party or to a third party according to the best interests of ward. Whichever parent has custody, the father is the guardian, unless he is unable to fulfill this role.

Succession is governed by classical law as outlined in Section III on Muslim succession in Book VII of Family Code.

The laws applicable to Muslim intestate succession include a provision for only granddaughters through predeceased sons not standing to inherit as residuary heirs from anyone else to receive one-sixth of the grandparent's estate.

Notable Cases

Law/Case Reporting System: Law reporting is through the *Journal Officiel.*

International Conventions (with Relevant Reservations): Senegal signed the ICCPR and ICESCR in 1970 and ratified them in 1978, without reservations.

Senegal signed the CEDAW in 1980 and ratified it in 1985, without reservations.

Senegal signed the CRC in and ratified it in 1990, without reservations.

Background and Sources: CEDAW, Concluding Observations: Senegal's Second Periodic Report to CEDAW, January 1995; Ndiaye, Le Divorce et la Sparation de Corps, Dakar, 1979; 1992; Redden, "Senegal," Modern Legal Systems Cyclopedia, Vol. 6.

Republic of Singapore

Legal History: [See also: Legal System/History of Malaysia]

The legal system is based on English common law. The Port of Singapore was founded in 1819 on the advice of Sir Stamford Raffles, Lieutenant-Governor of Java and employee of the British East India Company. It became part of the British Straits Settlement (of Malacca and Penang) in 1826. Singapore had a small population of Malay fishermen; Chinese and Indian settlement began after British rule. The Straits Settlements Act 1866 established Straits as a colony separate from British India, to be administered directly from London. In 1946, Singapore became a separate Crown Colony and Penang and Malacca joined the Malayan Union, which achieved independence as the Federation of Malaya in 1957. Singapore gained independence in 1959, and joined Malaysia (with Malaya, Sarawak and North Borneo) in 1963, but it withdrew from the federation after two years and became an independent city-state.

Singaporean Muslim personal status is governed by the Muslims Ordinance 1957 covering registration, *shariah* courts and property matters, and repealing the previous applicable Ordinance. It contained very limited substantive provisions, but the Ordinance did transfer jurisdiction over Muslim personal status to *shariah* courts from the regular judiciary. It was replaced by the Administration of Muslim Law Act 1966, providing more detailed regulations. The 1966 Act established the *Majlis Ugama Islam Singapore* (Singapore Islamic Council) to administer endowments and execute wills. The Council also has a Legal Committee consisting of the *Mufti* of Singapore, two other member of the *Majlis* and two non-members; the function of the Legal Committee is to issue *fatawa* on any point of Muslim law. The 1966 legislation also contains more substantive provisions than its predecessor. The Women's Charter, passed in 1961, superseded non-Muslim family law systems applied in Singapore. It imposed a monogamous marriage regime on all Singaporeans except Muslims, although Muslim men married to non-Muslims under the terms of the Women's Charter are prohibited from polygamy. Muslims are expressly exempted from certain provisions of the Women's Charter, for example, those relating to solemnisation, nullity, divorce, etc. The regular court system has jurisdiction over adoption, succession, and custody even for those married under Muslim law, and the Muslim wife may choose to go to the regular or the *shariah* judicial system to obtain maintenance order.

Schools of *Fiqh*: The majority of Muslims are Shafi'i. The majority of the population is Buddhist. The other religions represented are Christianity, Hinduism, Sikhism, Taoism, Confucianism, Zoroastrianism and Judaism.

Constitutional Status of Islamic Law: The Constitution was adopted on 3rd June 1959 and amended in 1965 when the Malaysian State of Singapore left Malaysia. The Constitution contains a number of provisions enshrining freedom of religion and prohibiting discrimination on grounds of religion. Article 153 under General Provisions states that "the Legislature shall by law make provision for regulating Muslim religious affairs and for constituting a Council to advise the President in matters relating to the Muslim religion".

Court System: There is one *Shariah* Court in Singapore; it may hear and determine actions in which all parties are Muslims or in which the parties involved were married under Muslim law (i.e., the husband is Muslim). The *Shariah* Court has jurisdiction over cases related to marriage, divorce, betrothal, nullity of marriage, judicial separation, division of property on divorce, payment of dowry, maintenance, and *mata'a*. Appeals from *Shariah* Court decisions or decisions of *kathis* lie with an Appeal Board, comprised of three Muslims chosen by the Registrar of the Supreme Court from a panel of seven nominated by President annually. Appeal Board decisions are final.

Notable Features: The minimum marriage age is 16 years for both parties. The *kathi* may permit the marriage of a girl under 16 years who has attained puberty under certain circumstances. The *wali* of the bride may solemnise her marriage according to Muslim law or may request the *kathi* to do so. The *kathi* may serve as *wali* where a woman has no *wali* or where he rules that the *wali*'s opposition to her marriage is unreasonable. Whether or not the *wali*'s agreement is required for validity of marriage is governed according to the classical position of the school of law applicable to the parties. In all cases, the *kathi* is directed to make an inquiry to determine that there are no lawful obstacles to a proposed marriage under either Muslim law or Administration of Muslim Law Act.

Marriage registration is obligatory. All Muslim marriages must be registered with a *kathi* or *naib kathi*. The President of Singapore appoints a Registrar of Muslim Marriages and all *kathis* and *naib kathis* are Deputy Registrars. Non-registration of marriage or divorce does not determine validity.

Polygamy is permitted, but marriage by a man who is already married must be solemnised by a *kathi* or with the *kathi's* written permission. Also, as with any Muslim marriage, the *kathi* is directed to make such inquiry as is necessary to determine that there are no lawful obstacles to the proposed marriage. The wife may apply to the court for a maintenance order; the sums and time period for which arrears may be claimed is not specified.

The registration of divorce and revocation of divorce is compulsory, and non-compliance is punishable by a fine. A *kathi* may not register a divorce without an inquiry establishing both parties consent. A *kathi* may not register any divorce by triple *talaq* and the case must be referred to the *Shariah* Court. The wife may be granted a judicial dissolution with her husbands consent. If the husband agrees to a *khul*, the Court will assess the amount of compensation to be paid by the wife according to the means and status of both parties. The wife may also apply for *faskh* on the following grounds: the husband's failure to maintain for three months; his imprisonment for three years or more; failure to perform marital obligations for one year; continued impotence since marriage; insanity or serious illness making cohabitation injurious to his wife; and cruel treatment (defined as habitual physical abuse or cruelty of conduct, associating with women of ill-repute, obstruction of wife's religious observance, unequal treatment of co-wives, cohabiting with another woman, or trying to force wife to lead immoral life). Before granting a decree of divorce or nullification, the Court may appoint arbitrators to attempt reconciliation.

The divorced wife may apply to the Court to order maintenance for her *idda*. If the former wife is not entitled to maintenance under classical law, the Court may award her maintenance in consideration of the particular circumstances of the case. Child custody is governed by the Guardians of Infants Act 1961. The Courts are directed to consider the religious and customary practices of the community to which the parties belong, but the best interests of the ward are of paramount consideration. The regular court system has jurisdiction over all custody cases.

The property of a Muslim dying intestate is to be divided according to Islamic law "as modified by Malay custom" although this appears to be a relic from pre-Independence legislation as commentators note that there have been no cases of such modification in the city-state of Singapore. Muslims may only dispose of property by will in accordance with the particular school of law to which they are subject.

Notable Cases

Law/Case Reporting System: Case reporting is through the *Singapore Law Journal* (formerly case reports were through the *Malayan Law Journal*). Law reporting is through the *Official Gazette.*

International Conventions (with Relevant Reservations): Singapore acceded to the CEDAW in 1995 with a number of reservations. The reservation to Articles 2 and 6 states that due to the multi-racial and multi-religious composition of the population and the respect for freedom of religion, "Singapore reserves the right not to apply the provisions of (said) Articles where compliance with these provisions would be contrary to (minority communities religious or personal laws".

Singapore acceded to the CRC in 1995, with declarations regarding the interpretation of Articles 12, 17, 19, 28(1a) 32 and 37. The declaration relating to Articles 12 and 17 states that the exercise of children's rights must be balanced against the authority of parents, schools, etc. and with regard for the customs and values of the multi-racial and multi-religious society of Singapore.

Background and Sources: Cheang, "Women and the Law in Singapore," pp. 76-94 in Women and the Law, Hooker, Islamic Law in South-East Asia, Singapore, 1984; Kum, Family Law in Singapore: Cases and Commentary on the Women's Charter and Family Law, Singapore, 1996; Mahmood, "Singapore" in Statutes of Personal Law in Islamic Countries, 2nd ed. New Delhi, 1995.

Somalia

Legal History

The Somali Republic was formed on 1st July 1960, upon the union of British Somaliland which gained independence on 26th June, and Italian Somaliland which gained independence from Italian-administered UN trusteeship on 1st July. Early legislation in British Somaliland was based on the importation of British-Indian legislation in the late nineteenth and earlytwentieth century. The British promulgated later promulgated the Natives Betrothal and Marriage Ordinance 1928 and *Qadis* Courts Ordinance 1937 specific to Somaliland. The Subordinate Courts Ordinance 1944 repealed 1937 Ordinance, limiting the jurisdiction of *Qadis* Courts to matters of personal status. Under Italian rule in the south, there was a well developed system of *Qadis* Courts which retained jurisdiction over civil and minor criminal matters.

Upon independence, the Republic was faced with the task of unifying legislation and judicial structures drawn from Italian, British, customary and Islamic legal traditions. After a military coup in 1969, the new regime embarked on a programme of legal reform based on scientific socialism. In the early to mid-1970s, debate regarding family law reform led to the appointment of a commission to prepare a draft code. The draft produced by the commission was enacted in 1975 with significant modifications made by President Siad Barre and the Secretary of State for Justice and Religious Affairs Abdisalem Shaykh Hussain. The Code aimed to abolish customary laws, and abrogated previous British and Italian era legislation relating to family law. Article 1 of the Family Code 1975 provides that the leading doctrines of the Shafi'i school and general principles of Islamic law and social justice are to serve as residuary sources of law.

Civil war ensued after the ousting of Barre in January of 1991, with competition for power between various factions. The collapse of the UN peacekeeping mission led to a final pullout of international troops in spring 1995. In August 2000, a majority of Somali leaders signed a transitional charter, to be in force for three years, and elected a parliament for the transition period. Fighting continues in the south with some orderly government established in the north.

Schools of *Fiqh*: The majority of Muslims are Shafi'i. There is a small Christian minority.

Constitutional Status of Islam(ic) Law: The current Constitution was adopted in August 1979. Article 3 (Section 1, Chapter 1) declares Islam the state religion.

Court System: After independence, the *shariah* and customary courts were formally recognised as Courts of *Qadis*. Their judicial role is very small and jurisdiction is limited to civil matters such as marriage and divorce.

The regular court system is constituted at four levels: Supreme Court, courts of appeal, regional courts and district courts. District courts have two sections, civil and criminal. The civil section has jurisdiction over all cases arising from *shariah* or customary law or civil cases where the matter in dispute does not exceed 3000 Somali shillings. Judges are directed to consider *shariah* or customary law in rendering decisions. Regional courts are divided into three sections, civil and criminal (first instance), assize, and labour. Courts of appeal are divided into two sections: general appeals and assize appeals.

Notable Features: The minimum marriage age is 18 years for both parties. The female party may marry at

16 years with her guardian's consent, and the Court may grant an exemption from the minimum age requirements in case of necessity. A girl who has reached 16 years but is under 18 years may be represented in the contract of marriage by her father (in the absence of the father, the guardians in order are: mother, grandfather, elder brother, uncle, a Court-appointed guardian or judge). The Court is also empowered to overrule the objection of a guardian to the marriage of a female ward between 16 and 18 years.

Marriage is to be registered at the nearest District Court or authorised office within 15 days (40 days for residents of rural areas); failure to register is punishable by a fine. The essential elements of marriage as outlined in Article 6 are: proposal and acceptance by the contracting parties before two witnesses. A marriage contracted under compulsion is invalid. A man may not contract a second marriage without the written permission of the District Court. The Court's authorisation requires ascertainment of one of the following conditions: sterility of the wife of which the husband was not aware at the time of marriage, attested by a panel of doctors; incurable chronic or contagious illness of the wife, certified by a doctor; the wife's sentencing to more than two years in prison; the wife's unjustified absence from the matrimonial home for more than one year; or the existence of social necessity (grounds for which are not defined).

The Family Code provides that marriage is based on equal rights and duties; the husband is declared the head of the family, the parties are obliged to cohabit, and the wife is obliged to follow her husband. Both parties are obliged to share the expenses of the matrimonial home in proportion to their incomes if they are able to do so. If either party fails in his/her duty to maintain and is not destitute, the other party may obtain a Court order for maintenance (the sums and time period for arrears of maintenance are not specified). The Court is empowered to award interim maintenance and authorise the claimant to contract debts against the defaulting partner if s/he finds it impossible to obtain maintenance from the defaulter.

The Family Code provides that the right of *talaq* belongs to the husband "subject to the authorisation by the competent court". The Court may authorise divorce only after reconciliation efforts (of up to 60 days) have failed, and the Court may not authorise more than one *talaq* at a time. Divorce by a minor or insane person, or pronounced under compulsion is declared invalid. Either party may seek a judicial dissolution on the following grounds: incurable disease of the other spouse making cohabitation dangerous or impossible; disappearance of the other party for a period of over four years; habitual failure to maintain by the responsible party; serious disagreement between spouses making conjugal life impossible (after reconciliation efforts of up to 60 days); perpetual impotence or sterility of the other party; and the other spouse's sentencing to over four years imprisonment. The wife is entitled to seek dissolution if the husband has been granted permission for polygamous marriage by the District Court, on condition that there are no children from the marriage. Where the reason for a *talaq* or *faskh* is deemed to be the husband's fault, the Court shall order him to maintain his former wife for three months to one year; if the wife is deemed to be at fault, the Court shall order her to pay her husband a sum not less than her dower in compensation. The mother is entitled to custody of male children until the age of 10 and female children until the age of 15, with the Court empowered to extend custody until age 18 for the male or female ward if s/he is not able to look after him/herself. If the mother remarries and the husband is within the prohibited degrees to the ward(s), or in case she is widowed and remarries, she may retain custody. Maintenance of children is the duty of both parents until the age of majority for sons and until marriage or until she is able to support herself through gainful employment for the daughter.

The power of the testator to make a bequest is limited to one-third of the estate, unless the consent of the heirs is obtained. A bequest in favour of an heir is similarly limited by requiring the consent of the other heirs. Article 158 states that "In conformity with the principles of the 1st and 2nd Charter of the Revolution females and males shall have equal rights of inheritance". Heirs are identified as: spouses, children, grandchildren, parents, grandparents, full siblings, paternal and maternal aunts and uncles. The widow or widower is entitled to half of the estate if there are no children or grandchildren, or one fourth if there are. Sons and daughters are entitled to equal shares, and the same applies to grandchildren. The shares of other heirs are also specified in the Code, as are grounds for inclusion or exclusion of heirs and reduction of shares.

Law/Case Reporting System: Laws are published through the *Official Gazette.*

International Conventions (with Relevant Reservations): Somalia acceded to the ICCPR and ICESCR in 1990, without reservations.

Background and Sources: Gavlak, "Somalia's New President Works to Build Peace," Christian Science Monitor, Sept. 14, 2000; Mahmood, "Somalia" in Statutes of Personal Law in Islamic Countries, 2nd ed., New Delhi, 1995; Nelson, ed., Somalia: A Country Study, 3rd ed., Washington, D.C., 1983; Pearl, A Textbook on Muslim Law, London, 1979; Redden, "Somalia" in Modern Legal Systems Cyclopedia, Vol. 6, Buffalo, NY, 1990

Democratic Socialist Republic of Sri Lanka

Legal History

Sri Lanka has been subject to centuries of Portuguese, Dutch and British domination. From the time of independence in 1948, the legal system of Sri Lanka has developed into a complex mixture of English common law and Roman-Dutch, Sinhalese, Muslim, and customary law.

Under Dutch rule in the late eighteenth century, the colonial administrators codified the rules of inheritance, marriage and divorce law in order to facilitate the application of Muslim family law. Preference was given to customary usage and the provisions of the Mohammedan Code over classical legal treatises. These special laws were preserved and adapted after the British defeat of the Dutch in 1799. The Code was initially applied only to the Muslims of the Province of Colombo, but its application was extended to the rest of the island by the late nineteenth century. Another piece of legislation, the Registration of Muslim Marriages Ordinance 1896, was enacted under the British, repealing parts of the earlier Code. The Muslim Marriage and Divorce Registration Ordinance 1929 replaced the 1896 legislation and further amended the Anglo-Dutch Mohammedan Code. The next item of legislation, the Muslim Intestate Succession Ordinance 1931, continues to be in force in Sri Lanka today, and the 1929 Ordinance was finally replaced by the post-independence Muslim Marriage and Divorce Act in 1951. The essential principle reinforced by the 1951 Act is that, in matters of personal status, the rights and duties of the parties involved are to be governed by the school of law to which the parties belong.

Schools of *Fiqh*: Sri Lankan Muslims mainly follow the Shafi'i or Hanafi schools. There are also Hindu and Christian minorities in Sri Lanka.

Constitutional Status of Islamic Law: The current Constitution was adopted on 16 August 1978. Article 9 falls short of establishing Buddhism as the state religion; rather, the provision gives Buddhism the "foremost place", making it the duty of the state to "protect and foster the Buddha Sasana," while assuring to all religions the rights enshrined in Articles 10 and 14(1)(e) of the Constitution. Those articles guarantee every person freedom of thought, conscience and religion, including the freedom to profess or adopt a religion or belief of his/her choice, and guarantee all citizens the freedom to manifest their religious beliefs in worship, observance, practice and teaching. These are the only provisions expressly relating to religion and implicitly to minority rights. No change to these provisions is put forward in the draft Constitution tabled in 1997. The draft has been the subject of heated debate but is unlikely to be passed into law in the near future due to the current composition of the parliament.

Court System: The Muslim Marriage and Divorce Act 1951 constitutes the main body of legislation relating to the application of Muslim family law, and also regulates the functions, qualifications and powers of the *Quazi* Courts applying that law. *Quazi* Courts are staffed by judges (*quazi*) appointed by the Judicial Services Commission. Male Muslims of good character and position and suitable attainments are eligible for appointment as *Quazi's*. Appeals from the *Quazi* Courts lie with the Board of *Quazis*, then with the Court of Appeal and ultimately with the Supreme Court. A board of three judges is required to hear appeals to the Board of *Quazi's*. The Board's other function is to furnish the Registrar-General or any *Quazi* that request such advice with a written opinion on any question of Muslim law that may arise in relation to the administration of the MMDA. The MMDA also delineates the limits of jurisdiction between the civil judicial system and the *Quazi* courts, as well as the powers of the *Quazi*. He has exclusive jurisdiction over the adjudication of *mahr* or maintenance claims, mediation between spouses upon application, adjudication of decrees of nullity, and a number of other administrative and judicial matters relating to Muslim personal law.

Notable Features: There is very limited legislation relating to Muslim personal status in Sri Lanka, following the characteristics of the application of Muslim personal law elsewhere in South Asia in that much of Muslim personal law remains uncodified. The legislation that does apply is largely of an administrative nature, and does not necessarily alter or reinterpret many of the substantive classical provisions of Islamic family law.

The Muslim Marriage and Divorce Act 1951 regulate matrimonial law for Muslims. The Act repealed the Muslim Marriage and Divorce Registration Ordinance 1929 and has been revised a number of times since its passage.

In 1995, the minimum age of marriage was raised to 18. However, the marriage age for Muslims is governed by the Muslim Marriage and Divorce Act, allowing for a girl to marry as young as 12 without the permission of a *Quazi*, and younger with the *Quazi's* permission after any such inquiry as he may deem necessary. With respect to capacity, the Act states that for any Shafi'i woman, no contract of marriage is valid under the law applicable to that sect unless her rightful *wali* is present at the time and place at which the contract is entered into and he communicates her consent to as well as his own approval of the contract. No person may knowingly act as a *wali* unless he is entitled to do so under the law governing the sect to which the bride belongs, and no marriage for which a person acts as a *wali* in contravention of that provision can be registered. The *Quazi* may inquire into any complaint by a woman against a *wali* who unreasonably withholds his consent to her marriage, and authorise the marriage and dispense with the necessity for his presence or consent if he rules in favour of the woman. He may authorise marriage in cases where a woman has no *wali* as well. The MMDA makes registration upon conclusion of the *nikah* mandatory and shares the responsibility of registration between the bridegroom, the *wali* of the bride (if a *wali* is required by the law governing the sect to which the bride belongs) and the person conducting the *nikah* ceremony. Nothing in the act renders an unregistered marriage or divorce invalid, so long as the marriage or divorce is valid according to the sect to which the parties belong. Every person responsible for registering a marriage or divorce who fails to do so is liable to a fine upon the first offence, and a fine or imprisonment or both for additional convictions.

The MMDA also requires notification in the event of a Muslim male wishing to enter into a polygamous marriage. He must give notice of his intention to the *Quazi's* of the area where he resides and the area where his wife (or wives) resides, as well as to the *Quazi* of the area where the intended bride resides at least thirty days before contracting the subsequent marriage. The notice provided to the *Quazi's*, in a prescribed form, must contain the full names and address of the husband and all prospective co-wives. It is the duty of each of the *Quazi's* to whom notice is given to post such notices at the *Jumma* (Friday) mosques within his area and in a "conspicuous place" at each address within his area that is specified in that notice. No polygamous marriage can be registered under the Act if the husband fails to go through this process before contracting the second or subsequent marriage.

The MMDA provides detailed rules regarding the registration of divorce by the husband and the wife. A husband who "intends to pronounce the *talaq* on his wife" shall give notice to the *Quazi* of the area where she is resident, and the *Quazi's* duty is to attempt to effect reconciliation, with the help of the relatives of both parties, as well as elders and influential Muslims of the area. If within thirty days no reconciliation is effected, the husband shall pronounce the *talaq* in the presence of the *Quazi* and two witnesses and the *Quazi* shall record the pronouncement and cause notice of it to be served to the wife if she is not present; the "alleged reasons" for which the husband seeks to divorce his wife are *not* to be recorded by the *Quazi*. It is the *Quazi's* duty, where conciliation proceedings have failed, to recover any unpaid *mahr* from the husband, whether or not the wife has claimed her outstanding dower debt. The remaining dower due her is deposited with the court in the name of the wife and the wife is served notice that such money is deposited in her name. If the husband does not appear on the dates he was called before the *Quazi* for the reconciliation process, the *Quazi* may, at any time after the expiry of three months from the date of the pronouncement of *talaq*, and upon the oath or affirmation of the wife, register the divorce.

The Act also outlines the procedure the Muslim wife must follow to effect a divorce from her husband, without his consent, on grounds of ill-treatment or on account of any act or omission on his part which amounts to a fault under the Muslim law governing the sect to which the parties belong. In such cases, the Muslim wife must apply for divorce to the *Quazi* of the area in which she is resident. The *Quazi* convenes a panel of three Muslim assessors to hear the application, and they must endeavour to effect an amicable settlement and remove the cause of the conflict between the husband and wife. If reconciliation efforts fail, the *Quazi* and the assessors proceed to hear the case for divorce and a decision is made according to the sect of the parties. (There is no provision relating to cases where the parties belong to different sects.) After the appealable time elapses, if there has been no appeal of the order of the *Quazi* allowing the divorce, or if the Board of *Quazis* or the Court of Appeal has decided to allow a divorce upon appeal, the *Quazi* shall register the divorce.

The MMDA contains provisions relating to maintenance, *mahr* and *kaikuli*. The time for the prescription of a suit or action for a woman's *mahr* (in whole or part), shall not begin until the dissolution of the marriage by death or divorce, and such suit or action must be commenced within three years from the date of such dissolution. The Act does not specify regulations for a woman claiming maintenance from her husband during the subsistence of their marriage, though there is explicit mention of the *Quazi's* powers to examine and decide upon claims by wives or divorced wives for *kaikuli* or lying-in expenses. The court may specify that maintenance arrears may be awarded from the date of the claim.

The Muslim Intestate Succession Act 1931 directs that the estate of any Muslim who dies intestate and who resided in Sri Lanka or owned any immovable property there at the time of his or her death shall devolve according to the Muslim law of the sect to which the deceased belonged. The same is the case for any donations (not involving usufructs and trusts) made by Muslims domiciled in Sri Lanka or owning immovable property there.

Law/Case Reporting System: Supreme Court and Court of Appeal decisions are published in *Sri Lanka Law Reports.*

International Conventions and Reports to Treaty Governing Bodies: Sri Lanka signed the CEDAW in 1980 and ratified it in 1981.

Sri Lanka acceded to the ICCPR and ICESCR in 1980.

Sri Lanka signed the CRC in 1990 and ratified it in 1991.

Sri Lanka did not submit any reservations or declarations upon signature, ratification or accession to any of the above instruments.

Background and Sources: Goonesekere, "Sri Lanka" in Lawasia Family Law Series, Watson and Sihombing, eds. Singapore, 1979; Mahmood, "Sri Lanka" in Statutes of Personal Law in Islamic Countries, 2nd ed., New Delhi, 1995; Tambiah and Markhani, eds., Muslim Law in Sri Lanka, Colombo, 1996; Redden, "Sri Lanka" in Modern Legal Systems Cyclopedia, Vol. 9, Buffalo, N.Y., 1990; Robinson, ed. The Cambridge Encyclopaedia of India, Pakistan, Bangladesh, Sri Lanka, Nepal, Bhutan and the Maldives, Cambridge, 1989.

Republic of the Sudan

Legal History

The legal system is based on English common law and Islamic law. Sudan came under Egyptian-Ottoman rule from the time of the Egyptian defeat of the Funj Kingdom in 1822. After the opening of the Suez Canal in 1869, European interest in the region increased; British General Charles Gordon appointed a governor of Egyptian Sudan in 1873. The Mahdist revolt led by Muhammad Ahmad al-Mahdi in 1880 led to the capture of Khartoum from the Egyptians in 1885. The British re-established control over the region in 1898 under General Horatio Kitchener. The British and Egyptians shared sovereignty during the Condominium period from 1899. An agreement to allow for a three-year transition period to independence in 1953 led to self-rule in 1956.

Civil war between the North and South continues to plague Sudan. Three extended periods of military rule have been punctuated by briefer periods of multi-party parliamentary rule. The last elected government was suspended after a military coup on 30th June 1989. Sadiq al-Mahdi was overthrown by the military and an Islamist coalition led by Lt. Gen. Umar al-Bashir and Dr. Hasan al-Turabi and martial law was imposed. From 20th January 1991, the Revolutionary Command Council imposed Islamic law on all residents of northern states regardless of religion.

On 1 July 1998, a new constitution came into force following a referendum the previous month. Lt. Gen. al-Bashir became President and Dr. al-Turabi became Speaker of the Parliament. On 12th December 1999, President al-Bashir dissolved Parliament and declared a state of emergency. In April 2000, the state of emergency was extended through the end of 2000.

Sources of law are Islamic law, consensus of the population, the constitutional, and custom. In family law, judicial circulars (*manshurat*) issued by Qadi al-Quda (first issued in 1916) served to institute reforms or instruct application of particular interpretations. Family Code passed in 1991, codifying *shariah* principles and interpretations of some *manshurat* and abolishing others. Section 5 of Code indicates Hanafi *fiqh* as residual source of law; Supreme Court (*Shariah* Circuit) vested with power to issue interpretations of Code. Sources of law are Islamic law, constitutional law, legislation, judicial precedent, and custom. In family law, judicial circulars (*manshurat*) issued by the Qadi al-Quda (first issued in 1916) served to institute reforms or instruct the application of particular interpretations. The Family Code passed in 1991, codified *shariah* principles and interpretations of some of the *manshurat* and abolished others. Section 5 of the Code indicates Hanafi *fiqh* as a residual source of law; the Supreme Court (*Shariah* Circuit) is vested with power to issue interpretations of the Code.

Schools of *Fiqh*: The Maliki School was the predominant *madhhab* in Sudan, although the dominant school is now the Hanafi, due to Egyptian and Ottoman influence.

Constitutional Status of Islam(ic) Law: The constitution came into force on 1 July 1998, after being approved in a referendum the previous month; Art. 1 states that Islam is the religion of the majority of the population, but does not proclaim it to be the state religion; Art. 65 identify the sources of law as *shariah*, the consensus of the people, the constitution, and custom. Prior to the enactment of the constitution, Sudan had largely been governed through a series of "constitutional decrees." Art. 137 repealed all of the constitutional decrees except Constitutional Decree No. 14, which provides for implementation of the 21 April 1997 Peace Accord.

Court System: The court system consists of a Constitutional Court, a High Court, Court of Appeals and courts of first instance. During the Islamisation campaign of 1983, the government reunified civil and *shariah* courts, which had been divided during the colonial period. There is nothing in the new constitution to suggest that there has been a change in the treatment of *shariah* in the courts.

Notable Features: The Muslim Personal Law Act 1991 requires that both parties to a marriage be past the age of puberty and be willingly consenting to the marriage. The male guardian marries adult women with their consent, although the *qadi* is empowered to act in this capacity if her guardian refuses his consent without justification. The guardian retains entitlement to seek dissolution on the grounds of lack of *kifa'a* of the husband, defined as *kifa'a* in religion and morals.

Classical rules apply to regulate polygamy. Provision is made for stipulations be inserted in the marriage contract. The wife is entitled to maintenance, assessed according to the circumstances of the husband; arrears can be claimed for up to three years preceding the date of submission of the claim at court. The wife loses the right to maintenance if she refuses to move to the marital home or leaves it without a *shariahh* justification, including if she works outside the house without her husband's consent, provided he is not being arbitrary in his prohibition on her working. The wife is required to obey the husband in accordance with the classical rules, but a ruling for obedience cannot be forcibly executed.

Reforms standard to the region to the rules on *talaq* have been introduced, affecting the validity of *talaq* accompanied by a number in word or sign, *talaq* in the form of an oath, *talaq* intended to induce someone to do something. In a further reform to classical law, the wife must be informed of the husband's revocation of a revocable *talaq* during her *'idda* period in order for the revocation to be valid.

The wife may seek judicial divorce on the grounds of the husband's incurable physical or mental illness rendering it impossible for the wife to continue to live with him without harm; the husband's impotence not curable within one year; the husband's cruelty, or discord between the spouses; the husband's inability to pay maintenance; and divorce by 'ransom' where a wife held disobedient by the court may waive her rights in return for a divorce and if the husband refuses to agree, arbitrators must be appointed and if the wife establishes that she suffers from remaining with him, a *talaq* will be ordered by the court.

After divorce the wife is entitled to maintenance for the *'idda* period and to *mut'a* to be assessed according to the means of her ex-husband to a maximum of six months' maintenance. This is unless the divorce was a judicial divorce by reason of the man's poverty and inability to pay maintenance or for some physical reason arising in the wife, or unless the divorce was by *khul'*.

A divorced mother is entitled to custody of her male children till they are seven years old and females till they are nine; the court may extend these period if it is proven to be in the interests of the wards, until the sons reach puberty and the daughters consummate marriage. The father or other male guardian is to maintain scrutiny of all matters related to the raising of the children in the custody of their mother. The court has certain discretion to allow a woman who marries a man not a *mahram* to retain custody if the interests of the ward so require. The custody of a woman of a different religion to the father ends when the child is five or earlier if there are fears for their faith being affected. Child support is the responsibility of the father until the daughter is married and the son is of an age when he is able to earn his own living.

In a reform to the law of succession, the *radd* has been extended to include the spouse relict after the fractional heirs and the succession of cognate relatives.

Law/Case Reporting System: Case reports are published in the *Sudan Law Journal and Reports*. Laws are published in the *Sudan Gazette.*

International Conventions (with Relevant Reservations): Sudan acceded to the ICCPR and the ICESCR in 1986, without reservations.

Sudan signed and ratified the CRC in 1990, without reservations.

Background and Sources: Amin, Middle East Legal Systems, Glasgow, 1985; Fluehr-Lobban, Islamic Law and Society in the Sudan, London, 1986; Hale, Gender Politics in Sudan: Islamism, Socialism and the State, Oxford, 1996; Mahmood, "Sudan" in Statutes of Personal Law in Islamic Countries, 2nd ed., New Delhi, 1995; O'Fahey, The National Front, Its Opponents and the Shariah Issue, Islam et society's au sud du Sahara, n. 11 (Nov. 1997): 55-65; Pearl, A Textbook on Muslim Law, 2nd ed., London, 1987; Redden, "Sudan" in Modern Legal Systems Cyclopedia, vol. 6, Buffalo, NY, 1990; Rubin and Cotran, eds. Annual Survey of African Law, Vols. I-VI (1967-1972), London; Safwat, "Islamic Laws in the Sudan," in Islamic Law: Social and Historical Contexts, al-Azmeh, ed., London, 1988; Safwat, "Sudan," Yearbook of Islamic and Middle Eastern Law, Vol. 1 (1994): 237-253; Women and the Law in Sudan: First and Second Reports, Women Living Under Muslim Laws, Vols. I-III (1997) and Vols. I-III (1999).

Syria (Syrian Arab Republic)

Legal History

Syria served as the centre of the Umayyad caliphate until the Abbasid Revolution of 756. After a succession of Arab, Crusader, Kurdish, and Mamluke rulers, Syria came under Ottoman control in 1516. Following the expulsion of the Ottomans after World War I, the League of Nations declared a French mandate over the region in 1922, from which Syria gained independence in 1946.

The Ottoman Law of Family Rights continued to govern matters of personal status until 1953. The *Qadi* of Damascus, Shaykh Ali al-Tantawi, drafted a comprehensive treatise on personal law, based on *takhayyur* according to principles most suitable to changing social conditions. After the publication of al-Tantawi's treatise, the government established a Commission to prepare a draft code of personal law. The Commission based its draft on principles from al-Tantawi's code, the OLFR, various Egyptian laws enacted from 1920 to 1946, and the unofficial code prepared by Egyptian jurist Qudri Pasha. The Syrian Law of Personal Status (*Qanun al-Ahwal al-Shakhsiyya*) 1953 produced by the Commission covers matters of personal status, family relations and intestate and testamentary succession and was the most comprehensive code issued in the Arab world to that date.

Article 305 of the SLPS directs that, for matters not specified in the text, resort shall be had to the most authoritative doctrine of the Hanafi school. Major amendments were made to the SLPS in 1975, particularly relating to the areas of polygamy, dower, maintenance, *mut'a*, cost of nursing, custody of children, and guardianship.

Schools of *Fiqh*: The Hanafi School is the predominant *madhhab* in Syria, and there are Ja'fari, Druze, Ismaili and Alawi minorities. There are also several Christian denominations and very small Jewish communities based in Damascus, Al-Qamishli, and Aleppo.

Constitutional Status of Islam(ic) Law: The Constitution was adopted on 13th March 1973. Article 3(1) declares that the religion of the President of the Republic shall be Islam. Article 3(2) declares Islamic jurisprudence a main source of legislation.

Court System: Courts having jurisdiction over personal status matters are *shariah* courts for Sunni and Shi'i Muslims, *madhhab i*courts for the Druze, and *ruhi* courts for Christians and Jews. There is one single-*qadi shariah* court of first instance per district (except Damascus and Aleppo where there are three each). Each of the three types of courts has its own appellate courts. Final appeal for all the religious courts lies with the Family Section of the Court of Cassation in Damascus, the highest court of the regular system.

Shariah courts have both general jurisdiction (relating to all Syrians without respect to religion and to non-Syrians originating from countries where Islamic personal status laws are applied- i.e., over matters of guardianship, succession, ascertaining capacity, missing persons, filiation, matrimonial issues, and maintenance of relatives) and special jurisdiction (relating to Muslim Syrians in matters of personal status including marriage, dissolution, *mahr*, custody and maintenance, and *awqaf*. The Code of Personal Status applied to Muslims by the *shariah* courts has specific exemptions for Druze, Christians and Jews.

Notable Features: The minimum marriage age is 18 years for males and 17 for females, with scope for judicial discretion for males of 15 years and females of 13 years if either the father or grandfather serving as *wali* consents and the parties appear physically able. If the court finds incompatibility in age between betrothed parties, the judge may withhold permission for marriage. Both parties require their *walis* permission for marrying under the age of full capacity, though a judge may overrule a *wali*s unreasonable objection to the marriage of his female ward (conditional upon equality of status or *kafa'a* between the betrothed parties).

Marriage registration is obligatory and applications for marriage must be submitted to the judge, requiring documentation attesting to identity, age, residence, guardian's identity, medical certificate, civil status, etc. of the betrothed parties. Marriages contracted out of court are not to be certified without such procedures with the exception of cases where the wife is pregnant or a child has been born, though extenuating circumstances do not prevent the application of legal sanctions for non-compliance with registration requirements.

The judge may refuse permission for a polygamous marriage unless the husband is able to establish lawful cause and financial capacity. The wife's financial rights are forfeit if she works outside the home without her husband's consent or if she is deemed disobedient due to leaving the matrimonial home without lawful justification or refusing to cohabit with her husband. Arrears of maintenance shall be awarded the wife from the date her husband fails to maintain her, up to four months prior to the date of the claim.

Talaq uttered while intoxicated, disoriented/enraged, under coercion, during death sickness or grave illness, or in order to coerce is ineffective. *Talaq* to which a number is attached shall be considered a single irrevocable repudiation (except the third of three).

The wife may seek a judicial divorce on the following grounds: a defect in the husband preventing consummation (though such right is forfeit if the wife accepted the defect except in the case of husband's impotence); husband's insanity; husband's absence without justification for one year; husband's sentencing to three years imprisonment, after he has served one year of the sentence; and the husband's failure to maintain if non-maintenance is due to the husband's inability to provide maintenance, the judge shall grant a grace period of up to three months. Either spouse may apply for a judicial divorce on grounds of discord causing such harm as makes cohabitation impossible (after reconciliation efforts). The divorced wife may be awarded compensation of up to three years maintenance (in addition to the maintenance owed her during her *idda* if the judge finds the husband's exercise of *talaq* to have been arbitrary. The divorced mother has right to custody over boys until the age of nine and girls until the age of eleven. The *qadi* may extend the mother's custody over girls until marriage or over boys or girls until they attain *rushd*, if the guardian is not the father, or if the court finds that the father is not to be trusted with the children.

The law relating to succession is based mainly on Hanafi *fiqh*, as embodied in the Code of Personal Status, although it is influenced by Egyptian reform legislation from the 1940s. The doctrine of *radd* (return) was extended to permit surviving spouses to share in the division of the residue of their deceased partners estates. Obligatory bequests have also been introduced to benefit orphaned grandchildren through predeceased sons.

Law/Case Reporting System: Law reporting is through the *Official Gazette*.

International Conventions (with Relevant Reservations): Syria acceded to the ICCPR and ICESCR in 1969, submitting the following reservations: the first reservation relates to non-recognition of the state of Israel; the second reservation (relating to Articles 48(1) and 26(1) of the ICCPR and ICESCR, respectively) states that these provisions are incompatible with the aims of the Covenants, as they do not allow all States "without distinction or discrimination" to become parties to the Covenants.

Syria signed the CRC in 1990 and ratifying it in 1993, with a general reservation to any provisions that are not in conformity with Syrian legislation or the principles of the Islamic *shariah*, with particular reference to Article 14 on children's freedom of religion, and Articles 2 and 21 concerning to adoption.

Background and Sources: Amin, Middle East Legal Systems, Glasgow, 1985; Anderson, "Syrian Law of Personal Status," Bulletin of the School of Oriental and African Studies, 17(1955): 25-59; Berger, "The Legal System of Family Law in Syria," Bulletin Orientales, 1997 (XLIX): 115-127; El Alami and Hinchcliffe, Islamic Marriage and Divorce Laws of the Arab World, London, 1996; el-Hakim, "Syria," Yearbook of Islamic and Middle Eastern Law, Vol. 1 (1994): 142-155; Mahmood, "Syria" in Statutes of Personal Law in Islamic Countries, 2nd ed., New Delhi, 1995; Nasir, The Islamic Law of Personal Status, 2nd ed., London, 1990; Pearl, A Textbook on Muslim Law, 2nd ed., London, 1987; Redden, "Syria" in Modern Legal Systems Cyclopedia, Vol. 5, Buffalo, NY, 1990.

United Republic of Tanzania

Legal History

The Bantu ancestors of the majority of current-day Tanzania's population settled in the region in approximately 500 CE. Arab settlers in the coastal regions introduced Islam to the region in the 9th and 10th centuries. European interest in the region began to increase with Portuguese explorers arriving in the region in the late 15th century, although the Portuguese never established settlements in Tanzania. In the late 19th century, Germany gained increasing control over the area from the coast inland to Rwanda and Urundi, establishing the Colony of German East Africa. Soon after in 1890, the islands of Zanzibar and Pemba were declared a British Colony. Following World War I, the League of Nations extended the British mandate to Tanganyika, while other parts of German East Africa (Rwanda and Burundi) were placed under a Belgian protectorate. A legislative council was established in 1926 and Tanganyika became a UN trust territory in 1946. The legislative council was expanded over the next decade in order to provide equal representation to Africans, Asians and Europeans. The Tanganyikan African National Union (TANU) established by Julius Nyerere in 1954 began calling for increasing African representation and by the late 1950s for full independence. TANU's appeal was clear from elections held in 1958 and 1960, and Tanganyika achieved its independence in December 1961, becoming a republic one year later. Zanzibar achieved independence in 1963, and the Sultan was overthrown the following year. The two states unified in April 1964 to form the United Republic of Tanzania. Both independent states had a single-party system and the two parties eventually merged to form the Chama Cha Mapinduzi (CCM). Under increasing internal and international pressure, the Tanzanian government introduced constitutional reforms permitting the establishment of opposition parties in 1992.

Under the federal agreement unifying Tanganyika and Zanzibar, the two units have separate legislative, executive and judicial institutions. Union matters are defined in the first supplement to the Constitution; personal status comes under those areas defined as "non-union matters", thus the Marriage Act that applies in mainland Tanzania is not applicable in Zanzibar. Prior to 1971, Muslims, Christian, Hindu and customary laws governed marriage and divorce, in addition to a civil marriage regime. The proposal of a new marriage law in 1967 aroused intense debate, especially relating to the role of the *shariahh in* matters relating to Muslim personal status. One of the proposals drawing most criticism related to the requirement of the first wife's permission for contracting a polygamous marriage. Despite much criticism and opposition, the uniform Marriage Act was passed into law in Tanganyika in 1971. The new Act integrated existing marriage laws while preserving the right to religious solemnisation and the option of polygamy. Elements that are uniformly applicable relate to the basic requirement of free consent, a common definition of permanent impediments to marriage, a minimum marriage age (although there is some leeway provided by grounds for judicial discretion and by the terms of the Penal Code), a common definition of void or avoidable marriages, and certain preliminaries such as a notice-period before marriage.

More recently, the Law Reform Commission of Tanzania has conducted several long-term studies, through its Family Law, Child Law and Succession Law Committees, on the reform of those applicable laws. The Committees have recommended such changes as raising the minimum marriage age to 18 for both parties, raising the 'tender age' presumption stating that women are the more appropriate custodians for children under 7 years to 14 years, harmonising succession laws, gradually eliminating the category of 'illegitimacy', etc.

Schools of *Fiqh*: The majority of Tanzanian Muslims are Shafi'i, with significant Hanafi, Ja'fari and Isma'ili communities and small Ibadi, Maliki, Hanbali and Ahmadi communities. The majority of Zanzibar's population is Muslim, with Christianity and indigenous religions predominant in Tanganyika.

Constitutional Status of Islamic Law: The Constitution was adopted on 25th April 1977, with major revisions in 1984 and the insertion of a Bill of Rights in 1988. It adopts no official state religion.

Court System: The judiciary is organised under the Magistrates' Courts Act 1963. There are primary courts in each of 25 administrative regions; the jurisdiction of primary courts includes all civil suits related to customary and Islamic law and all civil and Christian matrimonial suits. The next level of courts is District Courts, then Resident Magistrates' Courts, then two High Courts in Zanzibar and Tanganyika. The Court of Appeal serves as the highest court in judiciary.

Notable Features: The minimum marriage age under the Marriage Act 1971 is 18 for males and 15 for females. Courts may permit underage marriage of parties who have reached 14 years of age if specific circumstances make the marriage appear desirable. The Penal Code provides that persons of "African or Asiatic descent" may marry or permit marriage of a girl less than 12 years of age in accordance with their custom or religion so long as the marriage is not intended to be consummated before she attains 12 years. The Marriage Act only specifies the free consent of marrying parties for validity, and dispenses with the need for the guardian's consent if the have attained 18 years of age.

Marriage registration is obligatory and non-compliance is punishable by a fine, but will not render the marriage void. The Marriage Act provides for the licensing of religious functionaries as Marriage Registrars.

Polygamy is permitted with the consent of the first wife; the marrying parties must state in the notice of intention to marry whether the marriage is intended to be monogamous, polygamous or potentially polygamous. There is a rebuttable presumption that customary and Muslim marriages are potentially polygamous and others monogamous. It is also possible to "convert" a marriage to polygamous or monogamous by the spouses' joint declaration. This facility exists in the registration of civil marriages as well, although Christians married in church cannot do so as long as both parties remain Christian. Maintenance of the wife or wives is specified as the husband's duty, and becomes the wife's duty in cases where her husband is incapacitated and unable to earn a living. The Court may order the payment of maintenance in limited circumstances where the husband refuses or neglects to support his wife.

The Marriage Act provides that, except in extreme cases, no petition of divorce is to be heard before a marriage has subsisted for two years. Either spouse may apply for divorce on grounds of breakdown, but no decree of divorce can be granted unless the court is convinced of irreparable breakdown. The party seeking the divorce must first apply to the Marriage Conciliatory Board. The board must certify failure to reconcile parties before the divorce suit can be initiated. Evidence of irreparable breakdown of marriage for court's purposes must indicate one of the following grounds: mental or physical cruelty; willful neglect; desertion; voluntary separation; or change of religion that dissolves the marriage under the religious law the parties were subject to at the time of their marriage. *Talaq* is not recognised as an automatic dissolution of marriage, but a concession provides that any act dissolving a marriage under Islamic law is a compelling ground for divorce, but the act must have occurred after the Marriage Conciliatory Board has certified its failure to reconcile the couple. In dividing marital property and passing decisions on maintenance, courts must consider the customs of the parties' community, the contribution made by each party towards acquisition of the property in money, property or work, the debts owed by either party for acquiring property for their joint benefit, and the needs of infant children. Beyond that, the court may order maintenance for former wives in very limited circumstances, such as enforcing the Muslim wife's right to maintenance during *'idda*. In determining matters of child custody and guardianship, the Courts are directed to consider paramount the welfare of the ward. There is a rebuttable presumption that children should remain with the mother until the age of seven. Courts are also directed to consider the customs of the community to which the parents belong, the economic circumstances of both parents, the housing that both parents can provide, and the behaviour of the mother and whether or not she is considered to have contributed to the marital breakdown.

Succession is governed by statutory, customary, Islamic and Hindu law in Tanganyika. The Non-Christian Asiatic (Succession) Ordinance directs the application of the personal law of the deceased according to the individual's religion. Islamic law is applicable to African Muslims under the Judicature and Applications of Laws Ordinance empowering courts to apply Islamic law to matters of succession in communities that generally follow Islamic law in matters of personal status and inheritance. The Courts, in determining the appropriate legal regime to apply to cases where there is a conflict of laws (i.e., when there is a dispute over the division of the estate of an African Muslim who also came under a system of customary law) employ two tests: the "mode of life" and the "intention of the deceased" tests. In deciding between the applications of customary or statutory law, the "mode of life" test considers whether the deceased was part of a community where the customary law is widely accepted and applied. The "intention of the deceased" test considers statements and deeds of the deceased which could have indicated his/her preference.

Notable Cases

Law/Case Reporting System: Law reporting is through the *Gazette of the United Republic of Tanzania* and there are loose-leaf editions of the *Laws of Mainland Tanzania* issued periodically. Reports of High Court and Court of Appeals decisions are published in the *Tanzania Law Reports* which replaced the *High Court Digest* in 1975.

International Conventions (with Relevant Reservations): Tanzania acceded to the ICCPR and ICESCR in 1976 without reservations.

Tanzania signed the CEDAW in 1980 and ratified it in 1985 without reservations.

Tanzania signed the CRC in 1990 and ratified it in 1991 without reservations.

Background and Sources: Redden, "Tanzania" in Modern Legal Systems Cyclopedia, Vol. 6, Buffalo NY, 1990; Rwezaura, "Tanzania: Family Law and the New Bill of Rights," Journal of Family Law (University of Louisville), Vol. 29, No. 2 (1991): 453-461; Rwebangira, The Legal Status of Women and Poverty in Tanzania, Uppsala, 1996; Rwezaura, "Tanzania: Gender Justice and Children's Rights: A Banner for Family Law Reform in Tanzania," in The International Survey of Family Law, Bainham, ed., 1997: 413-443; Rubin and Cotran, "Tanzania" in Annual Survey of African Law, Vols. I-IV, 1967-1970; "Tanzania" in Women of the World: Laws and Policies Affecting Their Reproductive Lives-Anglophone Africa, Center for Reproductive Law and Policy and International Federation of Women Lawyers (Kenya Chapter), New York, 1997.

Republic of Tunisia

Legal History: The Legal system is based on the French civil law system and Islamic law.

As an autonomous province of the Ottoman Empire from 1574, Hanafi *fiqh* was influential, but never displaced the position of the Maliki School. Tunisia became a French Protectorate in 1881 and attained full independence in March 1956. The Law of Personal Status, inspired by unofficial draft codes of Maliki and Hanafi family law, was passed soon after independence. The TLPS was extended to apply to all Tunisian citizens in 1957, thus ending the application of rabbinical law to Jewish personal status matters and the French Civil Code to personal status cases relating to non-Muslim Tunisians. Among the most controversial provisions of the TLPS were those banning polygamy and extra-judicial divorce.

Schools of *Fiqh*: The Maliki School is the predominant *madhhab* in Tunisia.

Constitutional Status of Islamic Law: The Constitution was adopted 1st June 1959. Article 1 declares Islam the state religion, and Article 38 provides that the President of the Republic must be a Muslim.

Court System: *Shariah* courts were abolished in 1956. There are four levels of courts in the judiciary. Cantonal courts have limited criminal jurisdiction. Courts of first instance have civil, commercial, correctional, social and personal status chambers. Three courts of appeal (in Tunis, Sousse and Sfax) have civil, correctional, criminal and accusation chambers (the final one being similar to a grand jury). The Court of Cassation in Tunis is the highest court of appeal, with three civil and commercial chambers and a criminal chamber.

Notable Features

The minimum age of marriage is 20 for males and 17 for females. Marriage below these ages requires special permission from the courts, which may be given only for pressing reasons and on the basis of a clear interest or benefit to be realised by both spouses by the marriage. Marriage below the age of legal majority requires the consent of the guardian and (since 1993) of the mother; recourse may be had to the judge in the event of their refusal. The age of legal majority is 20 for both males and females, but marriage gives rise to legal majority for matters of personal status, civil and commercial transactions provided the party concerned is over the age of 17 (see Article 153). Marriage can proven only by official document as prescribed by law. Polygyny is prohibited, and offenders are liable to a prison sentence of one year and/or a fine.

During marriage, spouses are to treat each other well, to fulfil their marital duties as required by custom and usage and to cooperate in running family affairs, including the upbringing of children. As head of the family the husband is responsible for the maintenance of his wife and children, while the wife is to contribute to family maintenance if she has the means to do so.

Divorce is a strictly judicial matter; extra-judicial *talaq* has no validity. The occurrence of three divorces between a couple creates a permanent prohibition on their future remarriage.

The court may grant divorce based on (1) agreement of the spouses (2) a petition from one spouse by reason of injury caused by the other; or (3) the will of the husband or the petition of the wife. No divorce may be decreed until after the family judge appointed by the court has tried and failed to reconcile the couple. Where divorce is not by mutual agreement (i.e. in either of the last two cases) the court may award compensation for that injury. If the injured spouse is the wife, this may take the form of a lump sum or of regular alimony payments until she no longer has need of them that is, she dies or remarries or otherwise her social circumstances change.

If the marriage ends by death of one of the spouses, custody goes to the surviving spouse; if it ends by divorce, the judge is required to take the best interest of the ward into account in assigning custody either to one of the parents or to a third party. If the mother is awarded custody, she is authorised to exercise the prerogatives of the guardian in matters related to the ward's travel, education, and financial affairs; she may be granted full powers of guardianship if the guardian is unable or unfit to exercise them.

In succession, the obligatory bequest has been legislated for orphaned grandchildren through a pre-deceased father or mother, entitling them to the proportion of the dead parent's share to a maximum of one-third of the estate. The spouse relict share in the *radd* of the estate; daughters as well as brothers may exclude collaterals and other more remote male relatives of the deceased from inheritance.

Law/Case Reporting System: Law reporting is through the *Journal Officiel*.

International Conventions (with Relevant Reservations): Tunisia signed the ICCPR and ICESCR in 1968 and ratified them. No divorce may be decreed until after family judge has tried and failed in 1969 without reservations.

Tunisia signed the CEDAW in 1980 and ratified it in 1985 with a number of declarations and reservations. The general declaration states that Tunisia declares that it shall not take any organisational or legislative decision in conformity with the requirements of this Convention where such a decision would conflict with the provisions of chapter I of the Tunisian Constitution relating to general provisions as well as to fundamental rights and duties. Tunisia submitted the following reservations: the reservation to Article 9(2) states that the provision must not conflict with the provisions of chapter VI of the Tunisian Nationality Code; Tunisia also does not consider itself bound by Article 16(c), (d), (f), (g) and (h) and that paragraphs (g) and (h) of that Article must not conflict with the provisions of the Personal Status Code concerning the granting of family names to children and the acquisition of property through inheritance. Tunisia also submitted a declaration concerning Article 15(4), stating that requirements relating to women's right to choice of residence and domicile must not be interpreted in a manner which conflicts with the (relevant) provisions of the Personal Status Code as set forth in chapters 23 and 61 of the Code.

Tunisia signed the CRC in 1990 and ratified it in 1992 with a number of declarations and reservations. The first general declaration submitted by Tunisia states that it shall not adopt any legislation in conflict with the Tunisian Constitution in the implementation of the Convention. A further declaration states that implementation of the provisions of the CRC shall be limited by the means at Tunisia's disposal.The final declaration states that the Preamble to and provisions of the Convention (particularly Article 6) shall not be interpreted in such a way as to impede the application of Tunisian legislation concerning voluntary termination of pregnancy. Tunisia also submitted the following reservations: Article 2 of the CRC may not impede the implementation of the provisions of its national legislation concerning personal status, particularly in relation to marriage and inheritance rights; Article 40(2)(b)(v) on the review of judgements applying penal sanctions to minors is to be regarded as a general principle to which exceptions may be made by national legislation; and Article 7 of the CRC cannot be interpreted as prohibiting the implementation of the provisions of national legislation relating to nationality and, in particular, to cases in which it is forfeited.

Background and Sources: El Alami and Hinchcliffe, Islamic Marriage and Divorce Laws of the Arab World, London, 1996; Brand, Women, the State, and Political Liberalisation: Middle Eastern and North African Experiences, New York, 1998; Mahmood, Tunisia in Family Law Reform in the Muslim World, Bombay, 1972; A.E.Mayer, Reform of Personal Status Laws in North Africa, 49:3 *Middle East Journal* 1995; Nasir, The Islamic Law of Personal Status, 2nd ed., London, 1990; Nelson, ed., Tunisia: A Country Study, 3rd ed., Washington, D.C., 1988; Pearl, A Textbook on Muslim Law, 2nd ed., London, 1987; Tunisia, Combined Initial and Second Reports to CEDAW, 12 April 1994. See also website: www.jurisitetunisie.com

United Arab Emirates

Legal History

The UAE is a federation of seven Emirates: Abu Dhabi, Sharjah, Ajman, Fujayrah, Umm al-Qawain, Dubai and Ra's al-Khaymah. Sources of law are Islamic law, constitutional law, and legislation.

The area now known as the United Arab Emirates was known as the pirate coast by the early nineteenth century. From the 1820s, the British entered into a number of treaties with local rules in order to protect their shipping interests. A perpetual maritime truce signed in 1853 gave the British remit over handling of foreign relations for the region. Full independence was attained in December 1971, with Ras al-Khaymah, the last Emirate to join the federation, becoming a part of the Union the following year.

Schools of *Fiqh*: The majority of Emiriti nationals are Sunni Muslim; there is a significant Shi'a minority, as well as small Christian and Hindu minorities. The federation has a very high proportion of expatriates.

Constitutional Status of Islam(ic) Law: Article 7 of the Provisional Constitution adopted 2nd December 1971 and made permanent in 1996 declares Islam the official state religion of the Union, and affirms that Islamic *shariahh* shall be a principal source of legislation.

Court System: The Abu Dhabi Courts Law 1968 regulates the jurisdiction of *shariah* courts, though personal status law remains uncodified. The other six Emirates do not have similar legislation or organised judiciaries, so *shariahh* courts are not regulated. Important civil and criminal cases are brought before the ruler in person.

The Sharjah Courts Law 1971 created civil courts competent to hear commercial and labour disputes, with limited criminal jurisdiction. The Law Establishing the Union Supreme Court 1973 and the Union Law 1978 established the Union Courts of First Instance and Appeal and transferred jurisdiction from tribunals in Abu Dhabi, Sharjah, Ajman and Fujayrah to these courts. Union Courts of First Instance deal with civil, commercial and administrative disputes, including personal status cases, arising in the permanent capital.

Notable Features: Personal status law remains unlegislated.

The Ministry of Labour and Social Affairs has been made responsible for welfare payments to those who require such assistance. Under the 1977 Social Security Law, eligibility extends to widows, orphans, divorced women or women separated from their husbands, unmarried women, families of prisoners, women married to foreign nationals, etc. The Ministry also disburses funds to local women's organisations, including the main national umbrella-group, the UAE Women's Federation.

Notable Cases: Judgment no. 8/97: In 1997 the Dubai Court of Cassation ruled that a divorced mother who had remarried retained custody rights over children due to a written agreement between the parents whereby the father agreed not to claim custody even if his former wife remarried.

Judgment no. 16/15: In 1984 the Abu Dhabi Court of Cassation ruled that a Muslim wife has the right to a divorce where the husband has physically abused her and the dispute between them has not been resolved.

Law/Case Reporting System: Law reporting is through the *UAE Gazette*, with some of the Emirates having their own official gazettes (e.g., *Ra's al-Khaymah Gazette*, *Dubai azette*).

International Conventions (with Relevant Reservations): The United Arab Emirates acceded to the CRC in 1997 with the following reservations: the reservation to Article 7 states that "nationality is an internal matter whose terms and conditions are established by national legislation"; the UAE will be bound by Article 14 (relating to children's rights and freedoms) only to the extent that the provision "does not conflict with the principles and provisions of Islamic law"; Article 17 (on access to information and the functions of mass media) is to be applied in light of the requirements of domestic statutes; and the UAE does not consider itself bound by the provisions of Article 21 "given its commitment to the principles of Islamic law" in accordance with which "the UAE does not permit the system of adoption."

Background and Sources: Amin, Middle East Legal Systems, Glasgow, 185; El Alami and Hinchcliffe, "The Uncodified Law" in Islamic Marriage and Divorce Laws of the Arab World, London, 1996; Ballantyne, Commercial Law in the Middle East: The Gulf States, London, 1986; Mahmood, "Gulf" in Statutes of Personal Law in Islamic Countries, 2nd ed., New Delhi, 1995; Price and Al-Tamimi, United Arab Emirates Court of Cassation Judgments: 1989-1997, The Hague, 1998; Redden, UAE in Modern Legal Systems Cyclopedia, Vol. 5, Buffalo, NY, 1990.

Republic of Yemen

Legal History

Yemen was ruled by the Shi'i Zaydi dynasty of Sa'da, founded by Yahya ibn Husayn ibn Qasim ar-Rassi, from 897 CE until well into the current century, although the region came under nominal Ottoman control from 1517. The first period of Ottoman rule ended in 1636 when the Zaydi rulers reasserted their sovereign rule. The British established the Aden Protectorate in Yemen in 1839, and made a series of treaties with local rulers with the aim of extending British influence to southern Yemen. By 1849, the Turks reasserted control over all of the Yemen that was not in British hands. A revolt against the Ottomans led to the granting of autonomy to the Zaydi Imam in 1911, and the Turks retreated from the region altogether within the span of eight years. The British recognised Yemen's independence in 1925. The British succeeded in extending control as far as Hadhramawt by the 1950s, where a violet line separated Turkish Arabia and the South Arabian Protectorate. A military coup in 1962 led by Colonel Abdullah al-Sallal established the Yemen Arab Republic in the north and brought an end to centuries of Zaydi rule and ushered in an era of civil war between the Saudi-supported royalists and the Egyptian-backed Republicans. The civil war continued until Egypt's disengagement in 1967 and Saudi Arabia's extension of recognition of the YAR in 1970. By the 1960s, the British presence in southern Yemen was mainly confined to Aden, and guerrilla fighting throughout the decade hastened the British withdrawal from Aden in 1967, leading to the establishment of the People's Republic of South Yemen (later the People's Democratic Republic of Yemen), an Arab Marxist state. Relations between the two Yemens were strained, as evidenced by a series of border conflicts throughout the 1970s, but relations began to improve by the early 1980s, and a constitution was drafted with the aim of eventually merging to the two states. The proposed reunification did not take place until 1990, however, and not without disagreement over the terms of unification between the north and south resulting in a period of civil war in the summer of 1994.

Following the unification of the two Yemens, Republic Decree Law no. 20 constituting the Yemeni Law of Personal Status was passed in 1992. The legislation followed a Presidential Decree abolishing the 1978 code of personal status of the Yemeni Arab Republic and the 1974 code of personal status of the People's Democratic Republic of Yemen. The post-unification Law of Personal Status closely resembles the former-YAR's legislation. Article 349 provides that the strongest proofs in the Islamic *shariahh* are to serve as the residual source of law in absence of specific textual provision. The penal law of the unified Yemen also provides for the application of *hadd* penalties for certain crimes, although such penalties are not often applied in practice.

Schools of *Fiqh*: The Shafi'i and Zaydi schools are the predominant *madhahib* in Yemen.

Constitutional Status of Islam(ic) Law: The Constitution was adopted on 16th May 1991 and amended 29th September 1994. Article 1 declares Yemen an "Arab Islamic State". Article 2 declares Islam the official state religion. Article 3 states that "Islamic *shariahh* shall be the source of all legislation". Article 23 states that inheritance is regulated by *shariahh*. Article 26 states that the family is the basis of society and its pillars are religion, custom and love of the homeland. Article 31 states that women have rights and duties, which are guaranteed and assigned by *shariahh* and stipulated by law.

Court System: Courts of first instance in each district have jurisdiction over personal status, civil, criminal and commercial cases. Appeals go to the Courts of Appeal in each of the 18 provinces with Civil, Criminal, Matrimonial and Commercial Divisions, each consisting of three-judge benches. The Supreme Court is the highest court of appeal and sits in San'a. The Supreme Court has eight divisions: Constitutional, Appeals Scrutiny, Criminal, Military, Civil, Family, Commercial, and Administrative.

Notable Features: The minimum marriage age is 15 years for males and females. Marriage by coercion is invalid. The judge can overrule the guardian if his objection to the marriage of his ward is considered unjust, with the proviso that the wife receives her proper dower from her husband of equal status. The husband and *wali* are responsible for the registration of marriage within one week of the contract, with penal sanctions for non-compliance.

Polygamy is permitted subject to equitable treatment of co-wives, financial means, lawful benefit, and notification of prospective co-wives.

The wife may leave the marital home to work so long as there is no breach of honour or of her marital duties and her husband consents. Arrears of maintenance may be claimed for a period of up to one year prior to the date of the claim, unless the spouses had agreed to other conditions.

Talaq is ineffective if uttered while intoxicated or with intention to coerce. *Talaq* to which a number is attached is only effective as a single revocable repudiation (except the third of three).

Judicial dissolution is available to either spouse on grounds of defect (this right is forfeit if the defect was accepted explicitly or implicitly, except for such defects as insanity, leprosy and other communicable diseases difficult to cure); and inequality of social status. An annulment is to be effected if the husband becomes Muslim and the wife is not *kitabiyya* or if the wife becomes a Muslim and the husband refuses conversion to Islam, or on grounds of either party's apostasy. The wife may request a decree of dissolution (lesser irrevocable) on the following grounds: husband's non-maintenance; husband's absence or disappearance for one year if he left no provision for maintenance or two years if he provided for his wife's maintenance; husband's imprisonment for three years or more after one year of the sentence has passed; husband's breach of maintenance or accommodation obligations towards co-wives; incompatibility (after reconciliation efforts, and if the husband refuses to pronounce *talaq*, in exchange for the wife's return of her dower); husband's proved addiction to alcohol or narcotics. The wife may also obtain a *khul* in exchange for compensation. The husband is required to pay maintenance during the *idda*. The judge may award compensation equivalent to up to one year's maintenance to a wife who is arbitrarily divorced without just cause. The divorced mother maintains custody until the age of 9 years for boys and 12 for girls, and this period may be extended if it is considered to be in the best interests of the wards. As well, wards may choose which parent they wish to live with once the period of custody is over.

The YLPS provides for obligatory bequests for orphaned grandchildren by predeceased sons or daughters, up to the portion their dead parent would have received or up to the bequeathable one-third, depending on the circumstances of the heirs. That is, grandchildren through sons may inherit if they are poor and grandchildren through daughters if their father is poor. The YLPS allows Quranic heirs to share in the residue of an estate in proportion to their shares, but does not allow *radd* to the spouse relict.

Notable Cases

Law/Case Reporting System: Law reports or indexes of decisions were published in several law journals have been published by the law faculties of the Universities of San'a and Aden, the Jurists. Union and the Ministries of Justice in San'a and Aden, from the pre-unification period. Laws are now published in *al-Jarida al-Rasmiyya*.

International Conventions (with Relevant Reservations): The Republic of Yemen acceded to the

CEDAW in 1984 with a reservation to Article 29(1) relating to arbitration over interpretation or application of the Convention.

Yemen acceded to the ICCPR and ICESCR in 1987 with a general declaration pertaining to non-recognition of the state of Israel. Yemen also acceded to the Convention on Consent to Marriage, Minimum Age for Marriage and Registration of Marriages in 1987.

Yemen signed the CRC in 1990 and ratified it in 1991 without reservations.

Background and Sources: Amin, Middle East Legal Systems, Glasgow, 1985; El Alami and Hinchcliffe, Islamic Marriage and Divorce Laws of the Arab World, London, 1996; Mahmood, "North Yemen", "South Yemen" and "United Yemen" in Statutes of Personal Law in Islamic Countries, 2nd ed., New Delhi, 1995; Lackner, "Women and Development in the Republic of Yemen," pp. 71-96 in Gender and Development in the Arab World, Khoury and Moghadam, eds., London, 1995; Molyneux, "Women's Rights and Political Contingency: The Case of Yemen, 1990-1994," Middle East Journal, Vol. 49(3), 1995: 418-431; Redden, "North Yemen" and "South Yemen" in Modern Legal Systems Cyclopedia, Vol. 5, Buffalo, NY, 1990; Shamiri, "Yemen," Yearbook of Islamic and Middle Eastern Law, Vol. 1 (1994): 369-34; Worth, "A Sana'a Court: The Family and the Ability to Negotiate," Islamic Law and Society, Vol. 2(3), 1995: 320-340.

4

Conclusion

After studying the important aspects of codification of Islamic law in this research a very basic question arises that "Why is this gap between the existing Islamic laws and the reality on the ground in terms of solving problems and upholding the Islamic principles of justice and balance? Many Muslim women are revolting against some key provisions in the Classical laws, and some turning toward secular laws or challenging the traditional Islamic establishments to claim justice and seek a proper and relevant implementation of Islamic law. An important factor to help us understand these issues is that the Islamic law or fiqh lacks a systematic empirical foundation which is important while drafting any law in a particular society. The changing circumstances and social dynamics needs to be understood. The selfish approach of the religious leader is such that it resulted in problem of widespread poverty and destitution, outdated education and identity crisis being a minority. Any reform and change is been resisted sighting communal politics and the demands of the Hindu right wing to repeal all personal laws and to implement Common Civil Code. The Communalism no doubt challenging the Muslim minorities and its progress however when it comes to legal reforms within the community the problem in Muslim Personal Law mainly lies in its inception and the way it was drafted during the British period. In the first chapter we have seen how customary law also became an inevitable part of so called Muslim Personal Law or Shariah Law. But there is an ample evidence one can find in exploring the history of development of Shariah law that its mainly and human endeavour subject to change and varies from one scholar to another scholar of Fiqh (Jurisprudence).

Evolution of Islamic law clearly predicts the changes and reform is the nature of any law written whether today or centuries ago. It is an open fact that any Shariah Law can not be the law of one particular School of Thoughts like Hanafi, Shafi, Maliki and Hanbali. It is a compilation of Fiqh of all Madhhabs and is not restricted to particular School of Thoughts. Development of Fiqh proves that no single School of Thoughts or *Madh-habs* can claimed that they represent Islamic law in its totality. In other words any one school of thought acting alone does not determine Fiqh. All *Madh-habs* are equally important and necessary instrument for clarification and application of the Shariah law. Muslim regardless of their place, time and cultural background should make all efforts to develop further the science of Shariah catering to contemporary issues. Islam does not require a Muslim to follow a particular Madhhab (school of thought). Rather, we say every Muslim has the right to follow one of the schools of thought which has been correctly narrated and its verdicts have been compiled in its books.[1]

It also important to understand that in Islamic jurisprudence there are certain principles that allow adjustments even to pronouncements in sacred textual sources: *maslahat* (public interest), *istihsan* (juristic preference), *darurah* (necessity), etc.[2] Each of these secondary methodologies have provided some dynamism to the process of Ijtihad. Ijtihad had proved and even now will help in filtering the Fiqh from unauthentic or false ahadiths which had made its significant presence in formulating Islamic law. Ahadiths though made an important place in the Islamic jurisprudence but are questionable due its contents which contradict Quran. Especially the law pertaining to woman's rights has completely lost its Quranic spirit due to use of such unauthentic ahadiths.

First of all, Ahadith must be distinguished from the Quran in the following ways: Ahadith cannot be recited in acts of worship. Secondly, they were not meant to be compiled like the Quran which was memorised and written down on various items, such as leather and bone and then finally compiled in one authoritative book during Othman's leadership (mid-seventh century). The Prophet himself has been reported to discourage his companions from writing down his words, lest they be confused with the Quran. Lastly, they were not divinely preserved, as opposed to the Quran in which it states that God will preserve the Quran; therefore, they can be tampered with, as we have seen in several examples of the hadith.[3]

Ahadith should not contradict the Quran. Ahadith should be categorised as either those elaborating on revelations from God or those of personal opinions of the Prophet. It is agreed upon by many scholars, including Muhammed al-Ghazzali and Sheikh Mahmoud Shaltoot of al-Azhar that anything the Prophet said as a judge, ruler, medical person, his personal preferences and all other issues relating to natural human practices (mu'amalat), are not binding orders. If authentic, however, they may be taken as recommendations. Binding are those authentic sayings of the Prophet that refer to religious practice (ibadat), that elucidate the Quran, or the Prophet specifically mentioned he received as orders from God.[4]

Authentic ahadith should use specific wording such as "God prohibits" in order to qualify to be binding in making a prohibition. This is a well known teaching in usul-al-fiqh. Saying that it just isn't nice to do something, or that it's not nice to recommended, is not enough on its own to make the act prohibitive. Also Ahadith should be taken in their historical context.[5]

Ahadith that are *mutawatir* (relayed by a large group) are considered authentic, as opposed to ahadith that are based on individual chains of narration. Unfortunately, only literally a handful of *mutawatir* ahadith actually exist in the published hadith collections. For example, there are some ahadith where the Prophet uses the medical knowledge known during the seventh century. This was the extent of his knowledge and the knowledge of medicine for the Arabs at that time; the hadith should be judged against the medical information we have available to us today. Again, such a hadith should be judge by the capacity of the Prophet at the time is it his personal knowledge or a revelation from God.[6]

After the death of the Prophet, it was seen that the Caliphs Abu Bakr and Umar often were asked for advice by the Muslims and it is evident that the right of interpreting the Quranic regulations was not the privilege of any expert official body but could be exercised by anyone whose piety or social conscience dictated his discourse.

Today in many Muslim countries, Islamic decisions ranging from personal to political are made in the form of *fatawas*, where Islamic scholars render a decision on the morality or legality of an issue brought to them. *Fatawa* itself is a highly controversial tool in jurisprudence and cannot be relied on. During the Mongol invasion, the Muslim world lost many of its cultural and intellectual centres, including libraries, mosques and universities, not to mention the lives of hundreds of thousands of Muslims. The response of the Muslim community amidst this collapse was a withdrawal into a conservatism that resisted further change. Unfortunately, many of the practices of the time, which had resulted from acculturation of foreign customs and were contrary to Quranic values, were already associated with religion, and these, too, were preserved. This reaction, coupled with the 'closing of the door of Ijtihad' in law, resulted in the relative stagnation of the Muslim community and its jurisprudence.[7]

In the twentieth century, Muslim intellectuals concerned with questions of fiqh subjected the medieval versions of the Shariah which was critically reexamined and brought new interpretive approaches to the Shariah sources. Also with the spread of educational opportunities and the increase in literacy, many Muslims who are educated but have not pursued course in Madarasa are contributing interpretations of the Shariah. In other words, laypersons who belong to the modern educated elite do not necessarily feel that they must defer to the specialised knowledge of the fuqaha' and are prepared to challenge the monopoly formerly enjoyed by the fuqaha' to make authoritative statements on Shariah law. As a result, it has become very difficult to make generalisations about contemporary Shariah doctrines. While some contemporary Muslims, particularly those educated in traditional Islamic institutions like Darul uloom, consider medieval fiqh treaties authoritative, but there is a marked and growing tendency to treat such works as secondary legal sources. The old hierarchies of sources and the established methodologies for interpreting them are also questioned by contemporary thinkers and scholars.

In contemporary Muslim countries the desire on the part of the governments for legal modernisation combined with the need to show respect for the Shariah has resulted in various significant reforms. In the area of personal status, a number of reforms, by and large have been enacted in Muslim countries with a view to improving the status of women in matters of marriage, divorce, support, and child custody. The boldest reforms in this area were enacted in the Tunisian Code of Personal Status of 1956, the Iranian Family Protection Law of 1967 (since abrogated by the revolutionary government), and the South Yemen Family Law of 1974.

In Iran, the government has made a model marriage contract available to marrying couples that gives the divorced wife a right to half the property acquired during the marriage, provided she does not seek the divorce herself? And is not at fault? Another article of the contract consists of a power of attorney from the husband to the wife, permitting her to divorce herself on twelve different grounds. Regardless of the marriage contract; an Iranian man must secure the court's permission to divorce his wife. In 1994, the Iranian parliament enacted a law giving a divorced woman the right to monetary compensation for the years she worked in her husband's home as a mother and housewife. In 1997, a law was passed requiring courts to calculate the mahr payments husbands must pay divorced wives according to an index updated for inflation.[8]

In order to understand the scope and nature of the various statutes adopted in Muslim countries with the goal of reforming rules and laws concerning the family, a comparative approach is used by many thinkers and legal experts. Several comparative studies conducted also includes the rules on the family under the Hanafi doctrine, an Islamic school of law that developed in the Taqlid era and that historically had the largest influence on the Muslim law of these Islamic countries. It also shows the Hanafi rules to the extent to which many countries reforms departed from their historic *Taqlid* origins. Tunisia seems to have gone as far as to legislate liberalism in its family code in a manner that has no parallel in the Arab world. Tunisian lawmakers introduced terms such as "equality" in their legislation and made a concerted effort to abolish the structure of gendered reciprocity and complementarity inherited from Taqlid law. By comparison, the Egyptian legislature preserved gender reciprocity, while at the same time chiped away at the husband's surplus of powers in the family.[9]

Egyptian courts limited the husband's power in the marital relationship by restricting the interpretation of the wife's duty of obedience in the family, as well as expanding rather drastically the grounds available for her to request a divorce.[10]

Kuwait, for example, which codified personal status in 1984, remains closely linked to *shari'a* law, as does the law in Yemen, where Bill 20/1992 and amendments in 1998, 1999 and 2002, concedes little to reformist requests, unlike legislation in Southern Yemen that with its Bill 1/1974 established restrictions to polygamy and repudiation.

In Iraq by contrast, a first law enacted in 1959 had been approved for the definitely secular Personal Status Code, albeit not formally abrogating polygamy and repudiation it did, effectively, make both almost impossible. Following a legislative amendment dated 1978, polygamy was forbidden unless the first wife provided her explicit approval. Actually, according to a reformist interpretation, both polygamy and repudiation would not be admissible in the Arab world today, as the circumstances and reasons justifying them no longer exist in the current historical context. At the moment, however, there is a return to religious law in Iraq. In fact, in 2003 the *ad Interim* government abrogated the 1959 Personal Status Code, and Article 41 of the new Constitution refers all matters concerning Personal Status to denominational law.[11]

The most "revolutionary" results as we know are those achieved in Tunisia, a country that, with its 1956 Personal Status Code, formally abolished both polygamy and repudiation, thanks to courageous work of *Ijtihad* (interpretation), which resulted in the understanding that polygamy was implicitly forbidden by the Quran. In fact, a coordinated reading of chapter 4, verse-3 of the Quran says "And if you fear that you cannot act equitably towards orphans, then marry such women as seem good to you, two and three and four; but if you fear that you will not do justice (between them), then (marry) only one", with Chapter 4, verse 4, warns "You can never be equitable in dealing with more than one wife, no matter how hard you try", one deduces how it is effectively impossible to support many wives and treat them equally, and therefore polygamy cannot be practiced. Hence, Article 18 of Tunisian Personal Status Code not only contemplates a previous union among the obstacles to a marriage, but it also imposes a fine and a one year prison sentence, adding, in compliance with Article 21, that any second marriage entered into violates bigamy laws and it is to be considered invalid. As far as repudiation is concerned, an act that Islamic Law considers reprehensible (as stated in a *hadith* "God has permitted nothing more odious to Him than repudiation"), it has been abolished by Tunisian Law. Divorce - introduced in Tunisia almost twenty years before it became legal in Italy - is therefore the only way in which a marriage can be dissolved (Article 29 and following), and it is admitted only subsequent to the judge's attempt to reconcile the parties involved.[12]

Tunisia then continued its reforms, envisaging the possibility of adoption (Bill 27/1958) and persisting to reform its Personal Status Code. With Bill 74/1993, Article 23 was amended so as to guarantee equal rights for the bride and the groom, abolishing the wife's duty to obey and establishing the obligation for a couple to cooperate in managing family life. More recently, in March 2008, Article 56 of the Code has been changed, introducing Article 56, which addresses the custody of minor children and the right to housing paid for by the husband for the mother or the person having custody of the children (Bill 20/2008). Although Tunisia is now the only country that has formally forbidden polygamy and repudiation, many other Muslim countries are attempting to establish procedural obstacles to these practices. For example, codification in Syria (which in 1953 was the first Arab country to promulgate a general law on Personal Status, later reformed with Bill 34/1975), Jordan (with a first codification in 1956, reform in 1976 and other legislative interventions in 2001), and to a lesser extent Libya and Algeria (both dated 1984) have all established the possibility of including in the marriage contract a clause for monogamy, or require consent from the first wife or authorisation from a judge, both for polygamy and repudiation, thereby diminishing the traditionally preeminent position attributed to men.[13]

Morocco too recently changed its Family Law, promulgating in 2003 a new Personal Status Law, the *Mudawana*, which replaces the previous Code dated 1958 and the modest reforms implemented in 1993. Polygamist marriage, however, must be authorised by a judge, and authorisation is subordinated to the existence of an objective and exceptional justification as well as the petitioner having sufficient financial resources (Article 41). A second marriage may take place only on condition that the second wife understands and accepts the polygamist characteristics of the marriage. Furthermore, Article 40 establishes that authorisation cannot be provided if there is a risk that wives will not be treated fairly, and above all, if the first wife has included a monogamy clause in the marriage contract. In all events, the first wife has the right to ask for a divorce in case of a second marriage (Article 45). The reforms raise the minimum age of marriage for women from fifteen to eighteen; establish the right to divorce by mutual consent; place polygamy and repudiation (unilateral divorce by the husband) under strict judicial control; make the family the joint responsibility of both spouses; rescind the wife's duty of obedience to her husband; and eliminate the requirement of a marital tutor (wali) for women to marry.[14]

Although the Moroccan *Mudawana* includes the possibility of divorce, it is important to bear in mind that repudiation still exists (Articles 78-93), basically however in the form of divorce, since it must be authorised by a court following a written petition from either the husband or the wife. It would therefore appear that the right to unilaterally terminate a marriage has also been extended to women (Article 78). Actually, nonetheless, this is not automatic, but rather subordinated to the husband acknowledging such a right to the wife (Article 89).

Highlighting the reform in Egypt one has to understand that it is the country that has always been torn between reformist desires and attempts to reinstate Islamic traditions. The main characteristic of Egyptian reforms remains, however, the lack of a general codification of Family Law. Direct legislative interventions have been addressed for example, the wife's right to financial support (Bill 25/1920), minimum age required for marriage (Bill 25/1929) or the dissolution of a marriage (Bill 25/1929). Encouraged by Sadat, reforms continued during the Seventies with Bill 44/1979, which restricted polygamy, considered damaging to the first wife and hence grounds for divorce in the event of a second polygamist marriage. The conservative surge that followed Sadat's assassination resulted in a pause. The Bill was abrogated and then replaced by Bill 100/1985, which was however less liberal. In fact, the equation polygamy/damage to the wife vanished and to obtain a divorce it is now necessary to prove that one has suffered economic or emotional damage due to polygamy.[15]

The approval of Bill 1/2000 marked an important step forward in the modernisation of Egyptian Family Law. This law in fact not only made more accessible *khul*', i.e. the wife's right to petition for a divorce directly to the judge when renouncing financial benefits arising from the dissolution of marriage. It also envisages divorce for *'urfi* marriages (traditional non-registered marriages) and imposes restrictions on repudiation. This obviously resulted in strong reaction from those supporters of *Shari'ah* who consider a greater emancipation of women as a threat to family solidity. In spite of this, the modernisation process did not stop. Not only in 2003 did the Bill 1/2000 achieve constitutional legitimacy, but in 2004 the first secular courts specialised in Family Law opened in Egypt.[16]

Pakistan's Family Law Ordinance 1961 is one of the ideal law as far as matrimonial issues are concerned.The Muslim Family Laws Ordinance 1961 introduced reforms regarding registration of marriages and in default of such registration penalties of fine and imprisonment have been prescribed. Also in marriage according to the Hanafi School, an adult woman may contract her marriage without the consent of a *wali*. Government has also introduced some reforms in the law relating to polygamy. Now, a husband must submit an application and pay a prescribed fee to the local union council in order to obtain permission for contracting a polygamous marriage. Thereafter, the chairman of the union council forms an arbitration council with representatives of both husband and wife/wives in order to determine the necessity of the proposed marriage. In Divorce woman are empowered by judicial *khula* which is granted without husband's consent if wife is willing to forgo her financial rights.

India though not a Muslim country but Muslim minority like other minorities are free to practice their personal laws pertaining to Marriage, Property, Inheritance etc. In contemporary India Muslim Personal Law in relation to women is one of those concerns which time and again became a fodder to the communal elements and for those seeking electoral benefit. Post-independence no efforts been made to further reform or codify the Anglo-Mohammadan Law both by the religious body and government. Also the present Muslim Personal Law is not equivalent to 'Islamic law' as we have discussed in first chapter in the history of its formulation. Major transformation need to be carried out to give nomenclature as Shariah law. Islamic law as practiced in India does not reflect the reforms and progress made by Muslim majority countries with respect to women's right.[17] Indian Muslims in the absence of codified law seems to be mostly relied on Fatawas. It is another serious issue to be dealt with.

The Fatawas which is loosely promoted and projected as a part of Muslim Law by the orthodox clergy on one hand and the highlighting of unauthentic Fatwas by the media on the other has done great harm to the Quranic spirit of justice and equality. The Muslim community especially Muslims living in rural areas consult local Imam and seek his Fatwa on any issue related to marriage or divorce etc. Not only rural Muslims but urban educated Muslims too seek Fatwa thinking that it is a part of Shariah and hence also binding.The myth that Fatwa is binding is due to ignorance of the people and also due to deliberate tactics of Ulama to control the Muslim masses. Again the question arises who is authorised to give Fatwa? It is clear in the Islamic jurisprudence that a Mufti is the highest authority and is eligible to give Fatwa after thorough understanding of the issue and supporting his Fatwa (Opinion) with authentic sources like Quran and Sunnah. Since there is no homogenity in Islamic law then Fatwa on the same issue may differ from Mufti following Hanafi School to Mufti belonging to Shafi School of Thoughts. Different scholars have drawn different conclusion over the same issue.

Few years back a controversy over a Fatwa on Imrana's case shows the ambiguity within the Ulama's understanding of the issue and the secular law which define such act under criminal offence. Imrana was raped by her father-in-law and Fatwa, we have to make note of this point, that was not from the Mufti but it was opinion of the local semi-literate Imam who simply quoted a precedence without understanding the crime, says that Imrana after the rape incident, is now a mother of her husband and her marriage stands null and void with her husband. In this case of the Imrana, the clergy who followed the Hanafi doctrine annulled her marriage saying that she had become *haram* (prohibited) for her husband (as she was sexually assaulted by the husband's father). But, if the same matter had been referred to a scholars belonging to the Shafii School, primarily located in Kerala in India, they would not have given the same verdict and according to Shafi Fiqh any Prohibited or unlawful act will not cancel the permissible act or lawful act. Nikah is permissible or lawful act and rape is prohibited act and hence the Nikah remains valid. Here Imrana's marriage to her husband would not have been annulled and her father-in-law would have been punished for committing rape.

For those who might have forgotten the details of another case of Gudiya. Gudiya is the young woman from Mundali village in Meerut district, Uttar Pradesh. She thought her soldier husband Arif, who she had known for barely two weeks after her marriage, had died when he disappeared during the 1999 Kargil conflict. He was presumed to be dead or a deserter as his body was not found. In 2004, after four years, Arif came back to India as part of an exchange of prisoners between India and Pakistan. During his absence, Gudiya remarried. She was expecting a child from her new husband Taufiq when Arif returned. But this time Fatwa from the Darul Ifta Deoband gave the so-called ruling that she has to return to her first husband. However, she died in a year giving birth to a baby boy. There are thousands like Imrana and Gudiya happening every year. Many women's groups, organisation and Darul Qada witness numerous matrimonial cases but feel helpless and vulnerable due to lack of proper law and its high time that a codified law needs to be formulated and religiously implemented.

Muslim Personal Law is, after all, administered in secular courts by judges of all religions who do not specialise in the law of one tradition or another, and they cannot help but be influenced by that experience. The verdicts delivered by the high courts becomes the precedence and the large body of the existing law constitutes these judgements. Often the court fails to understand the position of women in Islamic law during the divorce and maintenance cases.

If we codify the present Muslim personal law, many shortcomings in the present law can be removed thus making it much more gender–just than it is at present. In fact, in its original spirit Islamic law in matters of marriage, divorce, inheritance etc. was most progressive and empowered women as no other law had done before. However, over period of time this original spirit was lost due to then prevailing social ethos and values. And customary laws acquired greater importance over Qur'anic and Prophet's (PBUH) pronouncements. Codification can remove these accretions over a period of time and restore original Qur'anic spirit. Rethinking Muslim personal law as prevalent in India is certainly not to violate divine injunctions as often maintained by some people but to bring in much closer to divine injunctions i.e. to infuse in them really divine spirit.[18] There is also a great need to make amendments and reforms to place it as Shariah law before the community. Several loopholes and arbitrariness in the application of Muslim law has led to gross injustice and destitution of women in the community. There is no standard practice though but every Muslim sect and Jamaat has their own bunch of customary law which is given priority over the Shariah law especially in matters of property and many Muslim women are forced to loose their Islamic rights.

Another important aspect in the codification is the demand for Standard Nikahnama for all the Muslims having clauses for terms and conditions. There is no uniform certificate of marriage and in some places the Nikah is a just an oral ritual without any writing work. A Nikhanama apart from constituting the entire detail of the bride and bridegroom it should also have a note on specific law on marriage, maintenance and divorce. This will also help in keeping check on divorce and polygamy.

For Muslim women, basically, the community dictates its own norms and restriction and sanctions it in the name of Islam. Also the economic and political circumstances determine the social attitude and perception of its people. The politicisation of religion post independence proved a major setback for the women of the minority communities especially Muslim women who are suppressed both outside and within the community. They are deprived of education, economic independence and legal rights sighting communal or religious ground. On the so called religious grounds, it is not the command of Islam, but their own norms and practices which are influenced by their customs and traditions loaded with patriarchal misogynist dictats. The awakening taking place across the globe among the Muslim women is forcing their local government to introduce reforms and empower them more with their legal rights. There are several issues cropping up in the world of Islamic feminism like Hijab, banning of customary law and practices, political representation, Legal rights, freedom for expression and participation of Muslim women in nation building is a clear pointer to the fact that reform is inevitable. A sound legislation having the consensus of the Ulama, Activists, legal expert and community member will definitely produce a positive result for the Muslim community in India suffering from socio-economic and political backwardness. The reformed and codified Muslim Personal Law not only will end the myth of Muslims being anti-progressive and anti-women but also it will lead to mass empowering of the fairer sex in every respect.

References

1. Mufti Mahmood Shaltoot, Cairo, On Intra Muslim Relation.
2. Abdul Hamid A. Abu Sulayman. Crisis in the Muslim Mind [Herndon, Virginia: The International Institute of Islamic Thought, 1993; Both Hanafi and Maliki school recognize the validity of *istihsan*. However, they differ in terms of the scope and nature of the notion. Muhammad Abu Zahrah. The Fundamental Principles of Fiqh.
3. *Ibid.*
4. www.ghazali.org

5-6. Abdul Hamid A. AbuSulayman. Crisis in the Muslim Mind [Herndon, Virginia: The International Institute of Islamic Thought, 1993

7. Abdul Hamid A. AbuSulayman. Crisis in the Muslim Mind [Herndon, Virginia: The International Institute of Islamic Thought, 1993
8. Dr. Esposito, Islam, p. 11.
9. Esfandiari, Haleh., Reconstructed Lives: Women and Iran's Islamic Revolution, 1997 Washington, D.C, The Woodrow Wilson Center Press. 3 Lama Abu-Odeh, Modernizing Muslim Family Law: The Case of Egypt, Georgetown University Law Center, la34@law.georgetown.edu
10. *Ibid.*
11. *Valentina M. Donini, Polygamy* and Family Law, 2009, www.resetdoc.org
12. *Ibid.*
13. *Ibid.*
14. Stephanie Willman Bordat and Saida Kouzzi. The Challenge of Implementing Morocco's New Personal Status Law, Global Rights, Originally published in the Carnegie Endowment for International Peace's Arab Reform Bulletin, Vol. 2, No. 8 (Carnegie Endowment for International Peace, 2004).

15. *Valentina M. Donini,* Polygamy and Family Law, 2009, www.resetdoc.org
16. www.pathwaysofempowerment.org
17. John Esposito, Women in Muslim Family Law, 2002, Syracuse University Press, pp. 116.
18. Asghar Ali Engineer, On Codification of Muslim Personal Law, 2 May, 2009 Secular Perspective.

Muslim Family Law (Draft)

Short Title – Family Law, Muslim Family etc.

Definitions

1. Qazi

Qazi is a judge ruling in accordance with the Shariah or Islamic law. Qazis' traditionally have jurisdiction over all legal matters involving Muslims.

2. Nikah

Nikah always means a religio-legal contract between a Muslim man and Muslim woman that regularises the lineage of this progeny and creates rights, duties, obligation and liabilities. Qur'anic vision Marriage (nikah) as a solemn and sacred social contract between bride and groom. This contract is a strong covenant (mithaqun Ghalithun). (Surah 4- Al-Nisa, Verse: 21). As equality and justice is central to Islam, in Nikah spouses shall enjoy equal rights and duties and support each other morally.

3. Darul Qada

Darul Qada is appellate or revisional court constituted by government in the said area, which shall deal with matters under 1937 Shariat Application Act.

4. Arbitration Council

"Arbitration Council" means a body consisting of the Chairperson and a representative of each of the parties to a matter dealt with the Family Law.

Provided that where any party fails to nominate a representative within the prescribed time, the body formed without such representative shall be the Arbitration Council.

5. Mahr

The Mahr is an amount of money or property that is given to the wife by the husband as a non-returnable dowry in the marriage contract. She may use it as she wishes. It may either be prompt (**Mu' ajjal**) or deferred (**Mu wajjal**)

6. Talaq-e-Ahsan

According to the Holy Prophet (PBUH), Talaq-e-Ahsan is the best mode of divorce. In this mode of divorce the husband pronounces single Talaq during the "Taha'r" period and in this situation and the wife waits for three menstrual cycles (if she menstruates) or three months (if she does not menstruate). If cordial agreement is reached during these three months the husband would call off his talaq and both can live together without renewing the Nikkah.

7. Talaq-e-Hasan

In this mode of divorce, the husband pronounces Talaq each coming month during the "Tuha'r" period. The husband can revert (Rajou') after pronouncing the 2nd Talaq but if he pronounces the 3rd Talaq the husband not only loses the right to revert but also he cannot perform Nikah with the same female unless she performs Nikah with another person who then divorces her or he is dead.

8. Talaq-e-Tafweed

In systems based on Muslim laws, a husband may delegate his unilateral right to talaq to his wife. He still retains his right of talaq but then also permits his wife to pronounce talaq upon herself. This agreement can be made through the marriage contract, or it can be negotiated subsequently. Talaq-i-tafwid is also commonly referred to in Arabic-speaking communities as 'esma, which simply means 'the permission or the option.'

9. Talaq-e-Mubarat

In *talaq-e-mubarat,* both spouses are desirous of separation and reach a mutual settlement that makes this possible.

10. Khul

Khul is basically a right for a woman to ask a divorce from the husband in certain circumstances. It could be defined as 'the separation of a husband from his wife, while receiving a return (of monetary gain from her) and using specific statements (to bring about the dissolution of the marriage).

11. Hiba (Gift)

The word Hiba literally means, the donation of a thing from which the donee derive a benefit. It must be immediate and complete. The most essential element of Hiba is the declaration, "I have given".

As per Hedaya, Hiba is defined technically as, "unconditional transfer of property, made immediately and without any exchange or consideration, by one person to another and accepted by or on behalf of the latter".

DRAFT

Nikah

The model Muslim marriage contract provides written proof of the marriage and of the terms and conditions agreed between the spouses.

There shall be three copies of the contract: one given to the bride, one given to the groom, and one kept by the mosque conducting the ceremony.

Written proof of the marriage helps prevent any future uncertainties about the marriage and its terms and conditions. Without a written marriage contract women often have difficulty in proving they were in a nikah, or that special conditions had been agreed between the spouses. It must include the amount of muqaddam/mu'ajjal mahr, and the amount of the muwajjal (deferred).

The model Muslim marriage contract emphasises the Qur'anic vision of marriage as a relationship of mutual love, mercy and kindness (mawaddah, rahmah, suku*n*.). "Among His signs is that He created for you mates from among yourselves, that you may dwell in tranquillity with them and as such He has created such a deep relationship between yourselves, as a means of actualisation of potentialities for both of you. Verily in that are signs for those who reflect." (Surah 30 Ar- Rum : Verse: 21)

Nikaah is a mutual contract between a man and a woman. (Surah : 4 An-Nisa, Verse: 21). As far as the mutual rights and obligations are concerned, the Quran has condensed it in one comprehensive sentence when it said: "The obligations of women shall be equal to their rights, one obligation against each right."(Surah Baqara: 2, Verse: 228).

The terms 'the wife' and 'the husband' are to be replaced by 'the spouses' as mentioned in Surah 53- Al Najm,Verse 45. Except in some places where there is need to address specifically term. There are several other changes as well:

- The husband is no longer the head of the family; spouses are equal partners, jointly running the matrimonial union with equal decision-making power;
- Spouses have equal rights over the family residence, and deciding where to live;
- Spouses have equal rights over property acquired during the marriage;
- Spouses have equal rights to enter into work;
- Spouses have equal powers to represent the family.

Registration of Nikah

(a) A Qazi or an officer appointed by the state government for registering Muslim marriage in accordance with this Act. He shall be an Indian national, professing religion of Islam and must be qualified.

(b) For the purpose of registration of Nikah the State Government shall grant licenses to one or more persons to be called Nikah Registrars.

(c) The form of Nikahnama, the registers shall be maintained by Nikah registrars, the records to be preserved by State Government. The copies of the Nikahnama shall be supplied to both the parties.

(d) The Nikahnama shall contain all the details like status of groom /bride – divorcee/widow/widower/ second marriage etc.

(e) In Nikah brides consent shall be obtained without which Nikah shall not be valid. Qazi shall make it mandatory that he himself hears clearly the acceptance of Nikah from the bride herself and not from any of her relatives whether mother or grandmother or sister, or cousin or aunt etc. The bride shall give her consent in her specific word either in front of two witnesses. Also most important point to be included is that bride shall utter the name of the Spouse to be and the amount of Mahr any asset by way of property, gold, shares etc. while giving her consent.

(f) The Bride will have to decide about her Mahr to be in currency or property or Gold or Silver.

(g) Age of Marriage- Baligh/ An adult as define in country's law.

Wali ('marriage guardian for the bride') not a requirement

The model Muslim marriage contract does not require a wali ('marriage guardian') for the bride. In classical jurisprudence, the scholars could not agree whether a wali was indispensable in classical sources. Hence the absence of the requirement for a wali in Muslim family law in countries following the Hanafi precedent such as Bangladesh and Pakistan. Wali is not a Quranic requirement for Nikah, it is contract between two adults.

Age of Marriage

By law the bride shall be 18 years of age and the age of the groom shall be 21 years. However, if a girl is married at a minor age, then under Islamic Law, there is a concept called **khiyar al-buloogh,** which means “the option of puberty”. It means that while a minor daughter’s marriage if arranged by an elder without taking into account the bride’s consent; she has the right to annul the marriage after reaching adulthood, if she doesn’t desire to accept the person as her spouse.

Mahr

1. The right bestowed to the wife at the time of Nikkah or during subsistence of marital life wherein the wife is given an amount of money or anything else is known as Zar-e-Mahr or Dower amount. Dower amount can be in the shape of cash, jewellery or property.

2. The Holy Quran has not ascertained the exact amount to be fixed as Zar-e-Mahr but has commanded the grooms to pay their wives from the assets they possess; hence, the Zar-e-Mahr depends upon wealth status of the groom. The Holy Quran has ordered men to pay Zar-e-Mahr to the wives at the time of Nikah (Al-Nissa-24), at another place the verse in the Holy Quran ordained men to pay Zar-e-Mahr to the wives pleasantly (Surah: 4 Al-Nissa, verse : 24). It might expand to a heap of gold (4:20). Some more verses on Mehr (Surah:2 Baqara:, Verse: 236-237).

3. The minimum Mahr amount shall be one year’s income of the bride groom or in kind payment equivalent to one year’s income.

4. The dower amount shall be the personal property of the wife therefore, parents of the wife or the groom or any other relative does not claim any right over it.

5. Furthermore, neither the parents or relatives nor the guardian shall have the authority to waive off the dower amount; however, the wife on her own free will can forgo or give up whole or part of the dower amount (Surah: 4, Al-Nissa, Verse: 4).

Prompt (Mua'jjal) and Deferred (Mu Wajjal)

Mua' jjal - As the names suggest, Mu ajjal dower means that the dower is payable immediately upon the marriage.

1. Prompt dower does not become deferred after consummation and the wife has the right to demand and sue for it any time.

Mahr-e-Muwajjal

Mahr-e-Muwajjal or Deffered payment shall be paid minimum within one year and maximum period shall not exceed by three years.

In some cases Mehr-e- Muwajjal or Ind-e-Talab shall be permissible only when the bride agrees.

Maintenance

1. If any husband fails to maintain his wife adequately, or where there are more wives than one, fails to maintain them equitably, the wife, or all or any of the wives, may in addition to seeking legal remedy available apply to the Chairperson who shall constitute an Arbitration Council to determine the matter, and the Arbitration Council may issue a certificate specifying the amount which shall be paid as maintenance by the husband.

2. A husband or wife may, in the prescribed manner, within the prescribed period, and on payment of the prescribed fee, prefer an application for revision of the certificate, to the Collector concerned and his decision shall be final.

3. Any amount payable if, not paid in the due time, shall be recoverable as arrears from husband's assets.

(Definition of Maintenance: Fatawa-e-Alamgiri 1986 Muslim Woman's Protection Act)

Divorce

Forms of Divorce

1. Talaq-e-Ahsan

2. Talaq-e-Tafweed (Delegated right to Divorce)
3. Talaq-e-Mubaraat
4. Khula
5. Faskh-e-Nikah (Dissolution of Muslim Marriage Act 1939.)

Oral Tripple Divorce

(a) Talaq-e-Biddat (Tripple Talaq in one sitting) should be abolished. Only valid form of divorce is Talaq-e-Ahsan as mentioned in the Quran.

(b) If Talaq-e-Biddat is pronounced then it should be taken as only one pronouncement.

Talaq-e-Ahsan

1. Any man who wishes to divorce his wife shall give the chairperson of Darul Qada a notice in writing of his intention to divorce his wife, and shall supply a copy thereof to the wife.

2. Talaq shall not be effective until the expiration of ninety days from day on which notice is delivered to the Chairperson of Darul Qada or Council.

3. Within thirty days of the receipt of notice the Chairperson shall constitute an Arbitration Council appointing two arbitrators one from groom's family and one from bride's family for the purpose of bringing about reconciliation between the parties, and the Arbitration Council shall take all steps necessary to bring about such reconciliation. (Sura: 4 Al-Nisa, Verse: 35)

4. If the wife be pregnant at the time of Talaq is pronounced, talaq shall not be effective until the period mentioned above or the pregnancy, whichever later, ends. (Surah 65: At-Talaq, Verse: 1)

5. Talaq should be executed at such a time from where Iddat can be counted. Divorced women shall wait concerning themselves three monthly periods. (Surah: 2: Baqara, Verse: 229) For those who are pregnant, their period

is until they deliver their burdens. (Surah: 65-At Talaq, Verse: 4)

6. Nothing shall debar a wife whose marriage has been terminated by talaq effective under this section from remarrying the same spouse, unless such termination is for the third time so effective.

While awarding separation of the spouses the Conciliation Committee or the Council shall also make provision about the:

- Amount of Mehr.
- Disbursement of all properties of the wife.
- Payment of compensation for Talaq (Muta-at-ul-Talaq).
- Maintenance during iddat, proper amount according to the status of wife.
- About the custody of children along with specific provision of maintenance to the children.

Talaq-e-Tafweez

1. *Nikahnama* (standard marriage contract form), the spouse may delegate the power of divorce to his wife with conditions arrived at by the parties.

2. In the event that the wife subsequently exercises this right, she is required to send the divorce notice to the Chairperson of the Arbitration Council, who issues a divorce certificate if reconciliation efforts from the platform of the Arbitration Council fail.

3. *Haq-e-Tafweez-e-Talaq* is another option for dissolution of marriage under which a woman is granted the right to annul her marriage. A broad consensus exists among Muslim jurists that Islam gives a woman the right to seek this power from her spouse, and it can be delegated by him to her both verbally as well as in writing, at the occasion of marriage solemnisation or afterwards, with different forms and conditions. If she has this right, she can divorce herself and dissolve the marriage. Once this right is delegated, it cannot

be repudiated. The husband's right of divorce remains intact even after he delegates it to his wife.

Talaq-e-Mubaraat

Talaq-e-mubarat, both spouses are desirous of separation and reach a mutual settlement that makes this possible.

Khul

1. A wife shall apply to the Court for divorce under khul.

2. The law provides that the wife shall apply to the Court for khul even without the consent from the husband.

3. The wife will have to sacrifice what would normally due to her under the talaq procedure and returns the advance portion of the dower.

Polygamy

What is important is justice and not the number. Polygamy is permissible but not a right and privilege and shall be allowed only in exceptional circumstances and only after seeking permission of the Council. Quran not only discourage polygamy but almost bans if its condition of rigorous justice are not followed. The verses 4: 3 and 4: 129 in Holy Quran must be read together.

The conditions are as follow:

1. No man during the existing marriage shall except with the previous permission in writing of the Darul Qada or Council, contract another marriage.
2. An application for permission shall be submitted to the chairperson in the prescribed manner, together with the prescribed fee and shall state the reasons for the proposed second marriage.
3. Permission of the first wife is compulsory to contract second marriage.
4. First wife shall be notified along with the Darul Qada or Council.

5. First wife shall be heard by the Darul Qada or Council and then the decision shall be given. Darul Qada or Council first must investigate before rendering any decision.
6. On receipt of the application the chairperson shall ask the applicant and his existing wife to nominate a representative each, and the Arbitration council so constituted may, if satisfied, that proposed second marriage is necessary and grant subject to such conditions, if any, as may deemed fit, the permission applied for.
7. In deciding the application the Arbitration council shall record its reasons for the decision and any party may, in the prescribed manner, within the prescribed period, on payment of the prescribed fee, prefer an application for revision to the District Magistrate concern and his decision shall be final and shall not be called in question in any court.
8. In considering whether another marriage is just and necessary during the continuance of an existing marriage, the arbitration council may, without prejudice to its general powers to consider what is just and necessary, have regard to such circumstances as the following amongst others-Sterility, physical infirmity, physical unfitness for the conjugal relations, willful avoidance of performing conjugal rights or insanity on the part of an existing wife.
9. Darul Qada or Council can only permits second marriage after knowing and verifying the financial capacity of the husband to maintain both the wives and to ensure justice and equity between both the wives.
10. It is must that the second wife should be either a widow or divorcee. And all their rights shall be intact.

Inheritance

Muslims inherit from one another as stated in the Qur'an Chapter 4; verse: 7. Hence, there is a legal share for relatives of the deceased in his or her estate and property. The major rules of inheritance are detailed in Qur'an and Fiqh.

1. The Shari'ah (Islamic Law) recognises the full property rights of women before and after marriage.

2. They may buy, sell or lease any or all of their properties at will. For this reason, Muslim women may keep (and in fact they have traditionally kept) their maiden names after marriage, an indication of their independent property rights as legal entities.

3. In Islamic law, female heirs suffers from no disability to succeed to land or real estates.

4. In case the daughter is crippled and has no possibility of marrying or otherwise cannot marry or do not want to marry or for some reason cannot earn her livelihood shall be given equal share.

5. A wife or a daughter contributing to the family income shall be given equal share or under Hiba provision shall be entitled to get more than her share in the inheritance as laid down in Shariah law.

(a) Fiqh-ul- Quran: Moulana Omar Ahmed Usmani takes clear stand that father can will his wealth to those daughters who are not married or who contribute to family wealth then she should get more than her share.

(b) Dowry which is not a part of Islam and expenses of Haj cannot be compared as share in the property.

(c) one-third of the property can be given as Hiba. Hiba would be compulsory for an unmarried daughter and if she contributes to family wealth then equal share.

When a Muslim dies leaving behind cash or property or both the same can be distributed among the heirs as per Shariah law after fulfilling these conditions:

1. Pay funeral expenses.
2. Pay debts.
3. Execute the testamentary Will of the deceased (which can only be a maximum of one-third of the property).
4. Distribute the remainder of estate and property to the relatives of the deceased according to Shariah Law.

*All contents are still under revision.

Index

J

K

S